Computer Simulation
in Management Science

Fifth Edition

Computer Simulation in Management Science

Fifth Edition

Michael Pidd

Department of Management Science
The Management School
Lancaster University

John Wiley & Sons, Ltd

Other Wiley Editorial Offices

John Wiley & Sons Inc., 111 River Street, Hoboken, NJ 07030, USA

Jossey-Bass, 989 Market Street, San Francisco, CA 94103-1741, USA

Wiley-VCH Verlag GmbH, Boschstr. 12, D-69469 Weinheim, Germany

John Wiley & Sons Australia Ltd, 33 Park Road, Milton, Queensland 4064, Australia

John Wiley & Sons (Asia) Pte Ltd, 2 Clementi Loop #02-01, Jin Xing Distripark, Singapore
129809

John Wiley & Sons Canada Ltd, 22 Worcester Road, Etobicoke, Ontario, Canada M9W1L1

Wiley also publishes its books in a variety of electronic formats. Some content that appears in print
may not be available in electronic books.

Coventry University

Library of Congress Cataloging-in-Publication Data

Pidd, Michael.
　Computer simulation in management science / Michael Pidd.—5th ed.
　　p. cm.
　Includes bibliographical references and index.
　ISBN 0-470-09230-0 (pbk. : alk. paper)
　1. Management science—Computer simulatin.　I. Title.
　T57.62.P53 2004
　658.4′0352—dc22　　　　　　　　　　　　2004003361

British Library Cataloguing in Publication Data

A catalogue record for this book is available from the British Library

ISBN 0-470-09230-0

Project management by Originator, Gt Yarmouth, Norfolk (typeset in 10/12pt Photina)
Printed and bound in Great Britain by TJ International, Padstow, Cornwall
This book is printed on acid-free paper responsibly manufactured from sustainable forestry
in which at least two trees are planted for each one used for paper production.

Contents

For Sally, Karen and Helen who have been a constant encouragement during the two decades since I first proposed this book.

Preface to the Fifth Edition

As in the previous editions, this book is aimed at management science students and practitioners who need to learn how to conduct computer simulation studies. As before, its main focus is on simulation *modelling* and all the material is organized to that end. Since 1997, when I wrote the fourth edition, progress in computing and in computer simulation has continued apace. Hence the changes in this edition aim to keep the book up to date, whilst making whatever other improvements seem sensible. When I started work on the first edition in 1982 I had no idea that I would be working on a fifth edition over 20 years later. Much as software and hardware are upgraded every so often, so, it seems, are books.

A number of people have helped me in producing this fifth edition by suggesting improvements to the third edition. They include David Lane, Joyce Brown, Sarah Cope, Robert Fildes and Nuno Melao. John Crookes, though now retired, stimulated many of my original ideas and I am grateful to him for that. I acknowledge the help and encouragement of Sarah Booth and her colleagues at John Wiley & Sons and also the cooperation of Lanner Systems, Micro Analysis and Design and the Simul8 Corporation. To all these, thank you for your help—but I take the blame for any mistakes that remain.

Thanks to small laptop computers and the appalling timekeeping of the Virgin West Coast train company, much more of this edition has been written on trains than I had ever thought possible. Perhaps if they made more use of the modelling approaches described here, things would be better?

As before, the book is organized around three parts.

PART I: FUNDAMENTALS OF COMPUTER SIMULATION IN MANAGEMENT SCIENCE

There are four chapters in Part I and they provide a general introduction to the principles of computer simulation. Chapter 3, *Computer Simulation in Practice* suggests how a simulation study might be conducted. Chapter 4 is wholly new and discusses the use of static Monte Carlo methods in managing risk and uncertainty. The whole of Part I is deliberately non-technical and makes little or no demand on computing or statistical knowledge, other than the ability to use spreadsheets. It serves as an introduction to those who wish to follow the rest of the book in detail, but is also aimed at MBA and undergraduate business majors who wish to gain an overview of the subject.

PART II: DISCRETE EVENT SIMULATION

This is aimed at those readers who need to know how to produce valid, working discrete event simulation models. It covers four important aspects of discrete event simulation methods.

(1) *Discrete event modelling*: Chapter 5 introduces the general terminology of discrete event simulation and shows, in some detail, how different approaches may be implemented. This is then continued in Chapter 6 to show how the internals of discrete simulations can be programmed. Chapter 12 discusses the important issue of model testing and validation, something that is so often squeezed out in practice.

(2) *Computing aspects*: Chapters 7, 8 and 9 cover different aspects of computing that are related to discrete simulation. Chapter 7 shows how a three-phase simulation model may be easily implemented in almost any programming language. To support Chapter 7 I have made a set of three-phase libraries available in C, C++, Visual Basic, Turbo Pascal and Java. These can be found at `http://www.lancs.ac.uk/staff/smamp/`. I retain copyright but accept no responsibility for their use or misuse. Chapter 7 introduces two commonly used Visual Interactive Modelling Systems—Micro Saint and SIMUL8. Chapter 8 provides a review of the main types of software available for discrete event simulation.

(3) *Statistical aspects*: Chapters 10 and 11 are concerned with the statistical aspects of discrete event simulation and form the final section of Part II. They describe how sampling methods can be built into simulation models and how to disentangle the problems of experimentation that follow in their wake. To follow these chapters properly, the reader needs to understand basic probability and statistics.

(4) Chapter 12 discusses the important issue of model testing and validation, something that is so often squeezed out in practice. This chapter could also sit in Part III, which is why it is placed at the end of Part II.

PART III: SYSTEM DYNAMICS

The methods of system dynamics as first propounded by Jay Forrester are, in my opinion, still the most widely used formal simulation methods in management science after discrete event methods. Hence I have devoted three chapters to the topic and have attempted to provide a general introduction to its methodology in Chapter 14. Chapter 15 discusses the detail of the approach and Chapter 16 describes work carried out by Brian Parker in using the methods to tackle managerial problems.

Part I

Fundamentals of Computer Simulation in Management Science

1

The Computer
Simulation Approach

1.1 MODELS, EXPERIMENTS AND COMPUTERS

Management scientists are not easily separated from their computers and for good reason. Since the 1960s, computers have become smaller, cheaper, more powerful and easier to use by non-specialists. In particular, the development of powerful and cheap portable machines with excellent graphics has opened up wide areas of work for the management scientist. Modern computers allow the analyst to explore the whole range of feasible options in a decision problem. These options could be explored without a computer but the process would be very slow and the problem may well change significantly before a satisfactory solution is produced. With a computer, large amounts of data can be quickly processed and presented as a report. This is extremely valuable to the management scientist. One way in which a management scientist uses a computer is to simulate some system or other. This is generally done when it is impossible or inconvenient to find some other way of tackling the problem. In such simulations, a computer is used because of its speed in mimicking a system over a period of time. Again, most of these simulations could (in theory at least) be performed without a computer. But in most organizations, important problems have to be solved quickly: hence the use of computer simulation in management science.

Computer simulation methods have developed since the early 1960s and may well be the most commonly used of all the analytical tools of management science. The basic principles are simple enough. The analyst builds a model of the system of interest, writes computer programs that embody the model and uses a computer to imitate the system's behaviour when subject to a variety of operating policies. Thus, the most desirable policy may be selected.

For example, a biscuit company may wish to increase the throughput at a distribution depot. Suppose that the biscuits arrive at the depot on large articulated trucks and, are unloaded and transferred onto storage racks by forklift trucks. When required, the biscuits are removed from the racks and loaded onto small delivery vans for despatch to particular retail customers. To increase the throughput, a number of options might present themselves to the management. For example, they could:

(1)   Increase the number of loading or unloading bays.
(2)   Increase the number of forklift trucks.
(3)   Use new systems for handling the goods, etc.

It would be possible to experiment on the real depot by varying some of these factors but such trials would be expensive and time consuming.

The simulation approach to this problem involves the development of a model of the depot. The model is simply an unambiguous statement of the way in which the various components of the system (e.g., trucks and lorries) interact to produce the behaviour of the system. Once the model has been translated into a computer program the high speed of the computer allows a simulation of, say, six months in a few moments. The simulation could also be repeated with the various factors at different levels to see the effect of more loading bays, for example. In this way, the programmed model is used as the basis for experimentation. By doing so, many more options can be examined than would be possible in the real depot—and any disruption is avoided: hence the attraction of computer simulation methods.

To summarize, in a computer simulation we use the power of a computer to carry out experiments on a model of the system of interest. In most cases, such simulations could be done by hand—but few people would wish to do so. Now that computers offer significant power for a minimal cost, a computer simulation approach seems to make even more sense in management science.

1.2   SOME APPLICATIONS OF COMPUTER SIMULATION

Though it is impossible to be sure which techniques are most commonly used in management science, the occasional surveys of practitioners usually report simulation methods in the top three. This section briefly reviews some of the main application areas.

1.2.1   Manufacturing

As markets for manufactured goods have become globalized, manufacturers have increasingly attempted to mass customize their products. That is, they have sought economies of scale by developing products that will have global appeal and should sell in many countries. At the same time they have had to ensure that the products themselves are suited to local preferences, which means they have had to produce local variants of the global designs. This mass customization, sometimes known as glocalization, has placed great pressure on manufacturers to develop and install manufacturing systems that can deliver high volumes of high-quality goods at low cost to meet local needs. This has led to huge investments in manufacturing plant and associated control systems. It is important to ensure that such systems operate as intended, and therefore computer simulation methods have found an important place in the process of designing and implementing these manufacturing plant and systems.

Examples of this use of computer simulation occur across most manufacturing sectors and include food manufacturing (Pidd, 1987), semiconductor wafer fabrication (De Jong, 2001), beverages (Harrell, 1993), automobile manufacture (Ladbrook and Januszczak, 2001), aerospace (Lu and Sundaram, 2002), shipbuilding (Williams *et al.*, 2001) and materials handling (Burnett and LeBaron, 2001). Simulation allows the comparison of alternative designs and control policies on the model before starting to build the physical plant. It helps to reduce the cost and risk of large-scale errors. Simulation approaches are also used on existing plant to find better ways to operate, and these studies might be one-off exercises or may be part of a periodic check on the running of the system.

1.2.2 Health care

As with manufacturing, there is also a need to make effective use of limited resources when providing and delivering health care. Thus, simulation approaches have found widespread application in health care systems around the world. Hupert *et al.* (2002) discuss the distribution of antibiotics and vaccines to dispensing centres in the event of a terrorist attack. Ceric (1990) describes how the methods were used to plan a system to move goods and equipment around a large new hospital in an effective and efficient manner. McGuire (1994) reports on the use of simulation for the planning of effective emergency departments. In all such simulations, the idea was to test different policies without putting patients to inconvenience or placing them at risk. Simulation is also used to assess the effect of different treatment programmes. For example, Davies *et al.* (2002) used simulation to investigate ways in which the eyesight of diabetic patients can be more effectively preserved and Jacobsen *et al.* (2001) used it to assess the value of paediatric immunization programmes.

1.2.3 Business process re-engineering

Recent years have seen an increasing concern by businesses to ensure that their core processes are operated effectively and efficiently, and this has been the aim of business process re-engineering (BPR). In BPR the idea is to take a fundamental look at the basic processes without which the business could not function and which contribute in a major way to both profit and cost. In some ways, the stress on BPR mirrors the shift in manufacturing from batch production towards flow-line manufacturing. An example of a BPR exercise might be an investigation of the various operations and activities involved in delivering goods to a customer, and in invoicing that customer and in receiving payment. In a traditional system, the paperwork and computer-based documentation might need to pass through several different departments. Taking a radical look at such processes might lead to great simplification and thus to reduced costs and to better service. The aim of BPR is to take an integrated view of such activities and to find ways to provide a better service at lower cost by more effective organization.

Dennis *et al.* (2000) summarize some applications in the telecomms industry. Bhaskar *et al.* (1994) identify computer simulation as one of the key approaches to understanding how business processes might be re-engineered to improve performance. Davies (1994) describes how simulation has been used in BPR in the UK financial services industry. Companies providing these financial services in the UK must meet legal time limits for their responses to customers and must also carry out a series of checks required by law—in addition to their own internal monitoring. Davies (1994) developed a simulation model known as SCOPE to enable organizations to organze their office processes so as to achieve target performance levels. SCOPE works by simulating the flow of documents through the organization.

1.2.4   Transport systems

Computer simulation is also used in a wide range of transportation systems. As with other applications, the idea is to ensure that the system operates as efficiently and as effectively as possible. In the aviation sector, simulation methods have, for example, been used to help plan large passenger terminals. Airport terminals include systems for moving baggage and for ensuring that passengers can get to the departure gates in time for their planes, and a number of simulations have been used to assess their performance (e.g., Joustra and Van Dijk, 2001). Also in the aviation sector, air traffic control systems are used to ensure that air space is used efficiently and safely. As part of this, the air traffic controllers must ensure that the movement of aircraft is planned in advance and then managed in real time. Simulation approaches have made a great contribution to safer and more cost-effective air traffic control (e.g., Lee *et al.*, 2001).

The shipping sector has also been a long-term user of computer methods. Indeed, one of the computer simulation programming languages (CSL; Buxton and Laski, 1962) was first developed by Esso (predecessor of Exxon) to support simulations of the movement of crude and refined oil around the world. Shipping applications continue to this day and an example is given in Heath (1993).

Salt (1991) reports how simulation methods were used to help plan the movement of traffic in the Channel Tunnel that links the UK and France. Though the introduction of this service was controversial, it is clear that one key to its future success is the reliability of the service that it offers. Unlike the ferries which also ply the route, bad weather should not prevent the operation of the tunnel service. It was therefore crucial that its operations were properly planned and managed. Salt (op cit) gives interesting examples of how this was supported by computer simulation approaches.

The road transport sector is also a major user of computer simulation methods both to plan individual companies' operations and to investigate road traffic systems in general. Traffic simulators are now a standard part of the armoury of road traffic planners (Pidd, 1995; Rathi and Santiago, 1990; Young *et al.*, 1989) since they permit possible road configurations and traffic management schemes to be refined before their physical implementation.

1.2.5 Defence

The defence sector is also a major user of simulation methods and the Proceedings of the Winter Simulation Conference usually include a range of papers discussing work in this area (e.g., see Robinson, 2001). Applications range from studies of logistics operations through to battle simulations, which investigate possible strategies and tactics to be used in defence or attack. Their appeal here is obvious; no battle commander wishes to be defeated and the chance to develop tactics beforehand and to prepare countermeasures is of some importance. Not surprisingly, the majority of defence simulations are not reported in the open literature.

1.3 MODELS IN MANAGEMENT SCIENCE

Models of various types are often used in management science. They are representations of the system of interest and are used to investigate possible improvements in the real system or to discover the effect of different policies on that system. This is not the place for a detailed exposition of modelling; for this the reader should consult Miser and Quade (1988), Pidd (2003), Rivett (1994), or White (1975). However, some mention of the topic is necessary.

The simplest type of model employed in management is probably a scale model, possibly of a building. By using scale models it is possible to plan sensible layouts of warehouses, factories, offices, etc. In a scale model, physical properties are simply changed in scale and the relationship of the model to the full-scale system is usually obvious. However, such simple scale models do have significant disadvantages.

First, a scale model is concrete in form and highly specific. No one would contemplate using the same scale model for a chemical factory and a school—the two require distinctly different buildings. More subtly, to experiment with a scale model always requires physical alteration of the model. This can be tiresome and expensive.

Second, scale models are static. That is, they cannot show how the various factors interact dynamically. For example, suppose that a warehouse is being designed. One issue that must be considered is the relationship between the internal capacity of the building and the number of loading or unloading bays provided for vehicles. Though it is easy to design a warehouse that always has enough internal space—simply make it too big—this is clearly a waste of money. Given that both the demand for the products and the production level will vary, the art is to design a building that balances the cost of shortages with the cost of over capacity. Such a balance will vary over time, particularly for seasonal products. No scale model could consider this.

Management scientists tend to employ mathematical and logical models rather than scale models. Mathematical models represent the important factors of a system by a series of equations that may sometimes be solved to produce an optimal solution. Many of the commonly employed techniques described in management science textbooks are of this form (e.g., mathematical programming, game theory, etc.). For computer simulation, logical models are usually required—though in the case of system dynamics (see Chapters 13 to 15) these are expressed in a mathematical form. The simplest way of thinking about logical models is to consider flow diagrams of various kinds. Industrial engineers often employ flow process charts in method study (Slack *et al.*, 1995) to display the various processes through which products pass in their manufacture and assembly. That is, the charts display the logic of the production process. Such a chart might show that a car body needs to be thoroughly degreased before any painting can begin. Instead of drawing a chart it is possible to represent the logic as a set of instructions. If these directions are clear and unambiguous, then they could be used to show someone how to do the job.

Modern digital computers are logical machines that obey a sequence of instructions, thus any sequence of instructions can form the basis of a computer program—which makes computer simulation possible. At some stage the simulation model, which may initially exist on scraps of paper, in agreed documents or in some formal set of flow diagrams, must be translated into a form that a computer can recognize and obey. Once in a computable form, the model may be easily modified so as to permit a wide range of options to be compared in simulation experiments.

1.4 SIMULATION AS EXPERIMENTATION

Computer simulation involves experimentation on a computer-based model of some system. The model is used as a vehicle for experimentation, often in a "trial and error" way to demonstrate the likely effects of various policies. Those that produce the best results in the model would be candidates for implementation in the real system. Figure 1.1 shows the basic idea.

Sometimes these experiments may be quite sophisticated, involving the use of statistical design techniques. Such sophistication is necessary if there is a set of different effects that may be produced in the results by several interacting policies. At the other extreme, the experimentation may be very simple, taking the form of "what if?" questions. Thus, if the simulation model

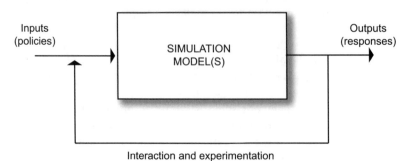

Figure 1.1 Simulation as experimentation

represents the financial flows in an organization over the next 12 months, typical questions might be:

- "What if interest rates rise by 3%?"
- "What if the market grows by 5% this year?"

To answer these questions, the simulation is carried out with the appropriate variables of the program set to these values.

1.5 WHY SIMULATE?

[Certainly, computer simulation is no panacea. Realistic simulations may require long computer programs of some complexity. There are special purpose simulation languages and packaged systems available to ease this task, but it is still rarely simple. Consequently, producing useful results from a computer simulation can turn out to be a surprisingly time-consuming process. In one way, therefore, computer simulation should be regarded as a last resort—to be used if all else fails. However, there are certain advantages in employing a simulation approach in management science and it may be the only way of tackling some problems.]

Assuming that a management scientist does not wish to make an instant "seat of the pants" judgement of a particular problem, various modes of approach are possible. First, it may be possible to conduct experiments directly on the real system. For example, the police may experiment with mock radar speed traps to see if this reduces the number and severity of accidents reported. Second, the analyst may be able to construct and use a mathematical model of the system of interest. For example, Thomas *et al.* (2001) describe how mathematical programming techniques are used in credit scoring and Wright (1994) describes how heuristics are used to timetable English cricket. A third possibility is to simulate the system.

1.5.1 Simulation versus direct experimentation

Then why simulate when it will be time consuming and there may be alternative approaches? Considered against real experimentation, simulation has the following advantages:

- *Cost.* Though simulation can be time consuming and therefore expensive in terms of skilled manpower, real experiments may also turn out to be expensive—particularly if something goes wrong!
- *Time.* Admittedly, it takes a significant amount of time to produce working computer programs for simulation models. However, once these are written then an attractive opportunity presents itself. Namely it is possible to simulate weeks, months or even years in seconds of computer time. Hence a whole range of policies may be properly compared.

- *Replication.* Unfortunately, the real world is rarely kind enough to allow precise replication of an experiment. One of the skills employed by physical scientists is the design of experiments that are repeatable by other scientists. This is rarely possible in management science. It seems unlikely that an organization's competitors will sit idly by as a whole variety of pricing policies are attempted in a bid to find the best. It is even less likely that a military adversary will allow a replay of a battle. Simulations are precisely repeatable.
- *Safety.* One of the objectives of a simulation study may be to estimate the effect of extreme conditions, and to do this in real life may be dangerous or even illegal. An airport authority may take some persuading to allow a doubling of the flights per day even if they do wish to know the capacity of the airport. Simulated aircraft cause little damage when they run out of fuel in the simulated sky.
- *Legality.* Even when not employed by the mafia there are times when an analyst may wish to investigate the effect of changes in legislation. For example, a company may wish to see what the effect would be on its delivery performance of changes in the laws that control drivers hours of work.

1.5.2 Simulation versus mathematical modelling

What, then, of the other possibility of building and using a mathematical model of the system? Here too there are problems. First, most mathematical models cannot satisfactorily cope with dynamic or transient effects and operate instead with average values. However, in any dynamic system, steady state values can be very misleading, particularly if there is statistical variation in demand. Even though average demand is met, this may not be true of peak demand. The challenge is to design such systems to meet reasonable demand without having idle resources "just in case". Thus, the model may need to take account of the statistical variation that is inherent in many systems. Second, though it is debatable (see Chapter 10) whether this is a good thing, it is possible to sample from non-standard probability distributions in a simulation model. However, queuing theory models permit only certain distributions and therefore cannot cope with many types of problem.

Computer simulation then may well be regarded as the last resort. Despite this, it is surprising how often such an approach is needed.

1.6   SUMMARY

Computer simulation methods allow experimentation on a computer-based model of some system. The model is built by carefully describing the ways in which the system changes state and the rules that govern its dynamic behaviour. Modelling is best planned on an incremental and parsimonious basis, with the expectation that the model will need to be enhanced as knowledge about the system develops. Once built, the model is used for experimentation, either interactive or classical or both.

EXERCISES

(1) Suppose that a public authority is considering various policies for checking whether goods vehicles are overweight as they arrive at ferry ports. Discuss whether it might be sensible to consider a simulation approach.
(2) In what types of situation would a simulation approach be unwise?
(3) Spreadsheet packages such as Microsoft Excel™ are widely used on personal computers. Discuss what type of simulation these packages allow.
(4) If you were the manager of a factory whose production operations were being simulated by a management scientist, why might you not be convinced that the simulation model was valid even if the production rates output from the simulation were the same as those of your factory?
(5) Consider the reasons why simulation approaches often form part of the process of designing new manufacturing systems.
(6) Computers are becoming easier to use by non-specialists. Should managers be encouraged to undertake computer simulations themselves or is there still a place for the specialist?

REFERENCES

Bhaskar R., Lee H.S., Levas A., Pétrakian R., Tsai F. and Tulskie W. (1994) Analyzing a re-engineering business processes using simulation. *Proceedings of the 1994 Winter Simulation Conference, December 1994, Lake Bueno Vista, Florida.*

Burnett D. and LeBaron T. (2001) Efficiently modeling warehouse systems. In: B.A. Peters, J.S. Smith, D.J. Medeiros and M.W. Rohrer (eds), *Proceedings of the 2001 Winter Simulation Conference, December 2001, Arlington, VA.*

Buxton J.N. and Laski J.G. (1962) Control and simulation language. *The Computer Journal,* **5**, 3.

Ceric V. (1990) Simulation study of an automated guided-vehicle system in a Yugoslav hospital. *Journal of the Operational Research Society,* **41**(4), 299–310.

Davies M.N. (1994) Back-office process management in the financial services—a simulation approach using a model generator. *Journal of the Operational Research Society,* **45**(12), 1363–73.

Davies R., Roderick P., Brailsford S.C. and Canning C. (2002). The use of simulation to evaluate screening policies for diabetic retinopathy. *Diabetic Medicine,* **19**(9), 763–71.

De Jong C.D. (2001) Simulating test program methods in semiconductor assembly test factories. In: B.A. Peters, J.S. Smith, D.J. Medeiros, and M.W. Rohrer (eds), *Proceedings of the 2001 Winter Simulation Conference, December 2004, Arlington, VA.*

Dennis S., King B., Hind M. and Robinson S.R. (2000) Applications of business process simulation and lean techniques in British Telecommunications plc. In: K. Kang, J.A. Joines, and R.R. Barton (eds), *Proceedings of the 2000 Winter Simulation Conference, Orlando, FL.*

Harrell C.R. (1993) Modeling beverage processing using discrete event simulation. *Proceedings of the 1993 Winter Simulation Conference, December 2000, Los Angeles, CA.*

Heath W. (1993) Waterfront capacity-planning simulations. *Proceedings of the 1993 Winter Simulation Conference, Los Angeles, CA.*

Hupert N., Mushlin A.I. and Callahan M.A. (2002) Modeling the public health response to bioterrorism: Using discrete event simulation to design antibiotic distribution centers. *Medical Decision Making,* **22**(Suppl.), S17–S25.

Jacobson S.H., Sewell E.C. and Weniger W.G. (2001) Using Monte Carlo simulation to assess the value of combination vaccines for pediatric immunization. In: B.A. Peters, J.S. Smith, D.J. Medeiros, and M.W. Rohrer (eds), *Proceedings of the 2001 Winter Simulation Conference, December 2001, Arlington, VA.*

Joustra P.E. and Van Dijk N.M. (2001) Simulation of check-in at airports. In: B.A. Peters, J.S. Smith, D.J. Medeiros, and M.W. Rohrer (eds), *Proceedings of the 2001 Winter Simulation Conference, December 2001, Arlington, VA.*

Ladbrook J. and Januszczak A. (2001) Ford's power train operations—changing the simulation environment. In: B.A. Peters, J.S. Smith, D.J. Medeiros, and M.W. Rohrer (eds), *Proceedings of the 2001 Winter Simulation Conference, December 2001, Arlington, VA.*

Lee S., Pritchett A. and Goldsman D. (2001) Hybrid agent-based simulation for analyzing the national airspace system. In: B.A. Peters, J.S. Smith, D.J. Medeiros, and M.W. Rohrer (eds), *Proceedings of the 2001 Winter Simulation Conference, December 2001, Arlington, VA.*

Lu R.F. and Sundaram S. (2002) Manufacturing process modeling of Boeing 747 moving line concepts. In: J.M. Charnes, E. Yücesan and C.-H. Chen (eds), *Proceedings of the 2002 Winter Simulation Conference, December 2001, San Diego, CA.*

McGuire F. (1994) Using simulation to reduce lengths of stay in emergency departments. *Proceedings of the 1994 Winter Simulation Conference, December 1994, Lake Bueno Vista, Florida.*

Miser H.J. and Quade E.S. (eds) (1988) *Handbook of Systems Analysis: Craft Issues and Procedural Choices.* John Wiley & Sons, Chichester, UK.

Pidd M. (1987) Simulating automated food plants. *Journal of Operational Research Society,* **38**(8), 683–92.

Pidd M. (1995) The construction of an object-oriented traffic simulator. *Proceedings of the 3rd EURO Working Group on Transportation, September 1995, Barcelona, Spain.*

Pidd M. (2003) *Tools for Thinking: Modelling in Management Science* (2nd edition). John Wiley & Sons, Chichester, UK.

Rathi A.K. and Santiago A.J. (1990) The new NETSIM simulation model. *Traffic Engineering and Control*, **31**(5), 317.

Rivett B.H.P. (1994) *The Craft of Decision Modelling*. John Wiley & Sons, Chichester, UK.

Robinson T. (2001) ODIN—An underwater warfare simulation environment. In: B.A. Peters, J.S. Smith, D.J. Medeiros, and M.W. Rohrer (eds), *Proceedings of the 2001 Winter Simulation Conference, December 2001, Arlington, VA.*

Salt J. (1991) Tunnel vision. *ORIMS Today*, **18**(1), 42–8.

Slack N., Chambers S., Harland C. and Johnston R. (1995) *Operations Management*. Pitman, London.

Thomas L.C., Banasik J. and Crook J.N. (2001) Recalibrating scorecards. *Journal of Operational Research Society*, **52**, 981–8.

White D. J. (1975) *Decision Methodology*. John Wiley & Sons, Chichester, UK.

Williams D.L., Finke D.A., Medeiros D.J. and Traband M. T. (2001) Discrete simulation development for a proposed shipyard steel processing facility. In: B.A. Peters, J.S. Smith, D.J. Medeiros, and M.W. Rohrer (eds), *Proceedings of the 2001 Winter Simulation Conference, Arlington, VA.*

Wright M.B. (1994) Timetabling county cricket fixtures using a form of tabu search. *Journal of the Operational Research Society*, **45**(7), 758–71.

Young W., Taylor M.A.P. and Gipps P.G. (1989) *Microcomputers in Traffic Engineering*. John Wiley & Sons/Research Studies Press, Chichester, UK.

2

A Variety of
Modelling Approaches

2.1 GENERAL CONSIDERATIONS

Before producing a dynamic simulation model and thus a computer program, the analyst must decide on the principal elements of that model, bearing two things in mind. The first is the nature of the system being simulated— obviously, the model needs to be a close fit, a good representation of the system. Needless to say, some modelling approaches are more suited to certain problems than to others. The second aspect is the nature of the study being carried out. That is, what are the objectives of the study, what is the point of the simulation, what results are expected? Considering both of these aspects will allow the analyst to decide what level of accuracy and detail is appropriate for the simulation. There is clearly little point in producing an extremely detailed simulation if only crude estimates are required. The practical decisions that need to be made concern the following, each of which will be considered in this chapter:

- Time handling.
- Stochastic or deterministic durations.
- Discrete or continuous change.

2.2 TIME HANDLING

One advantage of simulation is that the speed at which the experiment proceeds can be controlled. The essence of a dynamic simulation is that the state changes of the system are modelled through time. In management science it is usual to speed up the passage of time so as to simulate several weeks or months in a few minutes of computer time. Hence it is important to consider how time-flow might be handled within the simulation.

2.2.1 Time slicing

Perhaps the simplest way of controlling the flow of time in a simulation is to move it forward in equal time intervals. This approach is often described as

Table 2.1   Job shop order book

Job number	Batch size	Day order expected
1	200	1
2	400	8
3	100	14
4	200	18

"time slicing" and involves updating and examining the model at regular intervals. Thus, for a time slice of length dt, the model is updated at time $(t + dt)$ for changes occurring in the interval $(t$ to $(t + dt))$.

One obvious problem with this approach is that some decision must be taken about the length of the time slice before the simulation is carried out. For example, the activity levels within a supertanker terminal may necessitate a time slice of one hour, whereas for a civil airport the time slice may be more appropriately set to a half minute or less. Clearly, if the time slice is too large then the behaviour of the model is much coarser than that of the real system because it is impossible to simulate some of the state changes that occur. If, on the other hand, the time slice is too small then the model is frequently examined unnecessarily (when no state changes are possible) and this leads to excessively long computer runs.

As a simple example (based on an example in Jones, 1975)* consider a workshop with just two machines, A and B. Suppose that the time taken to complete a job on these machines depends on the size of the job. Thus the job times are:

- Machine A: (batch size$/50 + 1$) days.
- Machine B: (batch size$/100 + 3$) days.

Suppose too that the workshop only takes on jobs which must be processed on both machines and that each job must first pass through machine A as a complete batch and then through machine B as a complete batch. That is, no batch may be started on either machine until the previous batch is completed on that machine. If the workshop expects to receive the four orders shown in Table 2.1, when will the final batch be complete? The expected job times (days) are as shown in Table 2.2. Simulating the workshop using a time slice of one day leads to the times shown in Table 2.3. Thus job 4 is complete at the end of day 32.

Following this table through; on day 1, job 1 arrives and its processing immediately begins on machine A. Nothing new happens on days 2, 3 or 4 until the end of day 5 when machine A has finished job 1. Thus on day 6, machine B starts work on job 1.

On day 7 nothing happens. On day 8, job 2 arrives and machine A begins its

* This example is reproduced in revised form with permission from the Open University from T341 *Systems Modelling*: Unit 6 Simulation Modelling. © 1975 The Open University Press.

Table 2.2 Expected job times

Job number	Machine A	Machine B
1	5	5
2	9	7
3	3	4
4	5	5

Table 2.3 Job shop: time-slicing simulation

	Jobs queuing		Jobs in progress			Jobs queuing		Jobs in progress	
Day	For machine A	For machine B	Machine A	Machine B	Day	For machine A	For machine B	Machine A	Machine B
1	—	—	1	—	17	—	—	3	2
2	—	—	1	—	18	4	—	3	2
3	—	—	1	—	19	4	—	3	2
4	—	—	1	—	20	—	3	4	2
5	—	—	1	—	21	—	3	4	2
6	—	—	—	1	22	—	3	4	2
7	—	—	—	1	23	—	3	4	2
8	—	—	2	1	24	—	—	4	3
9	—	—	2	1	25	—	4	—	3
10	—	—	2	1	26	—	4	—	3
11	—	—	2	—	27	—	4	—	3
12	—	—	2	—	28	—	—	—	4
13	—	—	2	—	29	—	—	—	4
14	3	—	2	—	30	—	—	—	4
15	3	—	2	—	31	—	—	—	4
16	3	—	2	—	32	—	—	—	4

processing. This is obviously a tedious and inefficient way of simulating such a simple system, for there is little point in examining and attempting to update the model each day—on many days, nothing changes.

2.2.2 Next-event technique

Because many systems include such slack periods of varying length it is often preferable to use a variable time increment. In this case, the model is only examined and updated when it is known that a state change is due. These state changes are usually called events and, because time is moved from event to event, the approach is called the next-event technique.

Consider again the simple workshop. Table 2.4 shows the results of a next-event simulation of this system. Notice that the table is much smaller than that required for a time-slicing approach. The method focuses on the progress of each job as it passes through the workshop. The events are:

- A job arrives.
- Machine A starts a job.

Table 2.4   Job-shop: next-event simulation

		Machine A		Machine B	
Job No.	Arrival date	Start	Finish	Start	Finish
1	1	1	5	6	10
2	8	8	16	17	23
3	14	17	19	24	27
4	16	20	24	28	32

- Machine A finishes a job.
- Machine B starts a job.
- Machine B finishes a job.

Each of these events may occur a maximum of four times during the simulation, once for each job. In fact, as Table 2.4 shows, some of these coincide and the model need only be updated on 16 occasions. By way of contrast, Table 2.3 shows the inevitable 32 updates of a time-slicing approach. Though the halving of the number of state changes is only a feature of this example, a next-event model will usually require fewer state changes than one employing time slicing.

2.2.3   Time slicing or next event?

Thus, a next-event technique has two advantages over a time-slicing approach. The first is that the time increment automatically adjusts to periods of high and low activity, thus avoiding wasteful and unnecessary checking of the state of the model. The second is that it makes clear when significant events have occurred in the simulation. On the other hand, the simulation software that drives the simulation must be more intelligent, since it must manage a diary of future events. This means that it must hold more information than is needed for a time-slicing simulation. However, unless the actual events of a system do occur at regular intervals, a next-event technique is usually better. Of course, some systems have events that occur at regular intervals. For example, a superstore may check its stock levels at the same time each day and replenishment may similarly arrive at predictable times. In such cases it is quite adequate to update the model at regular intervals to allow for the intervening changes. Nevertheless, it should be noted that the next-event technique is more general since, if the events in a system occur at regular intervals (once per day, perhaps), the next-event technique will act as if it were a time-slicing approach. The reverse is not true.

2.3   STOCHASTIC OR DETERMINISTIC?

A system is deterministic if its behaviour is entirely predictable. Provided that the system is perfectly understood, then it is possible to predict precisely what will happen. A cycle of operations on an automatic machine may be deterministic in this sense. Each repeated identical cycle will take the same length of time unless the conditions influencing the cycle times are altered.

A system is stochastic if its behaviour cannot be entirely predicted, though some statement may be made about how likely certain events are to occur. For example, a lecturer may give the same lecture to several sets of students but the duration of the lecture may vary from occasion to occasion. Statistical statements may be made about the duration of the lecture: for example, that it is normally distributed with a mean of 50 minutes and a standard deviation of 3 minutes. Thus it is highly likely that the duration of the lecture will exceed 48 minutes. However, it is impossible to precisely state how long a particular delivery of the lecture will last unless the lecturer's behaviour can be completely controlled—and that of the class too!

In some senses, the distinction between stochastic and deterministic systems is artificial. It is more a statement of the amount of knowledge about a system or the amount of control over that system exercised by an observer. However, it is important to notice that both stochastic and deterministic simulations are possible.

2.3.1 Deterministic simulation: a time-slicing example

Any deterministic simulation model contains no stochastic elements and a simple example was the four-job simulation of the workshop of Section 2.2. As another example, this time one which can be formulated as a set of difference equations, consider the case of Big Al and his recruitment problems.

After his release from gaol (jail), Big Al, a well known gangster, decides to rebuild his mob for more assaults on the banks of Bailrigg County. This time he plans a large-scale operation and reckons that he would like to have 50 mobsters working for him within six months. He currently has none.

His previous experience in forming a mob suggests that he can recruit at a weekly rate equal to one quarter of the difference between his ideal mob size (50) and the number currently in the mob. His problem is that mobsters are caught by the cops with depressing frequency. Indeed, Happy Harry, chief of the Bailrigg County cops, boasts that his men will catch 5% of Big Al's active mobsters in each week and they receive gaol sentences of at least 12 months each. Fortunately, 10% of those in gaol escape each week and rejoin Big Al's mob. Big Al himself has other ways to satisfy the needs of the local police and does not expect to be arrested again. How large will his mob size be after 10 weeks?

One approach to Big Al's problem is to use a simple time-sliced simulation based on a two-part set of difference equations. To do this requires some variables to be defined.

Variables

Suppose that any 2-week interval can be represented as starting at time $t - 1$ (the first weekend), with an intervening weekend at time t and a final weekend at time $t + 1$. Variables of two types may now be defined.

(1) *Aggregated values at definite time points*
Consider the time point t

     Mob size $= MS_t$
     Number in gaol $= NG_t$

(2) *Variables which represent rates which are constant over an interval*
Consider the interval $t - 1$ to t

     Al's recruitment rate $= REC_{t-1,t}$
     The rate at which gangsters are arrested $= ARR_{t-1,t}$
     The rate at which gangsters escape from gaol $= ESC_{t-1,t}$
     The target mob size is a constant, $TARGET$

Hence, the following equations can be formulated:

(1) *Aggregated values at time t*

$$MS_t = MS_{t-1} + (REC_{t-1,t} - ARR_{t-1,t}) + ESC_{t-1,t}$$
$$NG_t = NG_{t-1} + (ARR_{t-1,t} - ESC_{t-1,t})$$

That is, the value of MS at time t is the value of MS at time $t - 1$, plus the changes that occur over the interval $t - 1$ to t. The latter is number of recruits, plus the number of escapees, minus the number of mobsters arrested over that interval.

(2) *Constant rates over the next week*

$$REC_{t,t+1} = (TARGET - MS_t)/4$$
$$ARR_{t,t+1} = MS_t{}^*0.05$$
$$ESC_{t,t+1} = NG_t/10$$

The system may now be simulated using a simple spreadsheet in which the columns represent the different variables and the rows represent the time points (weekends). The four constants, $TARGET$ and the three numerical parameters, can be placed as values on the spreadsheet to make experimentation rather easier.

The number in gaol and the mob size need to be specified for time point 0 (just before the start of week 1) and then the normal spreadsheet-linked computations can be employed. To check the computations by hand, do the following. Starting with time point $t = 0$:

(1) Write down the values of the mob size (MS) and number in gaol (NG).
(2) Write down the rates (recruitment, arrest, escape) over the next interval.

Move time to the next point ($t = 1$) and repeat; continue with $t = 2, 3, \ldots, 10$.

The results of the simulation for a 10-week period are shown in Table 2.5 and in Figure 2.1. Table 2.5 is slightly deceptive, for it hides the fact that the rates are actually computed over intervals of length dt, which is 1 week in this case, rather than at the time points 0, 1, 2, etc. Strictly speaking, these rate values should be printed in alternate lines, between the other values. It is

Table 2.5 Big Al's recruitment problem

Week	Recruit rate	Arrest rate	Escape rate	No. in gaol	Mob size
0				0.00	0.00
1	12.50	0.00	0.00	0.00	12.50
2	9.38	0.63	0.00	0.63	21.25
3	7.19	1.06	0.06	1.63	27.44
4	5.64	1.37	0.16	2.83	31.87
5	4.53	1.59	0.28	4.14	35.09
6	3.73	1.75	0.41	5.48	37.48
7	3.13	1.87	0.55	6.81	39.28
8	2.68	1.96	0.68	8.09	40.68
9	2.33	2.03	0.81	9.32	41.78
10	2.05	2.09	0.93	10.48	42.68

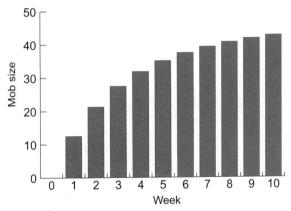

Figure 2.1 Big Al's mob size

clear that Big Al does not reach his target of 50 mobsters within ten weeks. Indeed, he may have trouble over a much longer period due to the fact that the recruitment rate is a function of the gap between the target and actual mob sizes. To get to 50 he may need to find other incentives.

There is one obvious problem about this model. It uses real values but even gangsters prefer to be treated as integers.

2.3.2 Stochastic simulation

Many systems behave stochastically and must therefore be simulated by a model with stochastic elements. This means that probability distributions are used in such stochastic simulation models. As the simulation proceeds, samples are taken from these distributions so as to mimic the stochastic behaviour. As an example, consider the following replacement problem.

A multi-user computer system includes two disk units which, being mechanical, are prone to failure. If a disk unit fails in service, users lose their files

Table 2.6 Probability of disk unit failure

Days since repair or maintenance	Probability of failure
1	0.05
2	0.15
3	0.20
4	0.30
5	0.20
6	0.10
>6	0.00

(and their tempers) which need to be restored. Restoration is achieved by copying on to the disk back-up copies of the files held on magnetic tapes. This restoration is inconvenient and so a new operating policy is being considered. At the moment, the disk units are repaired and restored as and when they fail. The proposal is to introduce a joint repair system. Table 2.6 shows the probability of a disk unit failing in the days following its last repair. That is, 5% of the units are expected to fail 1 day after repair or maintenance, 15% after 2 days, etc.

Under the current repair policy, it costs $50 per disk to repair and restore a failed unit. The joint repair system would operate as follows. When either unit fails, the failed unit is repaired and restored at a cost of $50 per unit. If operational, the other unit will be cleaned at a cost of $25. Cleaning a disk places it in a state equivalent to having been just repaired and restored. Is the new joint repair system cost effective?

This question can be answered by a simple stochastic simulation which involves random sampling from the failure distribution of the disks given earlier. Details of sampling methods are given in Chapter 10, but for present purposes a simple method can be used. Figure 2.2 shows a histogram of the disk failure distribution. In Figure 2.3, the data have been rearranged to show the cumulative probability of the various lives. For example, the probability of a disk lasting up to and including 3 days is 0.40

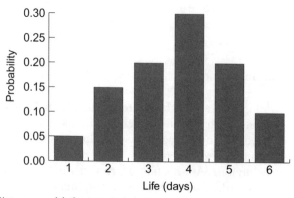

Figure 2.2 Histogram of failure probabilities

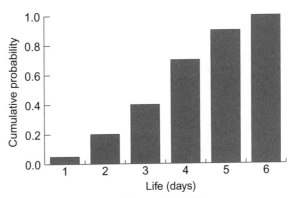

Figure 2.3   Histogram of cumulative failure probabilities

$(0.05 + 0.15 + 0.20)$. Using the cumulative form of Figure 2.3 and random number tables, random samples can be taken from the life distribution by associating a life (in days) with each random number.

An extract from a random number table is shown in Table 2.7, the values range from 00 to 99, and any number in that range has an equal probability of appearing at any position in the table. If these random numbers are divided by 100, so that their range is 0.00 to 0.99, then Figure 2.3 may be used to generate random samples as follows. The first random number in the table is 27 (i.e., 0.27); if this is marked on the vertical axis of Figure 2.3, then the corresponding point on the horizontal axis is 3 days. That is, 3 days is the life associated with the random number 0.27. In general, each life may be associated with a range of random numbers as shown in Table 2.8.

Table 2.9 shows a 50-day simulation of the two policies. In the case of the separate replacement policy, replacements of each of the two units have been

Table 2.7   Some random numbers

27	62	36	30	57	78	22	02	89	22
04	97	43	30	45	12	03	87	16	50
92	26	00	82	58	10	78	44	55	05
21	50	49	83	49	39	25	81	03	99
77	71	43	06	90	09	04	97	07	64
40	39	69	42	63	80	07	85	65	70
60	57	42	97	29	92	84	54	66	91
34	10	78	81	97	99	08	19	15	63
35	37	13	56	88	09	36	40	07	55
04	24	69	52	44	14	61	59	31	50
24	26	29	31	57	17	38	44	03	29
26	63	00	44	64	09	93	15	52	35
91	37	65	32	84	37	80	94	48	46
23	52	10	77	27	40	34	13	73	53
55	89	99	78	50	11	43	43	54	16

Table 2.8   Look-up table linking random numbers and disk life

Life (days)	Associated random numbers
1	0.00–0.04
2	0.05–0.19
3	0.20–0.39
4	0.40–0.69
5	0.70–0.89
6	0.90–0.99

Table 2.9   Next-event simulation of the disk repair policies

	Separate repair						Joint repair
	Unit A			Unit B			
	Random number	Life	Time of failure	Random number	Life	Time of failure	Time of failure
1	0.27	3	3	0.24	3	3	3
2	0.62	4	7	0.26	3	6	6
3	0.36	3	10	0.29	3	9	9
4	0.30	3	13	0.31	3	12	12
5	0.57	4	17	0.57	4	16	16
6	0.04	1	18	0.26	3	19	17
7	0.97	6	24	0.63	4	23	21
8	0.43	4	28	0.00	1	24	22
9	0.30	3	31	0.44	4	28	25
10	0.45	4	35	0.64	4	32	29
11	0.92	6	41	0.91	6	38	35
12	0.26	3	44	0.37	3	41	38
13	0.00	1	45	0.65	4	45	39
14	0.82	5	50	0.32	3	48	42
15	0.58	4		0.84	5	53	46
16	0.21	3		0.23	3		49
17	0.50	4		0.52	4		53
18	0.49	4		0.10	2		
19	0.83	5		0.77	5		
20	0.49	4		0.27	3		

simulated until the failure time (the cumulative life) of each is greater than or equal to 50 days. For this policy, unit A needed 14 repairs and restores; unit B needed 15. Hence, 29 units were used at a cost of $50 per unit, giving a total cost of $1450 over 50 days.

Exactly the same random numbers are used to simulate the second policy, which is also shown in Table 2.9. In this case, the units are considered in pairs. Hence, starting at time zero, the first A unit would last for 3 days if allowed to do so, as would the first B unit. In this case, therefore the first replacement takes place after 3 days. The second pair would last 4 days (in the case of A) and 3 days (in the case of B). Hence the second replacement will take place 3 days after the first (i.e., after 6 days). The simulation continues in this way until the replacement time (the joint cumulative life) is at or greater than 50 days. This shows that there were 17 such joint repairs in the period and that, of these 17, 9 involved both units in repair and restore (i.e., they both failed at the same time—coincidences). The other 8 of the 17 involved one unit in a repair and restore, whilst the other need only be cleaned. Hence, there were 26 repairs and restores at $50 per unit and 8 clean-ups at $25 per unit. Giving a total cost of $1500.

Thus on the basis of a single simulation, the new policy costs $50 more over a 50-day period. However, it would be wrong to assume that a separate repair policy is therefore more cost effective. If a different set of random numbers were used, the result could have been different for both policies and the new policy might appear cheaper. Chapter 4 returns again to this issue in its discussion of static Monte Carlo simulations.

In stochastic simulations, it is important to realize that the results are dependent on the samples taken. Hence it is usual to make several simulation runs each with a distinct sampling pattern before drawing any conclusions. Chapter 11 gives details. The sampling methods employed in stochastic simulations are well developed and documented. Commonly used methods are given in Chapter 10 and most simulation software systems have appropriate subroutines or procedures ready for use. Thus distribution sampling should not be a problem in model building. More likely, controlling the sequence of events is the major problem in model building. The interaction of the entities is responsible for the sequence of events, and in the above example these are trivial. But for complex systems a sensible structure is needed. Various common approaches are described in Chapters 5 and 6.

Distributions.

2.4 DISCRETE OR CONTINUOUS CHANGE?

In the job shop simulation, it was convenient to regard the system as moving from state to state through time. The concern with individual batches was whether their machining was complete or not, rather than with the rate at which the machining was proceeding. The variables included in a simulation model can be thought of as changing value in four ways:

(1) *Continuously at any point of time.* Thus, the values are changing smoothly and not discretely and the values taken are accessible at any time point within the simulation.
(2) *Continuously but only at discrete time points.* In this mode, the values again change smoothly but can only be accessed at predetermined times.
(3) *Discretely at any point of time.* In these simulations, state changes are easily identifiable but can occur at any point of time.

(4) *Discretely and only at discrete points of time.* The state changes can only occur at specified points of time.

Historically, computer simulation applications have tended to divide into those employing discrete change and those that allow the variables to continuously change value.

2.4.1   Discrete change

Consider an underground railway in which trains move from station to station, picking up and depositing passengers at each. Viewed from the perspective of discrete change there are a number of obvious system events. For example:

- Train stops at station.
- Doors now open.
- Doors now closed.
- Train starts to leave station.

Thus to simulate this system using a discrete model, the time taken to travel between stations or to open the doors would either be known deterministically or could be sampled from some appropriate distribution. Thus, for example, when the train starts to leave a station its arrival at the next station could be scheduled by referring to this "known" journey time. In a discrete simulation the variables are only of interest as and when they point to a change in the state of the system. Chapters 5 to 7 are devoted to the exposition of methods suitable for discrete simulation.

2.4.2   Continuous change

If the underground railway were to be simulated via a model that allowed continuous change, then the variables would be continuously changing their values as the simulation proceeds. Consider, for example, the train as it travels between stations. If the locomotive is electrically powered, its speed will increase smoothly from rest until it reaches an appropriate cruising rate. The speed does not change by discrete amounts. Thus, if the results of the simulation are to include the state of the system in relation to the continuous variable "speed", then a continuous change model is needed. These continuous changes could be represented by differential equations which would, in theory, allow the variables to be computed at any point in time.

In considering continuous change models it must be recognized that digital computers operate only with discrete quantities. Hence, changes cannot actually be occurring continuously within a "continuous" simulation on a typical computer. In system dynamics (see Chapters 13 to 15) the apparent continuity is achieved by allowing the variables to be inspected or changed at a multitude of fixed points in simulated time. This provides an approximation to continuous change, which is often good enough.

Continuous simulation "proper" is not covered in detail in this book because management scientists seem to be more often concerned with systems that can satisfactorily be simulated discretely. More often continuous simulations are the concern of economists in modelling the behaviour of economic systems via sets of differential equations, or the task of engineers designing equipment. Early continuous simulations were mainly carried out using analogue computers. Though these have some appeal for those with an interest in electrical hardware, they tend to be tedious to reprogram and of limited accuracy. Therefore, analogue digital simulators, such as CSMP (IBM, 1970), were developed. Early versions of these simulators employed the block diagram terminology of analogue computers, a description of the block diagram being the "program" from which a digital computer could simulate an analogue computer. Later versions allow systems to be directly represented as sets of differential equations that are integrated numerically.

2.4.3 A few words on simulation software

Chapter 8 introduces two commonly used dynamic simulation packages, Micro Saint (Micro Analysis and Design, 2003) and SIMUL8 (Simul8 Corporation, 2003). Both of these packages are based on a next-event simulation technique and both provide easy-to-use sampling routines that support full stochastic simulation with a minimal requirement for computer programming. Though it is possible to "bend" these packages for continuous simulation, this is probably unwise.

System dynamics simulations (see Chapters 13 to 15) are usually based on time slicing and this is evident in packages such as iThink/Stella (High Performance Systems, 2003), Powersim (Powersim Corporation, 2003) and Vensim (Ventana Systems, 2003). Though system dynamics packages do provide some stochastic sampling routines, these are best thought of as add-ins that are rarely used.

The vendors of simulation software systems realize that the separation of discrete and continuous simulation is somewhat artificial. Consequently, a number of simulation software systems allow the user to program discrete, continuous or mixed models. Recent examples include GoldSim (GoldSim Technology Group, 2003), AweSim (FrontStep APS, 2003) and Extend (Imagine That, 2003).

EXERCISES

(1) Use a spreadsheet program to simulate Big Al's problem as described in Section 2.3.1.

(2) Place the constants as values on the spreadsheet and vary these so as to carry out experiments. Use the graphing facilities to see how the mob size builds up.

(3) Try using your spreadsheet to model the disk failure problem. This is straightforward in the time-slicing case, but slightly more difficult in the next-event case.

(4) Check out your spreadsheet program to see what control, if any, it gives you over the random numbers which are produced. If it does give you proper control, then run the disk failure problem 10 times and try to understand the variation in the results.

(5) If you know a computer programming language, write a program to simulate the disk failure problem. Try the time-slicing case first, then the next-event case.

(6) Discuss why analogue computers are almost never used in management science despite the fact that many systems do change continuously.

REFERENCES

FrontStep APS (2003) http://www.pritsker.com/awesim.htm

GoldSim Technology Group (2003) http://www.goldsim.com/

High Performance Systems (2003) http://www.hps-inc.com/

IBM Corporation (1970) *Introduction to 1130 Systems Modelling Program II* (CSMP II, GH200848-1). IBM, White Plains, New York.

Jones L. (1975) Simulation Modelling (Unit 6, Course T341, Systems Modelling). Open University Press, Milton Keynes, UK.

Imagine That (2003) http://www.imaginethatinc.com/

Micro Analysis and Design (2003) http://www.maad.com/

Powersim Corporation (2003) http://www.powersim.com

Simul8 Corporation (2003) http://www.simul8.com/

Ventana Systems (2003) http://www.vensim.com/

3

Computer Simulation in Practice

3.1 PROCESS, CONTENT, PROBLEM AND PROJECT

3.1.1 Process and content

This chapter considers how computer simulation methods may best be put to use in management science. Most of the rest of this book is technical in nature, showing how ideas in computing and statistics can be combined to provide powerful ways to simulate different types of system. Much experience leads the author to believe that technical knowledge and proficiency, though necessary for successful simulation, are not sufficient. One obvious reason for this is that, in operational research and management science (OR/MS), problems do not come neatly labelled as mathematical programming, computer simulation or whatever. Instead, the OR/MS analyst needs to be aware that problem solving and analysis are more important than the blinkered, if enthusiastic, use of techniques such as computer simulation. In practice, OR/MS is usually judged by its impact on the organization rather than by technical criteria.

Planning, executing and completing a successful computer simulation study in OR/MS requires more than good computer programming. OR/MS methods were first used in business, commerce and the public sector in the 1950s and analysts have learned that to be successful, they must combine two sets of skills. Eden (1989) expresses this in the following neat relationship:

Outcome = Process × Content

It suggests that successful OR/MS depends on the correct deployment of skills related to process and to content. By *process*, is meant the manner in which a study is planned, conducted and completed. Managed properly, the process provides a bridge between the technical "world" of the analyst and the "real world" of the organization. By *content*, is meant knowledge related to the system being investigated and the simulation skills being employed to conduct the study. Of course, it is rarely possible to make such a neat distinction between process and content in practice. Nevertheless, the distinction is a helpful one if it serves to focus attention on important issues. The two aspects, argues Eden (1989), need to be properly integrated if an OR/MS study is to be successful. This chapter will explore how these ideas might be deployed so as to increase the likelihood that computer simulation methods are used successfully in OR/MS work.

3.1.2 Problems and projects

A second distinction, related to the one between process and content, is that between a problem and a project. Many OR/MS workers regard themselves as problem solvers, a view that Pidd (2003) discusses in detail. Such a view implies a focus that is sharply directed towards defined goals that may have technical solutions. Thus, some analysts who regard themselves as simulation specialists will happily speak of "interesting simulation problems" that they have tackled. As faced in OR/MS, problems do not have single correct solutions, for they are not like crossword puzzles. Instead, there may be many different ways of addressing the issues that make up a problem and there may be a range of acceptable solutions. Indeed, it is this fact that makes computer simulation one of the most commonly used tools within OR/MS, for it enables people to explore a whole range of possible solutions and scenarios.

It is important to realize, however, that though OR/MS problems can be solved in a technical sense, this may not be true in an organizational sense. This does not mean that OR/MS projects always end in disaster, it simply means that tackling a problem successfully may provide a way to *handle* the problem rather than actually *solving* it. In many organizations, the same problems crop up time and time again as the organization, its environment, its competitors, its partners and its customers change. Thus, most organizations face the need to manage stocks of different kinds and may need to explore the market for their goods and services. No project will solve these problems forever more, but good analysis may help the organization to manage things rather better.

Hence it is important to realize that OR/MS work within most organizations is managed by a series of projects. A project is, in some ways, an arbitrary thing. The boundaries set and the resources available are rarely determined in a detached or scientific manner but result from forces such as people's opinions, their power and the perceived degree of importance of the work to be done. Hence, though an analyst may dearly wish to be given a whole year to do a "proper job", it is important to realize that circumstances may dictate that only 3 months are available. If a tailor must cut a coat according to his cloth, so a simulation analyst must learn to do work within defined resource limits.

3.1.3 Two parallel streams

Figure 3.1 shows the need to manage process and content, and problems and projects—all simultaneously. This is, needless to say, not straightforward; but it is similar to the issues that, say, a doctor faces when treating her patients. The doctor must bring her technical knowledge to bear—and most countries have stringent rules to ensure that doctors are technically competent before they are allowed to practice. However, the doctor must also

Project management	Problem solving
Process skills and management	Content knowledge and skills

Figure 3.1   Content, process, problems and projects

learn what Miser and Quade (1988) following Schön (1982) term "craft skills". The surgeon must learn how to use her instruments and must know when risky interventions are needed. The psychiatrist must learn when to ask very personal questions, even when a patient is clearly distressed. In addition, they both must learn to manage the inter-personal side of their work—bedside manner is very important for doctors (pathologists excepted, perhaps).

This Chapter provides introductory coverage of some of these craft issues as they relate to computer simulation. Miser and Quade (1988) devote over 600 pages to this topic, which perhaps gives some idea of its importance and also indicates that in this chapter we only scratch upon the surface. Nevertheless, the hope is that the novice will gain enough guidance from this chapter to develop a personal style that is successful in its deployment of the craft skills needed for successful integration of process, content, projects and problems.

Figure 3.2 shows that, during a simulation study, the analyst needs to manage the technical work in which she is engaged as well as the project

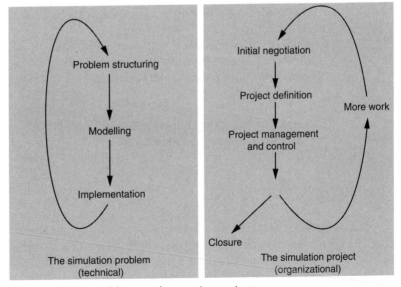

Figure 3.2   Solving problems and managing projects

within which the work is being done. The figure shows two parallel loops, one concerned with the project and one concerned with the technical side of the intervention. In a similar vein, Balci (1985) suggests that analysts should realize that simulation studies have life cycles (i.e., some activities may need to be carried out several times during a study). This chapter develops a simple model of the technical side of a simulation study based on the one discussed in Pidd (1991). It has three phases, one of which, *modelling*, is concerned with the technical material in the rest of this book. The project side of the figure will also be explored. Though the diagram looks rather neat and tidy, the actual experience of carrying out a simulation study is somewhat different. The neat phases shown in the figure overlap with one another and there is often backtracking. Thus, for example, the realization that the modelling is going wrong (which sometimes it does) may lead to a further attempt at problem structuring.

3.2   THE SIMULATION PROBLEM PART OF THE STUDY

This is represented by the left-hand side of Figure 3.2, it covers the technical work carried out during the simulation study and it has three phases as follows:

- *Problem structuring*. This is the attempt to take a "mess" and to extract from it some agreement about the particular problems that might be amenable to OR/MS. The hope is that this process of extraction will not remove all meaning from the "mess" itself.
- *Modelling*. This is usually taken as the technical heart of any simulation study and involves the use of statistical and computer methods to analyse the problems defined during problem structuring. The hope is that the modelling will not over-simplify the issues raised during problem structuring.
- *Implementation*. This is the attempt to put into practice any recommendations that emerge from problem structuring and analysis. It is expected to be a continuing process from which the OR/MS staff will need to withdraw at some stage.

The next sections of the chapter will discuss each of these three aspects in turn, as they relate to computer simulation.

3.3   PROBLEM STRUCTURING

Problem structuring is an attempt to understand the issues which are being addressed in the project in an effort to decide what detailed OR/MS methods will be appropriate. In one sense, therefore, it could be viewed as a mere preliminary to detailed modelling and computer work. However, deciding which are the problems to be tackled and trying to understand their linkages is as challenging a task as the detailed formulation and implementation of simulation models. The challenge in OR/MS is to be good at the full range of activities necessary for successful practice. That includes problem structuring and implementation skills as well as simulation modelling.

In most cases, the majority of problem structuring effort takes place at the start of a simulation project (i.e., problem structuring is the first phase of the work). How much time will be needed to do this is impossible to specify in general terms, it depends on a number of factors such as:

- The degree to which this is an entirely new area of work.
- The skills and knowledge of the OR/MS analyst.
- The requirements of the client.
- The time available.

Sometimes, relatively little time need be spent in problem structuring, at least in any formal sense. This happens when the work to be done is well established and there is clear agreement about the goals of the study. This may well be the case in organizations that make routine use of simulation methods (e.g., in designing manufacturing layouts). But even in these studies it is as well to ask some basic questions, even if they take a little time. Writing many years ago, John Dewey (quoted in Lubart, 1994) produced the maxim: "A problem well put is half solved". It seems as if he had in mind the fact that a problem which is poorly posed will be very hard, if not impossible, to solve. Hence it is best to spend a little time in problem structuring as it may save much anguish later.

Rosenhead and Mingers (2001) provide a good coverage of the formal methods of problem structuring which have come to be associated with management science. Pidd (2003) also covers some of this material and provides a discussion of problem structuring in the general context of management science modelling. Problem structuring is perhaps best regarded as a period of preliminary data collection, where the data includes qualitative as well as quantitative aspects. An old adage of management information systems is that "information is data plus interpretation". In a sense, problem structuring is an attempt to collect and interpret preliminary data so as to learn enough about the problem at hand so as to know how best to proceed. In parallel, of course, the project side of the study needs to be considered and, at this stage, this involves negotiation with a view to establishing a project definition that can be agreed by all concerned.

3.3.1 Problem structuring as exploration

As mentioned above, there are many formal approaches that are advocated as helpful in problem structuring, the author's experience is that rather simple ideas are often of great value. Two in particular will be mentioned here. The first is that this is best regarded as a process of learning and exploration. Most modern theories of organizational learning (see Argyris, 1983 and Kolb, 1983) are cyclic, as is the model of problem structuring shown in Figure 3.3.

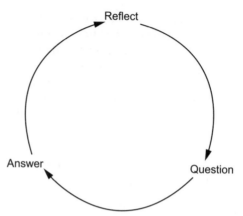

Figure 3.3   Problem structuring as exploration

This represents a view that this exploration proceeds almost in fits and starts as the analyst becomes gradually more comfortable with what may, initially, be new to her. As she learns, so she is able to explore more. The actual learning does not cease, but the priorities of the project side of Figure 3.2 ensure that a halt is called at some stage.

The second, very practical suggestion about problem structuring, is that six simple questions are often found valuable. These are captured in the well known verse of Rudyard Kipling from the *Just So Stories* ("The elephant's child"):

> I keep six honest working men
> (They taught me all I knew);
> Their names are What and Why and When
> And How and Where and Who.

Though all six questions are clearly interlinked, three (What? Why? and How?) relate to the system that may be modelled and three (When? Where? and Who?) provide much of the context. The idea is that the analyst should use these questions, not necessarily in a direct sense, but more as an aide memoir to consider the issues that must be faced in problem structuring.

The result of some of this questioning is likely to be useful data that, when interpreted, provides useful insights. For example, in what eventually became a computer simulation study (Pidd, 1987), a rough and ready analysis of limited data revealed that each 1% increase in the efficiency of a manufacturing plant would contribute an extra £10,000 of profit. This served as a spur to agreeing a more detailed analysis to try and achieve this pay-off. Limited preliminary data will also show the scale of the work likely to be needed and this will be useful in agreeing the scale of the projects that might emerge from the problem structuring.

At some stage during the problem structuring, someone must decide whether or not a computer simulation approach is likely to be fruitful. As has been explored in Chapter 1, there are many reasons why simulation approaches are often used. However, it is also true, as discussed in Chapter 1, that simulation projects can be very time consuming. If other ways forward are available, then they should certainly be considered.

3.4   MODELLING

Though much of this book addresses the detailed issues involved in developing a simulation model, it is worth touching on the main issues at this point. Figure 3.4 shows that modelling, in computer simulation studies, usually involves four tasks. As with problem structuring, modelling is a learning process that proceeds gradually and in a parsimonious manner. Chapter 5 recommends the use of the "principle of parsimony" in developing simulation models, which is similar to the idea of stepwise refinement and is further discussed in Pidd (2003). The idea is that a model should be developed gradually, starting with simple aspects that are well understood and moving step-by-step towards a more complete representation. At each stage, the analyst is conducting a partial validation of the model (see later in this section and in Chapter 12) and, finding the model wanting, adds extra features. As shown in Figure 3.4, there may even be limited experimentation with inadequate models on the way. Often, such experimentation demonstrates that the model needs further development.

3.4.1   Conceptual model building

Conceptual model building is an activity in which the analyst tries to capture the essential features of the system that is being modelled. Which features are deemed necessary will depend on two factors. The first is the method by which the system is to be simulated. If discrete simulation (the focus of Part II of this book) is being used, then the aim will be to identify the main entities of

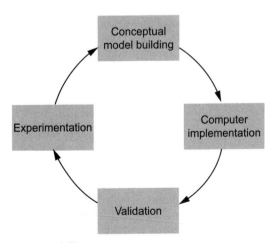

Figure 3.4   Simulation modelling

the system and to understand the logical ways in which they interact. Chapter 5 suggests that simple tools such as activity cycle diagrams are a great help in this regard. These and similar tools allow the modeller to map out the main interactions and principal behaviour of the entities in a system that is to be modelled using discrete simulation. Thus, if attempting to simulate an outpatient clinic, the main entities might be doctors, nurses, receptionists, patients and equipment. An activity such as a minor surgical intervention might be governed by conditions such as the availability of a doctor, a nurse, a room and specified equipment.

If system dynamics is being employed (the subject of Part III of this book) then different elements will need to be identified in the system of interest. System dynamics requires the modeller to understand the system in terms of flows (such as patient arrivals) and levels (such as the number of staff needed or the number of patients sitting in the waiting area).

This attempt to capture the essentials of the system is often known as conceptual model building and the resulting model is sometimes known as a *conceptual model*. It may exist as a set of flow diagrams, as a textual description or as a mix of the two. Its specification may form the basis of a contract on the project management side of Figure 3.2. In small-scale studies, such a conceptual model may not exist in any objective form other than in the mind of the analyst, since modern software, especially the use of Visual Interactive Modelling Systems (VIMS) mean that conceptualization can occur whilst developing the model at a computer screen.

Alongside the type of simulation approach to be employed, the second factor that affects the aspects to be included in the model is what Zeigler (1976) terms the *experimental frame*. This is the set of conditions within which the simulation model is to be used. As Chapter 12 makes clear, no model can be regarded as valid in any general sense, as models are constructed for particular purposes and these purposes should be captured within a formally described experimental frame. If a model is used within a frame that differs from the original intention, then there can be no guarantee that it will be suitable for the new frame, even if it was ideal for the original one. Thus, a model developed for monthly capacity planning in a factory may be useless for detailed machine and job scheduling. The experimental frame will determine, at least partially, the level of detail at which the system is to be simulated.

3.4.2   Computer implementation

The next box in the circuit of Figure 3.4 is labelled as *computer implementation*. If this book had been written before the mid-1980s, this box might have been labelled as *computer programming* as that was, until then, the way in which most conceptual models were implemented on computers. However, as much of this book makes clear, many simulations in OR/MS are conducted using what will later be defined as VIMS. These are computer packages such as Witness, ProModel and Micro Saint (for discrete simulation) and Stella/iThink for system dynamics. They enable the modeller to develop the computer model by selecting icons from an on-screen palette and linking them together to show the logical interactions that make up much of the model. Chapter 8 discusses the use of VIMS in discrete simulation and Chapter 14 shows how VIMS are used in system dynamics modelling and simulation.

These VIMS enable a computer-based model to be developed without recourse to "proper" computer programming. Instead, the detailed logic and parameters of the system are developed using menus and pull-down forms of the types familiar to users of windows-type operating systems. VIMS are not suitable for simulating all systems, however. Powerful though they are, they have their limitations and it is still necessary, sometimes, to implement conceptual models by developing computer programs as discussed in Chapters 6, 7 and 9. The need to develop a "proper" computer program arises for a number of reasons, such as:

- The simulation involves complex event logic or must include highly specific calculation (e.g., for scheduling purposes).
- The simulation is very large scale and may need to be maintained for a long period of time. There are many such examples in the defence sector.
- The simulation needs to run very fast (e.g., in real time).
- The organization has no wish to invest in specialist software when it already has considerable expertise in computer programming.

3.4.3 Validation

The third box of Figure 3.4 is labelled as *validation* and a detailed account of some of the issues is given in Chapter 12. Validation is the process by which the modeller and the client satisfy themselves that the model, as implemented on a computer, is suitable for use within its defined experimental frame. In the past it was usual to distinguish between validation and verification. Computer programs were verified by checking to see if they were a correct implementation of a model and the model was validated to see if it is appropriate for its experimental frame. However, the use of VIMS muddies the water a little, for in many such cases there is no real distinction between the model and the computer implementation. Hence, in many applications that use VIMS, it is best to think of validating the model and its computer implementation at the same time.

There are many approaches to this validation and extremely thorough accounts of the various techniques available are to be found in Balci (1994) and Sargent (1982). However, it is important to note that complete validation is never possible. This is because most simulation models are used to investigate things that are not understood. Hence, a model might be developed to simulate part of a hospital and it might be relatively easy to check that it is a valid representation of the way in which the hospital operates at the moment. In many cases, though, such a model will be used to estimate how the performance of the hospital might change under different conditions or under different management policies. A complete validation of the model under these new circumstances will be impossible. Does this mean that simulation approaches are, therefore, a complete waste of time? Not really. When used in this extrapolatory mode they are devices for thinking about how things might be and they need to be subject to the same rigorous analysis as would be any other proposals about possible futures.

3.4.4   Experimentation

The final box of Figure 3.4 is labelled as *experimentation* and it refers to the use of the model. The whole reason for building a simulation model is to carry out some experiments on it, and now we consider how such experiments are to be undertaken. Nowadays, most simulations are run either on workstations or on single-user computers. In both cases, the user has control over the running of the program (how much control will depend on the particular program and the operating system of the computer). Also, the program may display graphics and/or text output on-screen as it runs.

Whatever the form of experimentation, it is as well to be aware that the results of stochastic simulations are more difficult to interpret than those from deterministic models. This is because a stochastic simulation is, in effect, a complex sampling experiment in which samples from various distributions are combined as the model runs. Hence, the sampling processes themselves need to be well controlled so as to reduce the effect of sampling errors. At the very least, the use of pseudo-random numbers allows the experimenter to compare a set of policies, each using approximately the same random samples. Two different types of experimentation may be used—interactive or classical.

As argued earlier, applications best suited to simulation are complicated, highly variable and dynamic. This dynamic behaviour may be represented on-screen as the simulation runs by careful use of icons, diagrams and graphs. The changing state of the entities can be represented by icons that may change position, colour, orientation or size. The icons can be displayed against a backcloth of some stylized plan of the system being simulated and can be used to give a convincing representation of the system on screen. As an extension, state variables, such as waiting times, queue lengths and throughput, can be displayed in a graphical form and accessed through multiple windows.

Using such devices, the analyst can observe the dynamics of the simulation as it runs. Thus it is possible to see the build-up of queues, the movement of jobs, the delays suffered and the utilization of the entities without waiting until a simulation run is complete. Of course, such observations can be misleading, because the on-screen behaviour will be a function of the samples taken if there are stochastic elements in the model. If the samples are unrepresentative, then so will be the observed behaviour. Despite this caveat, the ability to view the dynamics as the simulation runs is a real benefit, as it links with the possibility of interacting with the simulation and operating it in a "gaming mode".

To provide interaction, the simulation software must permit some way in which the analyst can halt the simulation in its tracks, vary some of the parameters and continue the run under these new conditions. This Visual Interactive Simulation (VIS), is now the norm in OR/MS and it makes it easier for the analyst to experiment, to see logical errors (where did that crane go just then?) and to convince the client that the simulation is valid.

Sometimes, the VIS approach is not powerful enough, possibly because the system is simply too stochastic or because there are too many entities and variables to display meaningfully on-screen. Thus some classical form of controlled experiment is needed and which is carefully planned and executed. This is discussed in detail in Chapter 11.

The subject of experimental design is beyond the scope of this chapter, but the basics are simple enough. The experiment must be planned so that the various factors which may influence the results can be disentangled. In this way, the experimenter can determine statistically which factors give rise to which effects and may be able to draw appropriate conclusions about the effect on the system of the policies being simulated. To do this requires the experimenter to consider how long the experiment should be run in order to achieve statistically significant results. It also requires the investigator to be familiar with the appropriate statistical methods.

3.4.5 Implementation

As the old adage has it, "the proof of the pudding is in the eating." Within OR/MS, a simulation study is usually conducted because some benefit is sought from doing so. Hence, the issue of implementation cannot be ignored when discussing how simulation projects may be conducted. As with the other parts of the left-hand side of Figure 3.2, it is important to realize that implementation is not something that happens only at a single point in a simulation project—which is what the figure might be thought to suggest.

Broadly speaking, there are two types of implementation that may occur as a result of a simulation study, or indeed of any OR/MS study. The first, and most obvious, might be thought of as a *tangible product*. This occurs when, at some stage in the work (usually at the end) there are clear recommendations about whatever action should or should not be taken as a result of the study. These benefits are usually the official reason for conducting the study in the first place. "We want to find the best way to organize passengers as they flow through from the plane to the baggage hall via the immigration desks." The intended result of such a study will be a series of recommendations, based on simulation experiments that suggest how such flows may best be managed. This does not mean that the simulation team have necessarily come up with all the ideas themselves. In most circumstances, the model is used to check the implications of a range of policies suggested by different people. The intended tangible products of the simulation study are often documented in the contract that specifies the conduct of the study.

The second type of implementation that might occur is *improved knowledge and insight*. It happens when models and model building are used as tools for thinking (see Pidd, 2003). It commonly occurs at two points in simulation studies. The first occurs with problem structuring and asking questions of the "who, what, where ..." type. It is often the case that the type of data needed to build a model of some system is very similar to the data that would be needed to operate it properly in real life. Thus a common response when questioning during problem structuring is "... oh ... that's a good question ... I'm not sure if we know that ... but maybe we should ...". Thus the problem structuring and model building processes may serve to explicate important features of the system that is to be simulated and the information that emerges may be immediately used in the real world without waiting for the study to end.

The second point at which this often occurs is during experimentation. It is not unusual for these experiments to throw up unexpected results. Sometimes, sadly, these surprises are because the model is invalid, but this is not always so. Forrester (1961) wrote about the "counter-intuitive behaviour of systems". By this he meant that our mental models of how things behave may turn out to be wrong when compared with a thorough attempt to model something explicitly. Thus the spin-off results produced on the way to proper experimentation may allow the participants in the study to develop improved insight. This can be a very valuable benefit, but the relationship of process and content suggested at the start of this chapter is absolutely crucial. The insight will not occur unless the process is properly managed.

3.5   THE PROJECT PART OF THE STUDY

Alongside the technical work in which the analyst must engage is the project by which the work is managed and this section will review some aspects that are particularly relevant to computer simulation studies. The main points are shown on the right-hand side of Figure 3.2 and these will serve as the basis for the discussion here. It should be noted that most large organizations have their own procedures for managing projects and hence the comments made here will need to be interpreted in the light of specific circumstances.

The parties involved will vary greatly and examples include the following, in order of complexity:

(1)   Projects in which one person does all the work for themselves and is, therefore, analyst, project manager and client rolled into one.
(2)   Projects in which there is one or more analyst and a client who takes responsibility for the work.
(3)   Projects in which there is one or more analyst, a client who takes responsibility for the work and other people who serve as day-to-day contacts.
(4)   Large-scale projects that involve teams of people, long timescales and decision makers who are far removed from the technical work of the study.

Types 1, 2 and 3 are common in business and type 4 is common in some public sector work, especially in defence.

Just as the *problem* side of Figure 3.2 is shown as a cycle, so is the *project* side.

This is because many projects stem from previous efforts, sometimes in the same area, or sometimes because of a reputation made elsewhere. Though both process and content are important on the project side, it is perhaps the case that process may dominate content, whereas the reverse may be true on the problem side of things.

3.5.1   Initial negotiation and project definition

All projects seem to require some terms of reference that specify the expectations of the various parties involved in the study. The idea of the problem structuring on the problem side of Figure 3.2 is to decide, in technical terms, how to go about the study. The idea of these two phases on the project side is to ensure that there is agreement about this and other aspects right at the start of the study. The initial negotiation may, of course, happen before the simulation analyst is involved in the work and this may present a few problems—especially if the problem structuring suggests that simulation may not be appropriate in a particular case.

Hence, where possible, it makes sense to have initial negotiation and project definition occur in parallel to problem structuring. This may mean that the work is done under a two-part contract, the first of which is very short and covers these phases of work. The contract to go on to the rest of the study may thus depend on the outcomes of the problem structuring, the initial negotiations and the project definition. The aim of these phases is to agree, between all concerned, a number of fundamental aspects of the work to be done. Obvious examples of these aspects are:

(1)   A specification of the experimental frame for the modelling work. The experimental frame, discussed above, specifies the conditions under which the model is to be used and the intended purpose of its construction. If this is ignored then it is hard to see how the study can be a success.

(2)   An agreement about the timescale for the work. This can be very problematic since many simulation studies are, by their nature, exploratory. Hence, it may not be easy in some circumstances to say, in advance, how long the work will take. Perhaps the best way to cope with this is to agree a series of milestones for the project. These will be specific near the start of the project and the later ones may be re-negotiated as time proceeds. The milestones specify what work will be done and when it will be done. This can be very difficult to specify and it breaks what some cynics feel is a cardinal rule of economic forecasting—never give a number <u>and</u> a date, just one or the other!

(3)   A specification of the resources needed for the study. As with the timescale, this can also be tricky when the simulation study is intended to be exploratory. The same way of coping with the difficulty presents itself—use milestones and agree tight specifications for the early ones and negotiate the others as work proceeds. The resources required covers aspects such as costs, manpower, computer hardware and software.

It might be tempting to assume that it is always possible to write a proper requirements specification for a simulation model, however this is rarely the case. This is another reason why this book argues that the principle of parsimony should drive the modelling process.

In essence, this stage of the project process aims to produce a contract between the various parties so as to support the work and so as to allow its progress to be monitored as work proceeds. The more that these things are considered at the early stages of a project then the less likely it is that unforeseen problems will occur later. However, once again, it must be borne in mind that many simulation projects are not like computer systems development work and attempts to be too bureaucratic should be avoided.

3.5.2 Project management and control

It should be clear from the previous section that there are two key elements in managing and controlling a simulation study. The first is in managing the expectations of the various parties involved in the work. The aim of the initial contract definition is to specify what these are at the start of the work and this presents a useful beginning to the management of the project. However, there is a second aspect, the use of milestones, to cope with the dynamic progress of the technical and other work on the project.

The initial milestones can be specified in the initial contract documents, but it is crucial for all to realize that these milestones may have to be shifted as the project proceeds. There are many reasons for this, such as:

- As mentioned earlier, one result of a simulation (and of any OR/MS) study is that there may be spin-offs en route. The emergence of these spin-offs may be as valuable as the intended final results of the study and they must be attended to as the work proceeds. Meetings agreed for the milestones may be used to review progress and to consider how realistic the later milestones now seem to be.
- A second problem is that, except in routine applications (such as sometimes occur in manufacturing) the simulation work maybe involve some novelty and the project hence begins to resemble a research and development effort. Thus, some shifts in the milestones may be inevitable in all but the most straightforward of work. However, some of these shifts should be positive, when progress is faster than expected.
- A third problem may be due to difficulties with the data that is needed to build the model. This data may not be available as and when it is needed and it may turn out to be faulty in one way or another. This may happen even when the data requirements were specified in the initial contract documents.

For these, and for other reasons, the use of meetings and reports related to milestones seem to be the key to managing the completion of simulation projects.

It should also be noted that inter-personal skills are vital in managing successful simulation projects. The ways in which the various parties perceive one another plays an important part in the assessment of simulation projects and this cannot be ignored. Robinson and Pidd (1998) discuss this in depth and suggest how some ideas of Total Quality Management (TQM), initially developed in the service sector, may be employed to enhance the chance of successful simulation projects.

3.5.3 Project completion

The final stage on the right-hand side of Figure 3.2 is the idea of project completion, which is shown as leading to either of two routes—closure, or more work. Like any human activity, simulation projects come to an end and it seems important that they do not just dribble out. Instead, an important role in their management is to ensure that the various parties agree that the project is now complete, or that it will lead on to more work.

In a sense, milestones serve a similar purpose. They enable the work so far to be reviewed, they enable those involved to comment on it and to make suggestions and they allow people to decide whether to continue or to cease the work. The difference is that the project completion phase should cover the work in the full glare of the experimental frame that has been agreed for the simulation model. The completion phase may decide that the modeller should play some part in the implementation of the study or that other people will take responsibility for this. If the project was one that resulted in a simulation model that other people will use, then this presents one extreme. On the other hand, the final result may be a model that requires considerable technical expertise in its use and maintenance—this is common in the defence sector. Finally, the result may be a set of recommendations and insights that will lead to action by other people.

EXERCISES

(1) Find a case study that describes a simulation application and try to understand how the process and content aspects of the project were managed.

(2) Find a case study that describes a simulation application and try to decide whether some approach, other than simulation, might have been more appropriate.

(3) Find a case study that describes a simulation application and try to understand how the experimentation was planned and controlled.

(4) Find a case study that describes a simulation application and try to understand how the model was validated. See if you can uncover its experimental frame from the descriptions that are given.

REFERENCES

Argyris C. (1983) Productive and counter-productive reasoning processes. In: S. Srivasta (ed.), *The Executive Mind*. Jossey-Bass, San Francisco.

Balci O. (1987) Credibility assessment of simulation results: The state of the art. *Proceedings of the Conference on Methodology and Validation, Orlando, FL* (pp. 19–25), SCS, San Diego, CA.

Balci O. (1985) *Guidelines for successful simulation studies* (Technical Report TR-85-2). Department of Computer Science, Virginia Tech, Blacksburg, VA.

Balci O. (1994) Validation, verification and testing techniques throughout the life cycle of a simulation study. In: O. Balci (ed.), *Annals of Operations Research, Vol. 23: Simulation and Modeling*. J.C. Balzer, Basel, Switzerland.

Eden C.L. (1989) Using cognitive mapping for strategic options development and analysis (SODA). In: J. Rosenhead (ed.), *Rational Analysis for a Problematic World*. John Wiley & Sons Ltd, Chichester, UK.

Forrester J.W. (1961) *Industrial Dynamics*. MIT Press, Cambridge, MA.

Kolb D.A. (1983) Problem management: Learning from experience. In: S. Srivasta (ed.), *The Executive Mind*. Jossey-Bass, San Francisco, CA.

Lubart T.I. (1994) Creativity. In: R.J. Steinberg (ed.), *Thinking and Problem Solving* (2nd edition). Academic Press, London.

Miser H.J. and Quade E.S. (1988) *Handbook of Systems Analysis: Craft Issues and Procedural Choices*. John Wiley & Sons Ltd, Chichester, UK.

Pidd M. (2003) *Tools for Thinking: Modelling in Management Science* (2nd edition) John Wiley & Sons, Chichester, UK.

Pidd M. (1991) OR/MS method. In: M.F. Shutler (ed.), *Operations Research in Management*. Prentice Hall, Hemel Hempstead, UK.

Pidd M. (1987) Simulating continuous food plants. *Journal of Operational Research Society*, **38**(8), 683–92.

Robinson S.L. and Pidd M. (1998) Provider and customer expectations of successful simulation projects. *Journal of Operational Research Society*, **49**(3), 200–9.

Rosenhead J.V. and Mingers J. (eds) (2001) *Rational Analysis for a Problematic World Revisited*. John Wiley & Sons Ltd, Chichester, UK.

Sargent R.G. (1982) Verification and validation of simulation models. In: F. E. Cellier (ed.), *Progress in Modelling and Simulation*. Academic Press, London.

Schön D.A. (1982) *The Reflective Practitioner. How Professionals Think in Action*. Basic Books, New York.

Zeigler B.P. (1976) *Theory of Modelling and Simulation*. John Wiley & Sons, Chichester, UK.

Static Monte Carlo Simulation

4.1 BASIC IDEAS

Chapter 2 showed how a series of samples taken from a probability distribution can be used to simulate the performance of systems in which there is stochastic behaviour. In these systems we cannot be sure exactly what will happen or when it will occur, though we can represent this using probability distributions. The example used was of computer disk units that fail from time to time and about which someone had collected data from which a probability distribution could be formed. Repeated samples from this distribution formed the basis of a simulation of two different policies for replacing failed components. If the repeated simulations have been properly designed, statistical methods can be used to decide which of the two policies is the best; or to decide that there is no significant difference between them. How this can be done is discussed in Chapter 11.

4.1.1 Risk and uncertainty

In daily life, the words "risk" and "uncertainty" are often used to mean the same thing. We are uncertain about something and there is a risk that things may not turn out as we hope. Though this casual usage is fine for everyday life, it can be helpful to distinguish between the two. It seems that Knight (1921) was the first to make a rigorous distinction as part of an analysis of profits and their origins. Since then, the same idea has been used to differentiate between choice (decision making) under risk and under uncertainty. In both cases, we cannot be sure what will happen and the distinction is based on what can be known in some objective sense.

A risky decision is defined as one for which, even though we cannot be sure what will happen, we have enough evidence to construct a probability distribution of the outcomes. A small-scale example would be a fair game of roulette; we do not know what numbers or colours will come up, but it is possible to compute the probabilities of each outcome. The replacement problem simulated in Chapter 2 is, in these terms, an example of decision making under risk. Of course, leaving aside examples such as roulette, the probability distribution of outcomes from a decision will not be perfectly known. Thus, decision making under risk applies when we have enough information to estimate the probability distribution. In general, an outcome will be the result of a repeated set of actions, otherwise there is no objective evidence from which to construct the probability distribution. Thus, most events that recur non-deterministically can be considered as risky.

Understanding this helps us to appreciate what is meant by choice under uncertainty, which deals with events for which there is no objective way to construct the probability distribution. In general, these are events that are not repeatable. Most of us deal with such events all the time and some, gamblers in particular, enjoy doing so. A horse race is an example of an unrepeatable situation in which there is great uncertainty. The race may be re-run, but it will not be the same race since the jockeys will have extra experience and the conditions on the course will not be identical. In the business arena, investment decisions are good examples of choices under uncertainty. Though it is possible, for example, to buy the same machine twice, the circumstances are likely to differ between the two purchases, since the world will have moved on in the interim.

Simulation approaches are an effective way of managing both risk and uncertainty. Using a simulation to do so does not guarantee anything, since no one can be sure what will happen. However, understanding how the different risks and uncertainties may occur and may interact, helps people to develop strategies and approaches that will cope with risk and uncertainty. Using a simulation approach it is possible to run repeated simulations to estimate the most likely outcomes. From this, we may develop appropriate policies.

4.1.2   The replacement problem: a reprise

Section 2.3.2 used a simple stochastic simulation to compare two replacement policies. Running a single pair of comparative simulations for 50 weeks showed that replacing a disk unit when it failed was $50 cheaper than replacing a failed unit and also cleaning the other to restore both to pristine condition. However, this conclusion applies only to a single comparative pair of runs. Will this conclusion hold if the simulations are repeated many times?

We have no need for expensive simulation software to further analyse this problem. Figure 4.1 shows a histogram that summarizes the result of running this simulation 50 times using Microsoft Excel. Interestingly, it shows that to conclude that separate replacement is the best policy, might be wrong. Table 4.1 reveals an average cost difference of only $19, but in favour of the new, joint repair policy. It also shows a standard error of about $9, which means that any advantage offered by the new policy will, in the long run, be very small. In effect, we cannot clearly say that one policy is better than the other after 50 simulations, each of 50 weeks. The table and histogram also show that the cost difference was once as high as $125 in favour of the old, separate repair policy and once as high as $200 dollars in favour of the new, joint repair policy.

Spreadsheet software such as Microsoft Excel provide a very useful basis for conducting static Monte Carlo simulations. In particular, there are add-ins available that provide the extra functionality needed to run multiple replicates

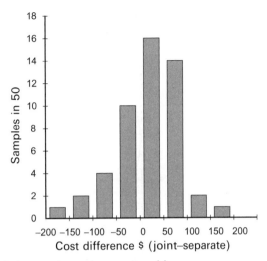

Figure 4.1 Simulation results: replacement problem

Table 4.1 Replacement problem: results from 50 runs

Average	−19
Standard deviation	63.40
Standard error	8.97
Maximum	125
Minimum	−200

of the same simulation. They include extra functions for taking random samples from a range of probability distributions, extended analytical tools for analysing the output and help with deciding which probability distributions should be used. Widely used Excel add-ins of this type include Crystal Ball (Decisioneering, 2003), @Risk (Palisade, 2003), XLSim (Analycorp, 2003) and Simtools (Myerson, 2003). It is, of course, possible to develop this extra functionality by writing Excel macros in Visual Basic for Applications.

4.1.3 Static Monte Carlo simulation defined

Strictly speaking, the Monte Carlo method is a way of performing numerical integrations of functions that are impossible with direct analytical approaches. It seems to have got its name when used in the Manhattan Project—part of the World War 2 effort to build atomic weapons in the USA. The method was used to understand complex shapes needed for such weapons. As a simple example, consider the problem, which many people tackle at high school, of estimating the area of a circle without knowing the value of π. This can, in turn, be used to estimate π. One way of doing this is to draw the circle with a unit diameter on graph paper and bound it with a unit

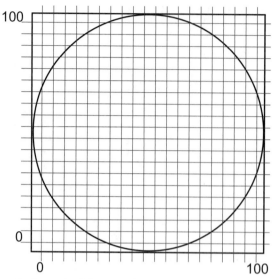

100

0

0   100

Figure 4.2   Monte Carlo method for a circle

square as shown in Figure 4.2. Counting the number of small squares that fall within the circle allows us to compute the value of π as follows.

If there are n small squares within the large square and m lie inside the circle, an estimate of the area of the circle is m/n multiplied by the area of the square. Hence, if A_c is the area of the circle and if the area of the square is A_s, then $A_c = A_s\, m/n$. If r is the radius of the circle, we know that $A_c = \pi r^2$ and $A_s = 4r^2$; hence $\pi = 4m/n$. The greater the number of small squares, the greater the precision of this estimate of π.

The Monte Carlo method uses a similar approach, but with random numbers. It works rather like the rejection sampling as introduced in Section 10.4.2. For a 2-D problem, random numbers are generated in pairs and are used as coordinates of points inside the large square area on the graph paper. Enough pairs of random number are generated to produce a reasonable coverage of the unit square. We count the number inside the circle and use this, as if counting squares, for the estimation. The accuracy of the final estimate depends on the number of random numbers used. Using similar methods it is possible to estimate the area within many strange and irregular shapes.

Strictly, it is incorrect to refer to random sampling methods from probability distributions as Monte Carlo sampling. Nevertheless, the name has stuck and many people refer to sampling from risk and uncertainty distributions as Monte Carlo sampling. The term "static" is used here because there is very little dynamic interaction in the simulations that follow. They usually have a time dimension, but this is usually handled via a time-slicing approach with little in the way of complex logic. By contrast, Chapters 5 onwards deal with simulations in which the dynamic interactions can be complex and modelling them properly is crucial for successful simulation modelling.

4.2 SOME IMPORTANT CONSIDERATIONS

4.2.1 Subjective probabilities

What do we mean when we say that an event (e.g., that it will rain tomorrow), has a probability of 0.7? Basic though this question is, answering it provides the grounds for supporting decision making under uncertainty as well as under risk. In both cases, we do not know what the outcome will be, but under risk we have some objectively developed probability distribution. Probability theory is based on fundamental assumptions and these provide several ways of defining a probability. Three of these are relevant to this discussion:

(1) *The a priori argument.* This is relevant when we have perfect information about all outcomes and also are sure about how these outcomes are produced. Rolling a fair six-sided die is such an example; we know the outcomes (1, 2, 3, 4, 5, and 6) and we are sure that they are equally likely to occur. Hence, for each roll of the die, we can state that the probability of any outcome is 1/6. Since, in statistical terms, the outcome distribution is uniform with discrete values, we can also compute the mean as being 3.5 and the variance as being 2.92. It is important to realize that the a priori argument does not rely on all outcomes being equally likely. If we had a six-sided die in which the faces were marked as 1, 2, 3, 3, 5, and 6, the distribution of the outcomes is non-uniform but we can still compute its mean as 3.33. We can also say that the probabilities of the outcomes (1, 2, 5, and 6) are all 1/6 and the probability of a value of 3 is 1/3.

(2) *The relative frequency argument.* This is relevant when we do not really understand the process that is producing the outcomes but we do have enough data to compute their relative frequency (i.e., the process producing the outcomes is treated as if it were a black box from which the values emerge and can be recorded). Whereas the a priori argument assumes that we have perfect knowledge, this argument is essentially based on continuity and regularity. Though we have only a sample of outcomes, we assume that they are representative of all possible outcomes—though we should, of course, check this if we can. This is likely to be the way in which the life histogram of Table 2.6 will have been calculated (i.e., a data collection exercise may have covered, say, 1000 breakdowns, and from this, the respective probabilities have been computed). Clearly, the reliability of such a distribution will depend on the sample size from which it is computed.

(3) *The subjectivist view.* One way to understand this is to regard it as an extension of either the a priori or relative frequency approaches. Underlying both approaches are assumptions about knowledge. Consider, for example, the view that if a coin is tossed, the probability of a head is 0.5, as is the probability of a tail. On what is this view based? Anyone who repeatedly tosses a coin to check the relative frequencies will find that the two outcomes do not occur with equal frequency. One outcome will

dominate the other, though probably by only a small amount. Why, then, do we infer that the probabilities are equal at 0.5? We do this by bringing another assumption to bear—our beliefs about the coin. If we believe it to be unbiased, then we infer that the probabilities are 0.5 and we find that the observed relative frequencies are close enough to these values. If 1000 such tosses led to 600 heads and 400 tails, we might revise that view. Thus, the subjectivist view is based on beliefs that may be revised in the light of information. It does not rest on a view that any such probability values will do. Estimating the probability of non-recurring events is essentially subjective.

Three important points need to be noted. The first is that, though the above discussion refers only to discrete probability distributions (ones in which the outcomes take only defined, discrete values) the same argument applies to continuous distributions as defined in Chapter 10. For example, instead of thinking about whether it will rain tomorrow and spoil the wedding, we could try to estimate the amount of rainfall. This would occupy a continuous scale from zero up to some likely maximum. We could then apply at least the last two types of probability to consider the probability distribution for the amount of rainfall.

The second point is that, unless we have perfect information about the process that produces the outcomes, any probability distribution of outcomes will involve some element of subjectivity. This is either because the event is unrepeatable, as in a horse race and most capital investments, or because the distribution stems from the analysis, albeit rigorous, of a sample of data. Bayesian statisticians have made it their business to develop methods that build on the ways in which the subjective elements of probability can be rigorously treated so as to revise estimates as more information becomes available. Lindley (1980) provides an excellent and non-technical introduction to Bayesian methods.

The third point is that the use of rigorously defined subjective probabilities allows us to use the same analytical methods to consider situations that involve uncertainty as well as those that involve risk. This means that it may be better to regard risk and uncertainty as extreme points on a spectrum rather than as wholly distinct situations. It is, though, sensible to be extra careful in situations in which uncertainty, as earlier defined, dominates risk.

4.2.2   Repeatability

Knight's (1921) distinction between risk and uncertainty reflects, in part, a discussion about whether it is possible to hedge against occurrences that may or may not happen. Most of us engage in such hedging when we buy insurance against common risks. We do this to cushion ourselves against possible outcomes we can regard as undesirable. It is economically rational to pay an insurance premium when the cost of doing so is less than the risk of not doing so. Insurance works by pooling risks so that players who face the same risks, but who will experience different outcomes, all pay into a common fund. This fund then pays out against the outcomes. Paying the insurance premium reduces the value of a desirable outcome by the amount of the premium. However, in doing so we reduce the cost of undesirable outcomes.

For repeatable events, actuaries have standard ways of computing the risks using statistical theory. Hence there are life tables for computing premiums for life assurance, given the age and health of the applicant. In recent years, insurance companies have put great effort into increasing the precision of their risk estimates so as to reduce their own risk exposure. In general, this increased precision is due to the availability of better, more accurate and more up to date data about the population applying for insurance.

Returning to the world of management science, it should be obvious that frequently recurring events can be analysed using sampling methods and standard statistical theory. This is why Chapter 2 uses the example of the component failures. It was reasonable to compare the policies by repeatedly running a simulation for long periods, since the real life failures would also recur. This means that the probability distribution of the outcomes had some real life correspondence.

What of non-recurring events? These are inherently uncertain and, applying the argument developed earlier, we may apply at least the same methods and analysis as for recurring events (i.e., we may simulate the event many times and produce a probabilistic estimate of the outcomes). But what does this mean, given that the events do not recur and the resulting probability distribution has no real life correspondence? The best that we can say is that estimates will be consistent, given the subjective probabilities on which they are based. However, as we shall see, even this can be very useful.

4.3 SOME SIMPLE STATIC SIMULATIONS

This section provides two examples of the ways in which a spreadsheet may be used for static Monte Carlo simulation. Both are deliberately simplified so as to demonstrate some of the basic ideas, but they provide an indication of the things that can be done using this common software technology.

4.3.1 The loan repayment

One of the biggest mistakes that we can make is to think that, because something is OK "on average", then it will be OK. As a simple example, suppose that we need to borrow £100,000, re-payable over 25 years, to buy a house. Suppose, too, that current interest rates are 7%, paid annually, on the reducing balance of the mortgage. Is it better to take out a fixed-rate loan or one that can vary with a mean value of 7%? In both cases, the annual payment would be fixed at the same amount. It seems obvious that the result should be the same, but this is not the case.

As mentioned earlier, spreadsheet software such as Excel can be used for most static simulations, and the fixed and variable mortgage loan will be used to illustrate this. The annual payment can be computed using the PMT()

	A	B	C	D	E	
1	LOAN REPAYMENTS, VARIABLE INTEREST, repeated trials					
2	Mean rate	7%	Term (yrs)	25		
3	Interest rate variation		3%			
4	Payment	£8,581.05				
5						
6			INTEREST		CAPITAL	
7	YEAR	PRINCIPAL	RATE	PAID	REPAID	
8	1	£100,000.00	5.38%	£5,384.45	£3,196.60	
9	2	£96,803.40	9.14%	£8,849.91	-£268.86	
10	3	£97,072.26	4.13%	£4,013.69	£4,567.36	
11	4	£92,504.90	6.67%	£6,170.61	£2,410.44	
12	5	£90,094.46	8.42%	£7,583.61	£997.44	
28	21	£23,058.67	5.00%	£1,153.34	£7,427.71	
29	22	£15,630.96	4.51%	£704.89	£7,876.16	
30	23	£7,754.80	6.31%	£489.16	£8,091.89	
31	24	-£337.09	8.29%	-£27.95	£8,609.00	
32	25	-£8,946.09	4.54%	-£406.20	£8,987.26	
33		-£17,933.35	Debt after 25 years			
34						
35		Average rate	6.41%			
36						

Figure 4.3   Mortgage simulation: single run

function of Excel, which computes the payment for a loan based on constant payments and a constant interest rate. This gives a fixed annual payment of £8,581.05, which reduces the balance to approximately zero after 25 years if the interest rate is constant at 7% pa.

Figure 4.3 shows part of an Excel spreadsheet for the mortgage, with an annually variable rate that has a mean value of 7% but can vary by ±3%, such that any value between 4% and 10% is equally likely. (Note that rows 13 to 27 have been hidden to reduce the size of the figure.) The annual payment, though, is constant at £8,851.05 as in the fixed interest case; therefore, if the sampled interest rate (in column C) is less than 7%, more capital will be repaid that year and less will be repaid if it is higher. In this spreadsheet, random numbers have been used to generate an interest rate each year. The result shown is pleasing, for it shows that the variable rate mortgage will lead to total repayments of almost £18,000 less than the fixed rate mortgage over 25 years—because the average interest rate turned out to be only 6.41%.

However, it is important to realize that, if different random numbers were used, a different result would be obtained. Repeating the same calculations with another 50 different sets of random numbers leads to the statistics

Table 4.2   Mortgage simulation: results from 50 runs

Average	−£3,189
Standard deviation	£17,526
Standard error	£2,479
Maximum	£43,018
Minimum	−£29,744

shown in Table 4.2 for the end-of-term debt. These repeated simulations show that, on average, the variable rate mortgage will cost over £3,000 less than the fixed rate mortgage. However, that is not the end of the story. In one of the simulations, the end-of term position was disastrous—a debt of over £43,000. In another, the end of term position was very cheering, with a positive end result of almost £30,000. If we do not wish to run the risk of a final debt of over £43,000 then we should stick with the fixed rate mortgage. In fact the simulation is inconclusive. Though, on average, the variable rate mortgage is over £3,000 cheaper, there is much variation in the results. As Table 4.2 shows, the standard error is almost £2,500, which means that after 50 simulations we cannot be sure that the true saving is significantly different from zero.

4.3.2   An investment decision

As with loan repayments, it is convenient, but wrong, to assume that average values will be what happens in practice. To cope with this, many people resort to developing scenarios—of which the use of optimistic, pessimistic and average are typical. Presented with figures in these terms, a decision maker must decide which scenario will dominate the decision process, most likely this will depend on how risk averse they are. Using a static simulation, we can do better than this.

Suppose a business is considering the investment of $10,000,000 in a new facility to make a consumer product. How might it decide whether this is sensible? An obvious way to do this is to compare the expected costs and receipts over some reasonable time period. To allow for the time value of money it is usual to apply a discount factor, related to the cost of capital, in making such calculations. The calculations involved are simple; whereas making estimates of the likely costs and benefits is difficult. Initially, suppose that a combination of experience and analysis leads them to believe that the likely annual net receipts over the next five years will be as shown in Table 4.3.

To calculate the present values of the net receipts we simply invert the normal calculation for compound interest. If we invest a capital sum X at a compound interest rate of $r\%$ per annum, then the value of the investment at the end of n years is simply $X(1 + r/100)^n$. Using a similar argument, the present value of receiving a payment of Y in n years time is $Y/(1 + r/100)^n$, if a discount rate of $r\%$ is applied. Hence we can produce Table 4.4, which shows the net present value of the entire investment of $10,000,000— assuming the net receipt projections are accurate and with a 10% discount

Table 4.3   Investment decision: expected net receipts

Year	Expected net receipts ($ million)
1	3.00
2	4.00
3	3.00
4	2.50
5	2.00

Table 4.4   Investment decision: NPVs using expected net receipts

Year	Present values ($ million)
0	−10.0000
1	2.7273
2	3.3058
3	2.2539
4	1.7075
5	1.2418
NPV	*1.2364*

rate. It reveals that the net present value (NPV) of the investment should be over $1.2 million, after applying a discount rate of 10%. Thus, if the business requires its investments to earn 10%, this one looks good. However, a basic question must be asked: how accurate are the forecasts of annual net receipts?

Rather than assuming that the forecasts are accurate, someone might suggest computing the NPV of the investment under three scenarios: optimistic, most likely and pessimistic. If so, it makes sense to use the previous annual net receipts as the most likely values. Suppose that Table 4.5 shows the resulting scenarios and their net present values. Hence, taking an optimistic view, the investment could have a NPV of about $4.3 million if all goes

Table 4.5   Investment decision: pessimistic, most likely and optimistic net receipts

	Expected net receipts ($ million)			Present values ($ million)		
Year	Optimistic	Most likely	Pessimistic	Optimistic	Most likely	Pessimistic
0				−10.0000	−10.0000	−10.0000
1	3.50	3.00	2.00	3.1818	2.7273	1.8182
2	5.00	4.00	2.50	4.1322	3.3058	2.0661
3	4.00	3.00	2.00	3.0053	2.2539	1.5026
4	3.50	2.50	1.50	2.3905	1.7075	1.0245
5	2.50	2.00	1.00	1.5523	1.2418	0.6209
NPVs	—	—	—	*4.2622*	*1.2364*	*−2.9676*

well, but could be disastrous and lead to a negative NPV of almost −$3 million, both after applying a discount rate of 10%. Now things look a little less certain. They could have a very good investment, but there is a possibility that things could go very wrong indeed. The problem is that they do not know how likely they are to experience the optimistic or pessimistic scenarios—or something in between. A static Monte Carlo simulation can help the managers to think this through.

Since this will require repeated samples to be taken, it is best to use one of the Excel add-ins for this purpose, such as those listed in Section 4.1.2. Since it is available at no charge, the example here uses the free version of XLSim (Analycorp, 2003). Like SimTools (Myerson, 2003), XLSim does not have the full functionality of products such as Crystal Ball (Decisioneering, 2003) or @Risk (Palisade, 2003) but is good enough for the examples in this chapter. In fact it has far more power than can be demonstrated here.

The three scenarios explored in Table 4.5 are presented as if these were deterministic figures (i.e., as if we were sure what would happen under defined conditions). This is not so and it is helpful to use some probability concepts instead. We need a probability distribution of the likely net receipts in each of the five years and it seems very unlikely that this is known for sure. Johnson (1997) discusses situations of this type and suggests that a triangular distribution can be safely used. How samples are taken from a triangular distribution is discussed in Section 10.4.1, and Figure 10.8 shows such a distribution. Note that the distribution is continuous (i.e., x takes any value between known minimum and maximum values). A triangular distribution has three parameters: a minimum value (a), a maximum value (c) and the mode (the most likely value; b). Triangular distributions are often used in probabilistic project planning with PERT, as well as in risk analysis of this type.

XLSim is very simple to use and Figure 4.4 shows a screen dump of an Excel spreadsheet that is ready to use XLSim. This includes the data of Tables 4.3 to 4.5, plus an extra table in cells F14:F22—these are simulation results from one simulation run. The formula used to calculate cells F17:F21 uses the gen.Triang(Min, Mode, Max) function provided with XLSim. Each value in cells F17:F22 reads the values in the correct row of cells B17:D21 and takes a sample from the appropriate triangular distribution. It then applies the discount rate to the resulting sample. Hence, the formula for cell F18 is: gen.Triang(D8,C8,B8)/(1 + B2)^A18. Figure 4.4 shows that a single run of this simulation, based on one sample for each of the years 1 to 5, results in a final NPV of over $310,000—which is encouraging. However, this result is dependent on the samples taken, which in turn depend on the random numbers used. Each time the F9 key is pressed in Excel leads to a different result and, as in Section 4.1.2, we could then write down each result. However, XLSim, and similar packages, automate this process.

The free version of XLSim will run up to 100 replicates of a simulation and the summary result for doing so with this example are shown in Table 4.6. This shows the same estimators as in Table 4.1 (for the disk replacement problem), but with values resulting from the investment simulation. It shows that the expected value of the NPV is about $870,000—which is encouraging. Since the standard error is about $65,000, this means that the simulation

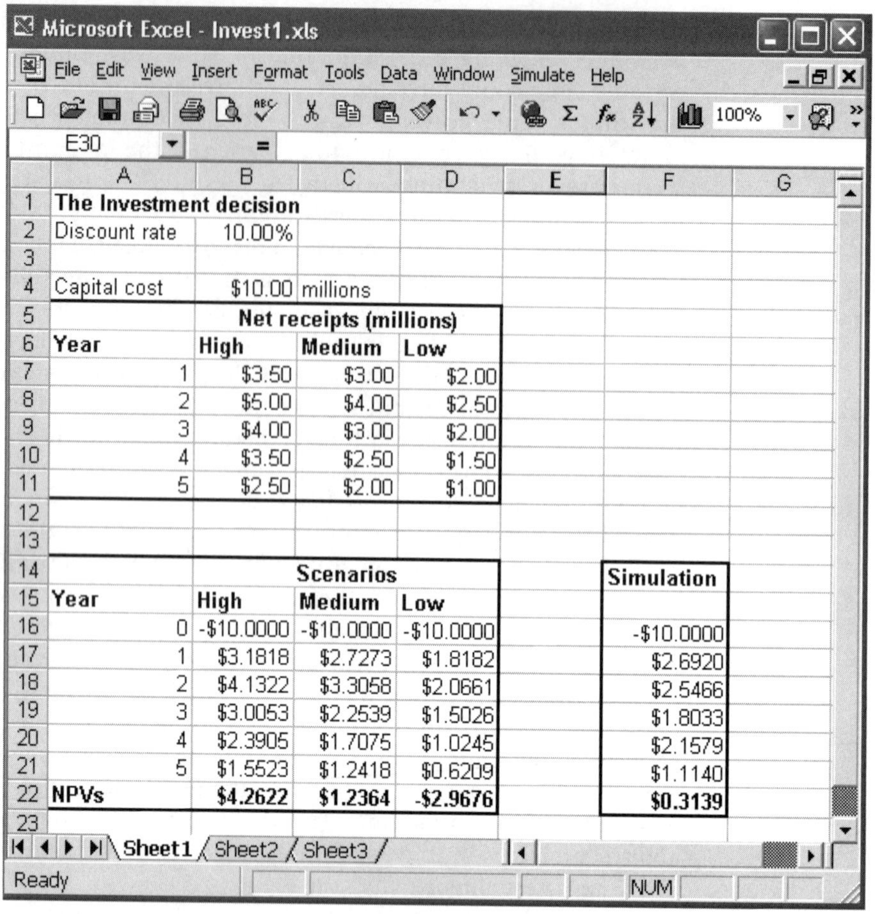

Microsoft Excel - Invest1.xls

	A	B	C	D	E	F
1	The Investment decision					
2	Discount rate	10.00%				
3						
4	Capital cost	$10.00	millions			
5		Net receipts (millions)				
6	Year	High	Medium	Low		
7	1	$3.50	$3.00	$2.00		
8	2	$5.00	$4.00	$2.50		
9	3	$4.00	$3.00	$2.00		
10	4	$3.50	$2.50	$1.50		
11	5	$2.50	$2.00	$1.00		
12						
13						
14		Scenarios				Simulation
15	Year	High	Medium	Low		
16	0	-$10.0000	-$10.0000	-$10.0000		-$10.0000
17	1	$3.1818	$2.7273	$1.8182		$2.6920
18	2	$4.1322	$3.3058	$2.0661		$2.5466
19	3	$3.0053	$2.2539	$1.5026		$1.8033
20	4	$2.3905	$1.7075	$1.0245		$2.1579
21	5	$1.5523	$1.2418	$0.6209		$1.1140
22	NPVs	**$4.2622**	**$1.2364**	**-$2.9676**		**$0.3139**

Figure 4.4 Investment decision: single run

Table 4.6 Investment decision: results from 100 runs

Average	0.8683
Standard deviation	0.6471
Standard error	0.0647
Maximum	2.4359
Minimum	−0.7037

indicates that the expected return is very likely to lie between $1 million and about $750,000. This is also encouraging—if we believe the estimates on which it is based. It is usually worth digging a little further than this, so as to examine the probability of different outcomes.

One way to do this is to plot the cumulative probability of the range of outcomes found in the simulation. XLSim will do this automatically and the result for the 100 replicates is shown in Figure 4.5. The vertical axis shows the probabilities as percentages and the horizontal axis shows the range of

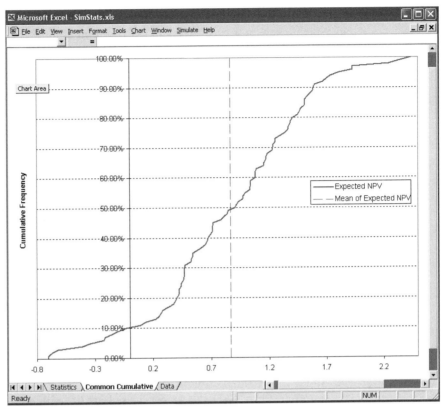

Figure 4.5   Cumulative probability plot from XLSim

values. As would be expected from Table 4.6, this runs from about −$700,000 up to about $2.4 million. The dashed vertical line shows the mean vale of about $870,000. From the graph we can immediately see that there is about a 10% chance that the investment will generate a zero or negative NPV (i.e., there is a 90% chance that it will generate a rate of return of at least 10%). As it happens, the NPV distribution is almost symmetric about its mean—which is not surprising given the values used for the minimum, mode and maximum of the distributions of net receipts. Were the NPV distribution to be asymmetric about its mean, then that would indicate a skewed risk or uncertainty profile.

4.4   SIMULATION ON SPREADSHEETS

Spreadsheets are probably the most widely used analytical tools in management and are usually the basis on which MBA students are introduced to the analytical tools of management science. Several authors, for example Powell and Baker (2003), provide a range of applications and models to demonstrate their value in management science. In the parallel field of risk analysis, Evans and Olsen (2001) provide a similar service. As the preceding sections make clear, conducting static Monte Carlo simulations on spreadsheet software is straightforward, especially when using a properly designed spreadsheet add-in. Spreadsheet software exists for all common computer operating systems including Microsoft Windows, unix and its linux cousin, and Mac OS. Some, such as Microsoft Excel, which has been used for the examples in this chapter, run on at least two platforms.

Seila (2002) provides a discussion of the general issues to be faced when using spreadsheets for simulation purposes and Grossman (1999) suggests ways in which they can be used in teaching students to understand queuing problems. Another common application includes manpower planning for organizations in which staff move from grade to grade in a system of progression. Each staff member has a probability of remaining in a grade, of leaving the organization and of promotion to another grade. As the simulation runs, samples are taken from appropriate probability distributions to model the stochastic movement of staff between grades. In this way, it is possible to experiment with manpower policies to develop a plan to meet manpower targets. Spreadsheet simulations work well when a rectangular matrix is the natural way to represent the system being simulated and when there is limited interaction between the entities in the simulation.

Part II of this book, which comprises Chapters 5 to 12, shows how to develop simulations of complicated dynamic systems in which entities interact to produce the behaviour of the system. It is certainly possible to develop a simulation model of some of these systems on a spreadsheet, but it is unwise to do so. Spreadsheets are difficult to debug, even when automated by Visual Basic for Applications and do not provide a natural way to link dynamic entities to one another. Chapters 13 to 15 comprise Part III, which is devoted to system dynamics modelling. A simple system dynamics model was developed in Section 2.2.1 (Big Al's problem) and is easily implemented on a spreadsheet. However, as with stochastic simulations, once the interactions start to get complicated, a spreadsheet runs out of steam and specialist software is preferred.

EXERCISES

(These assume that you have installed one of the spreadsheet add-ins referred to in the chapter).

(1) Set up the replacement problem (Section 2.3.2) on a spreadsheet and use this to compare the two options as discussed in Section 4.1.2.

(2) Set up the loan repayment problem (Section 4.3.1) on a spreadsheet and compare your simulation with that given in this chapter.

(3) Edit your loan repayment spreadsheet so that the variable interest rate follows a normal distribution with mean 7% and standard deviation of 1.5%. What difference does this make to the simulation results and to your view of the best mortgage?

(4) Edit your loan repayment spreadsheet so that the variable interest rate follows a triangular distribution with a mode of 7%, minimum of 4%

and maximum of 10%. What difference does this make to the simulation results and to your view of the best mortgage?

(5) Set up the investment decision (Section 4.3.2) on a spreadsheet and compare your simulation results with those of this chapter.

REFERENCES

Analycorp (2003) `http://www.analycorp.com/`

Decisioneering (2003) `http://www.decisioneering.com/`

Evans J.R. and Olsen D.L. (2001) *Introduction to Simulation and Risk Analysis*. Prentice-Hall, Englewood Cliffs, NJ.

Grossman T.A. (1999) Teachers' forum: Spreadsheet modeling and simulation improves understanding of queues. *Interfaces*, **29**(3), 8–103.

Johnson D.G. (1997) The triangular distribution as a proxy for the beta distribution in risk analysis. *Journal of the Royal Statistical Society—Series D (The Statistician)*, **46**(3), 387–98.

Knight F.H. (1921) *Risk, Uncertainty and Profit*. Houghton Mifflin, Boston.

Myerson R. (2003) `http://home.uchicago.edu/~rmyerson/addins.htm`

Lindley D.V. (1980) *Making Decisions* (2nd edition). John Wiley & Sons, New York.

Palisade (2003) `http://www.palisade-europe.com/`

Powell S.G. and Baker K.R. (2003) *The Art of Modeling with Spreadsheets: Management Science, Spreadsheet Engineering, and Modeling Craft*. John Wiley & Sons, New York.

Seila A.F. (2002) Spreadsheet simulation. In: J.M. Charnes, E. Yücesan and C.-H. Chen (eds), *Proceedings of the 2002 Winter Simulation Conference, December 2002, San Diego, CA*.

Part II

Discrete Event Simulation

Discrete Event Modelling

5.1 FUNDAMENTALS

As the name suggests, a discrete event simulation is one that employs a next-event technique (Section 2.2.2) to control the behaviour of the model. Many applications of discrete event simulation involve queuing systems of one kind or another. The queuing structure may be obvious, as in a queue of jobs waiting to be processed on a machine, or in a stack of aircraft waiting for landing space at an airport. In other cases, the queuing structure may be less obvious, as in the deployment of fire appliances in a large city. In this case, the customers are the fires needing attention and the servers are the firefighters together with their associated equipment.

As another example, consider a car body paint shop in which the bodies pass through a series of processes such as spray booths, ovens and rectification areas. They move from area to area on lifts, conveyors and other transfer machines until, satisfactorily painted, they reach the painted body store. In some cases (e.g., immediately after a vertical transfer in a lift) the bodies may not be processed straightaway but may enter a temporary storage area to wait with other bodies. Because of this part-finished stock, a lift breakdown would not immediately bring the succeeding process to a halt (i.e., the stocks are used to decouple two processes). This stock can be thought of as a queue and, in the simplest case, the queue would operate with a first in first out (FIFO) discipline. The car bodies are waiting for the next process.

Quite a variety of systems can be regarded as having a queuing structure and as such they lend themselves well to discrete event simulation. The purpose of this chapter is to introduce some general terminology that may be used to build models suitable for discrete event simulation. A particular modelling device, the activity cycle diagram, is then introduced as a way of developing the structure of a model.

5.2 TERMINOLOGY

There is no agreed terminology in discrete simulation, which leads different writers to occasionally use the same term to mean different things and this can lead to some confusion. The terminology defined here is fairly standard and is deliberately quite limited to try to minimize confusion. It is divided into two parts. The first set provides labels for the objects that constitute a system to be simulated. The second set defines the operations in which these objects engage over time.

5.2.1 Objects of the system

- *Entities*. These are the individual elements of the system that are being simulated and whose behaviour is being explicitly tracked. Examples might include machines in a factory, patients in a hospital or aircraft at an airport. Within the simulation, the computer program maintains information about each entity and therefore each one can be individually identified. As an entity changes state in the simulation, the computer program keeps track of these state changes. The overall system state is a result of the interaction of the individual entities. The number of entities in a model gives some idea of its complexity and may give some idea about how fast it will run.

- *Resources*. These are also individual system elements but they are not modelled individually. Instead, they are treated as countable items whose individual behaviour is not tracked in the computer program. Examples might be the number of passengers waiting at a bus stop or the number of boxes of a product available in a warehouse. Thus, a resource consists of identical items and the program keeps a count of how many are available, but their individual states are not tracked. The number of resource types in a model is another clue to its complexity and this is not the same as the number of resource items.

Whether a system element should be treated as an entity or as a resource is something that the modeller must decide. The decision will depend, mainly, on the purpose for which the simulation is intended. Consider a simulation of a bus network in which passengers board and leave at bus stops. If we need to know how long each passenger takes to complete a bus journey in which different passengers have different trips in mind, then we will treat passengers as entities. If, on the other hand, we are only interested in the number of people on each bus at any time, then we may be able to use a counter such as *NumberOnBus* for this purpose. Section 5.3 gives examples of simulations, some of which treat all elements as entities and some of which use a mixture of entities and resources.

When elements are represented as entities, some software requires further distinctions to be made. A common distinction is between permanent and temporary entities. Permanent entities are ones that are created at the start of a simulation and which will exist throughout a run. Temporary ones are created and may be destroyed during a run. Temporary entities may often be better modelled as resources.

The other distinction that is sometimes required is between active and passive entities. This distinction is most common when simulating client–server systems in which entities cooperate in some task or other. One entity is regarded as active—it seizes the other; and the other is regarded as passive—it is seized. This distinction is, of course, wholly arbitrary. In another realm, when two people meet and fall in love, it doesn't really matter which one made the running in the first place!

5.2.2   The organization of entities

Although entities are individually modelled within a discrete event simulation, it is convenient to think about them in groups, some of which are permanent and some of which are temporary.

- *Classes*. These are permanent groups of identical or similar entities. Bus passengers might be such a class, as might commercial aircraft. The classes can be subdivided into more detailed subclasses in some software. Within a class, each entity can still be identified as an individual but the class provides a convenient way to refer to similar entities that engage in similar behaviour.
- *Sets*. These are temporary groups of entities that are often used to represent entity states or queues. Thus, those bus passengers currently on bus number 37 could be regarded as being in a set *OnBus37*. Or those waiting in a queue at the depot could be a set *WaitingAtDepot*. Entities move from set to set during a simulation as they change state. Entities within a set may be held in a particular order, such as FIFO, LIFO (last in first out) or according to some priority scheme, or they may be unsequenced.
- *Attributes*. These are items of information that belong to each entity and they are used for two purposes. First, they are used to distinguish between members of the same class of entity. Thus, the intended route of a bus passenger might be such an attribute, as might the length of time since she left home. The second use for attributes is to control the behaviour of an entity. In this sense, attributes may be used instead of sets to represent the state of an entity. Hence, for example, a machine in a factory might have an attribute such as *Condition*. If *Condition* is OK, then the machine may process a job, but not otherwise.

Clearly, there is some redundancy in the above terms. For example, the state of an entity might be represented as its current set membership or as the current value of one of its attributes. Nevertheless it can sometimes be useful to maintain both sets and attributes.

5.2.3   Operations of the entities

As the simulation proceeds, the entities cooperate and thence change state. Some terminology is needed to describe these operations and also to describe the flow of time in the simulation.

- *Event*. This is an instant of time at which a significant state change occurs in the system, such as when an entity enters or leaves a set, or some operation begins. Note that it is up to the analyst to define whether an event is significant or not in the context of the objectives of the simulation.

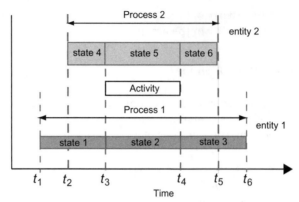

Figure 5.1   Events, activities and processes

In the paint shop, the start or completion of an operation such as rectification may be regarded as an event.

- *Activity*. Entities move from set to set because of the operations in which they engage. The operations and procedures that are initiated at each event are known as activities and these activities are what transform the state of the entities. For example, in a car body paint shop, the activity "rectification" transforms a body from the state "awaiting rectification" to the state "waiting for spray".
- *Process*. Sometimes it is useful to group together a sequence of events in the chronological order in which they will occur. Such a sequence is known as a process and is often used to represent all or part of the life of temporary entities. For example, a car body arrives, is degreased, hot dipped, primed, etc.
- *Simulation clock*. This is the point reached by current simulated time in a simulation. Hence in a simulation where the time unit is minutes, the test "is clock = 240?" might be used to test whether a lunch break is due. If so, appropriate activity could then be initiated in the simulation.

The relationship between events, activities and processes is shown in Figure 5.1.

5.3   ACTIVITY CYCLE DIAGRAMS

In a discrete event simulation the various entities interact through simulated time and these interactions can be described in the terms introduced in Section 5.2. In order to build a model suitable for discrete event simulation, it is necessary to:

- Identify the important classes of entity.
- Consider the activities in which they engage.
- Link these activities together.

From this skeleton, the fine detail of the model can be built up.

While considering the topic of simulation modelling, it is as well to bear in mind the "principle of parsimony". This requires the analyst to begin model building with the well understood and obvious elements of the system of interest. Once these are properly modelled and validated, then the more complicated and less well understood elements can be added later. In most modelling there is an overwhelming temptation to dive straight into the complicated features. This temptation is to be resisted.

Activity cycle diagrams are one way of modelling the interactions of the entities and are particularly useful for systems with a strong queuing structure. They were popularized by Hills (1971) and are normally associated with the activity and three-phase approaches described in Chapters 6 and 7. However, Mathewson (1974) points out that they are just as useful for other modelling approaches such as event-based methods or process-based methods also covered in Chapter 6 and can be useful however the simulation is to be implemented. Though they have been used as the basis of automated program generators, they are best regarded as a quick way of capturing some of the major interactions to be included in the model. In most cases they cannot include the full complexity of a system being simulated, but they do provide a skeleton that can be enhanced later.

Activity cycle diagrams make use of only two symbols and these are shown in Figure 5.2. The diagram itself is a map that shows the life history of each class of entity and displays their interactions. Each class of entity is considered to have a life cycle that consists of a series of states. The entities move from state to state as their life proceeds in a sequence of alternate active and dead states. Time moves forward in the simulation as entities spend time in these states.

An active state usually involves the cooperation of different classes of entity. The duration of an active state can always be determined in advance, either because the state duration is deterministic or by taking a sample from an appropriate probability distribution if the duration is stochastic. The basic idea of random sampling was introduced in Chapter 2 and is given more rigorous treatment in Chapter 10. In a queuing system, a service is one such active state because it involves the cooperation of a server and a customer. An appropriate probability distribution or histogram for the service time can be sampled to determine the duration of the active state.

On the other hand, a dead state involves no cooperation between different classes of entity and is generally a state in which the entity waits for something to happen. Dead states are sometimes treated as sets or queues. The length of time that an entity spends in a dead state cannot be determined in advance. It depends on the end of the immediately preceding active state and on the start of the next active state. This is why the life cycle of an entity

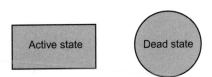

Figure 5.2 Symbols for activity cycle diagrams

is modelled as an alternate sequence of active and dead states in an activity cycle diagram. For example, in a simulation of a car body paint shop, the time spent by a car body in the dead state "waiting for rectification work" depends on when its painting was finished and on when its rectification begins. The latter, as an active state, may depend on when resources are available to carry out the rectification.

Drawing an activity cycle diagram involves listing the states through which each class of entity passes, and normally these are drawn as alternate dead and active states. The complete diagram consists of a combination of all the individual cycles.

5.3.1   Example 1: a simple job shop

Consider a simple engineering job shop that consists of several identical machines. Each machine is able to process any job and there is a ready supply of jobs with no prospect of any shortages. Jobs are allocated to the first available machine. The time taken to complete a job is variable but is independent of the particular machine being used. The machine shop is staffed by operatives who have two tasks:

(1)   Reset machines between jobs if the cutting edges are still OK.
(2)   Retool those machines with cutting edges that are too worn to be reset.

Thus there are two classes of entity (see Figure 5.3):

(1)   The operatives.
(2)   The machines.

The operatives

These are responsible for the two tasks RETOOL and RESET as described above. In addition an operator may be unavailable while attending to personal

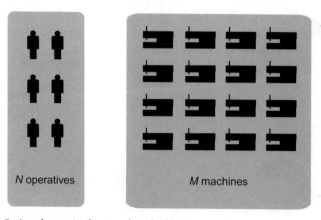

Figure 5.3 Entity classes in the simple job shop

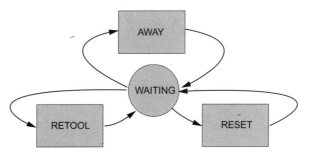

Figure 5.4   The operatives' activity cycle

needs. Obviously, a real job shop would be much more complicated—however, this example is aimed solely at introducing the concepts of activity cycle diagrams. With this information, the activity cycle for the operative class is as shown in Figure 5.4. This shows three active states: AWAY, RETOOL and RESET.

Obviously, RETOOL and RESET are carried out in cooperation with the machines (the other class of entity) and are therefore active states. If not deterministic, their durations could be simulated by sampling from appropriate probability distributions. The distributions themselves might be obtained by observing the actual times taken by the operative to carry out these tasks. AWAY is also an active state because such a probability distribution could be used to determine its duration and thus it meets one of the conditions for an active state.

When not in any of these active states, the operative is in the dead state WAITING and is available for work of some kind, or is able to attend to his personal needs. In practice he may be in this dead state for quite some time or he may merely pass instantaneously through this state between two active states.

Notice, therefore, that the diagram consists of alternate active and dead states (i.e., the operative must pass through a dead state when moving between active states).

The machines

These have three active states: RETOOL, RESET and RUNNING. The latter active state represents the time when the machine is satisfactorily processing a job. Hence the activity cycle for the machines is as in Figure 5.5.

Following the convention for activity cycle diagrams, the active states have been separated by three dead states. After a machine stops RUNNING (i.e., a job is complete) it moves into the dead state STOPPED, from which it may move to:

- RESET. If its cutting edges are serviceable.
- RETOOL. If the cutting edges are too worn.

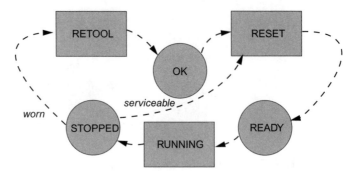

Figure 5.5   The machines' activity cycle

During a simulation, an attribute may be used to decide whether a machine moves to RESET or RETOOL on each occasion.

After RETOOL, a machine is OK (another dead state) and is then RESET. Now the machine is READY (another dead state) following which it is RUNNING again. In real life, the dead states OK and READY may not exist, as the operative may move smoothly between the three active states. OK and READY are included here for two reasons. First, they maintain the convention of alternate active and dead states. Second, they would allow the model to be enhanced so as to consider, say, two operatives, one of whom is responsible for RETOOL and the other for RESET.

The two cycles may now be combined into the complete activity cycle diagram shown in Figure 5.6. Note that the dead states are unique to each

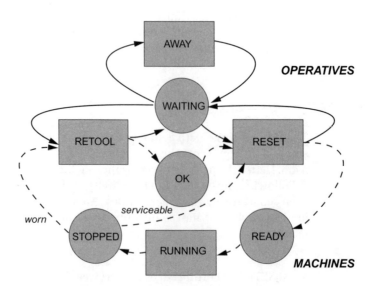

Figure 5.6   The job shop activity cycle diagram

class of entity. Only the operative can be WAITING and only the machines can be OK, STOPPED or RUNNING. On the other hand, at least two of the active states involve cooperation between the two classes of entity.

Activity cycle diagrams provide a graphical way of describing the interactions which must be built into the skeleton of the simulation model (i.e., they show the logic of the system). Thus, they allow precise specification of the conditions that must hold before state changes can occur. For example, before RETOOL can begin there must be at least one machine STOPPED and in need of a retool and the operative must be available (i.e., WAITING) to do the work. The next example will show in more detail how these diagrams may be used as the basis of a simulation model—this time, of an explicit queuing system.

5.3.2   Example 2: the harassed booking clerk

A theatre employs a booking clerk during the day. The clerk is employed to sell tickets and to answer any enquiries which may arise. Seat bookings are accepted only if the customer turns up in person at the theatre and pays for the tickets. Enquiries can come either from someone there in person or from someone phoning the theatre. The clerk is instructed to give priority to personal customers—after all, they may hand over some cash. Thus, if the phone rings just as a customer arrives in person, then the personal enquirer is served first. Thanks to a sophisticated phone system, incoming calls can queue on a FIFO basis until answered. Phone callers never ring off in frustration.

There are three classes of entity:

(1)   A single booking clerk.
(2)   Personal enquirers.
(3)   Phone callers.

We will consider each of these in turn.

The booking clerk

The booking clerk clearly has two active states:

- SERVICE. Serving personal enquirers by selling tickets, answering questions or both.
- TALK. Speaking to phone callers.

When not engaged in these active states, the booking clerk is in a dead state IDLE. Thus the activity cycle for the clerk is as shown in Figure 5.7. As before, the clerk goes through a sequence of alternate active and dead states. On occasions, the clerk will spend zero time in the dead state between two active states. This illustrates another point about simulation modelling: it

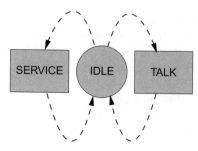

Figure 5.7   The booking clerk's activity cycle

can sometimes be useful to have an entity to occupy a state even if the time spent in that state is zero.

Personal enquirers

These are initially OUTSIDE the theatre. They then ARRIVE, QUEUE for service and the SERVICE begins. After the clerk has completed their service, they leave the theatre and are once again OUTSIDE.

First, consider the state SERVICE. This is a cooperative state that requires an enquirer and the clerk if it is to occur. There is therefore no doubt that this is an active state according to the earlier definitions. Second, consider the state QUEUE. As its name suggests, this is the state in which the enquirers wait until they are at the head of the queue and the booking clerk is able to serve them. Thus, as it is not a cooperative state and its duration clearly depends on the duration of the previous customer's service, it is a dead state.

This means that ARRIVAL is an active state, although why this should be so is probably not clear. To understand this, it may be helpful to imagine a machine that somehow transfers personal enquirers one at a time from OUTSIDE the theatre into the QUEUE. It returns for the next enquirer once it has safely placed an enquirer into the QUEUE. This arrival machine takes a finite time to execute this transfer and the enquirers are considered to be in the ARRIVAL state during that time. Hence, the duration of the ARRIVAL state becomes the interval between successive arrivals. In this way, the arrival process may be modelled as an active state provided that the inter-arrival time is determinable. Two obvious ways of doing this would be to use a timetable of arrivals or to take samples from some appropriate probability distribution.

If the inter-arrival times are taken as samples from some probability distribution, then the arrivals are usually controlled by a bootstrapping process. This works as follows:

If enquirer N arrives at time T, then take a sample from the distribution of inter-arrival times and use the sample as the interval t between customers N and $N + 1$.

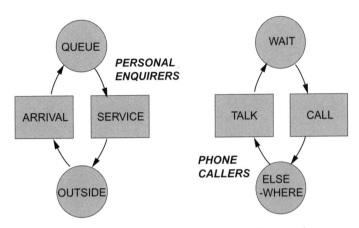

Figure 5.8   The personal enquirers' and phone callers' activity cycles

Thus customer $N + 1$ arrives at time $T + t$. Clearly, this process must begin with a prior determination of the arrival time of the first enquirer. However, once that is done, the method allows successive arrivals to be modelled as active states.

Finally, consider the dead state OUTSIDE. This represents the world outside the theatre from which the enquirers emerge and to which they return after SERVICE. It constitutes the environment of the system being modelled; in effect, the arrivals are quasi-exogenous events. OUTSIDE is inserted for two reasons:

- To give the personal enquirers the sequence of active and dead states required by the conventions of activity cycle diagrams.
- Because it is normal for all cycles to be closed loops. This is obviously artificial in one sense as the number of potential enquirers is virtually infinite.

The left-hand side of Figure 5.8 shows the resulting activity cycle.

Phone callers

This cycle parallels that of the personal enquirers. This time the arriving "customers" are phone calls to the theatre which are allowed to queue until the phone is answered. The interval between successive calls is modelled by the active state CALL and the active service state is TALK. The activity cycle is shown in the right-hand side of Figure 5.8 in which the dead states WAIT and ELSEWHERE separate the two active states. As before, ELSEWHERE represents the environment of the theatre from which phone calls emerge.

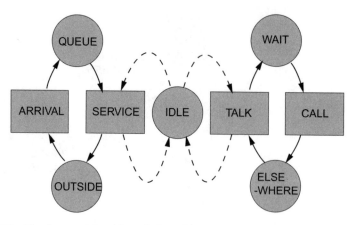

Figure 5.9   The harassed booking clerk problem: complete activity cycle diagram

The complete diagram

The three cycles may now be combined to form the activity cycle diagram shown in Figure 5.9.

5.3.3   Example 3: the delivery depot

A delivery depot serves two functions. First, goods are received from the factory on large lorries and are held in stock. Second, they are delivered to customers by small vans which collect their loads from the stock held at the depot. At the moment, the depot has two unloading bays for the lorries and four loading bays for the vans. The same labour force is used for loading and unloading, either operation requiring a gang of two men. There are 10 men available at the moment. The owners of the depot wish to know how many loading bays are needed to meet the current demand.

To complicate matters, the depot is on a rather awkward site as shown in Figure 5.10. Access to the site is gained from the main road and at the entrance there is a vehicle park in which lorries or vans may wait. To get to either loading or unloading bays, the vehicles must be driven along a narrow access road. Its narrowness means that two lorries cannot pass one another—even if they are travelling in opposite directions. However, there is room for two vans to pass—although not for a van to pass a lorry. At the moment, the site manager operates with a rule that gives top priority to lorries leaving the site over any other vehicles on this road. Second priority is to lorries moving towards the unloading bays. Vans have the lowest priority.

This system could be modelled in a number of ways. It will be used here to illustrate the use of entities and resources, whereas the previous examples have just used entities. Assume that we wish to study the delays suffered by the vans and lorries to see if delivery performance can be improved. This

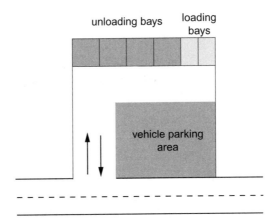

Figure 5.10   The delivery depot: site plan

suggests that vans and lorries should be treated as entities and that it may be possible to treat the rest as resources. Hence, the system might be modelled with the following:

ENTITY	Vans	An unlimited number, arriving and leaving
CLASSES	Lorries	An unlimited number, arriving and leaving
COUNTABLE	Unloading bays	Two available
RESOURCES	Loading bays	Four available at the moment, but we wish to vary this
	Labour	Five gangs available
	Road in	One available
	Road out	One available

Note that the access road, which serves the site, has been split into two resources, *roadin* and *roadout*. Lorries fill the entire road when they move and will thus require both *roadin* and *roadout*. Vans need only the *roadin* when they arrive and *roadout* when they leave.
Considering each entity and resource in turn:

- *Lorries*. Since these are to be treated as an entity class, they have their own activity cycle and this is shown in Figure 5.11. The lorries come from OUTSIDE, they ARRIVE and then join a QUEUE in which they wait to MOVE to an unloading bay until both *roadin* and *roadout* are free. Once it is at the unloading bay, *roadin* and *roadout* become free again. Having arrived at the unloading bay, a lorry must wait there until there is a free gang of labour available and, when this condition is met, it may UNLOAD. Once unloaded, the gang of labour is released and the lorry waits in the state EMPTY until both *roadin* and *roadout* are free and it may then LEAVE the site. Once it has left, *roadin* and *roadout* become free again.

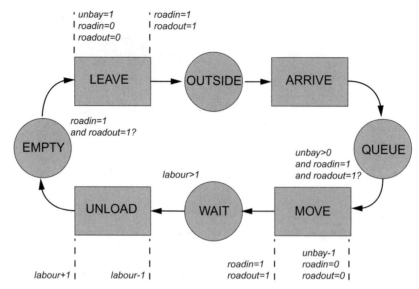

Figure 5.11   The lorries' activity cycle

- *Vans*. These have a very similar activity cycle to the lorries and this is shown in Figure 5.12. The main difference, apart from the names given to the states, is that ENTER needs only the *roadin* and EXIT needs only the *roadout*.
- *Unloading bays*. These are modelled as a resource, which might be represented as a variable called *unbay* that is initially set to a value of 2, to indicate that both are available at the start of the simulation. As an unloading bay is occupied, the variable *unbay* is decremented by 1 and then incremented by 1 when the lorry leaves the bay.

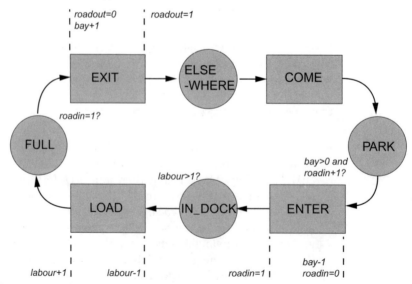

Figure 5.12   The vans' activity cycle

- *Loading bays.* These are rather like the unloading bays, except that they are used by vans. If there are four available at the start of the simulation, then we might represent them by a variable such as *bay*, which is initially given the value of 4.
- *Labour.* If labour is also represented as a resource, we might employ a variable such as *labour*, which is given the value 5 initially and then reduced or increased in value as required by vans and lorries.
- *Roadin.* These are also resources and might be represented by a variable such as *roadin* that takes a value of 0 or 1. Thus, when the road is free it might have the value 1 and might take the value 0 if it is occupied. Alternatively, *roadin* could be a Boolean variable.
- *Roadout.* These are also resources and might be represented by a variable such as *roadout* that takes a value of 0 or 1. Thus, when the road is free it might have the value 1 and might take the value 0 if it is occupied. Alternatively, *roadout* could be a Boolean variable.

5.3.4   Using the activity cycle diagram

As described so far, activity cycle diagrams are simply a way of showing the interactions between the various classes of entity involved in the system. It would be possible to consider these interactions using lists, but most people find some sort of flow diagram helpful at the early stages of simulation modelling. In drawing these diagrams, the analyst is also forced to consider the events which occur as the system changes state. Initially it is useful to imagine that events occur at the beginning and end of activities. Thus, using the theatre booking clerk as an example, the following changes of state are evident:

SERVICE BEGINS   SERVICE ENDS
ARRIVAL BEGINS   ARRIVAL ENDS
TALK BEGINS   TALK ENDS
CALL BEGINS   CALL ENDS

For instance, when SERVICE BEGINS the following changes occur:

- The booking clerk is no longer idle but engaged in service.
- The queue of waiting enquirers is reduced by 1.

Needless to say, the event will only take place if:

- There is at least one enquirer in the queue.
- And the clerk is free (i.e., idle).

Though eight events are listed above, some of them will always coincide. Consider the active state ARRIVAL, which has two associated events ARRIVAL BEGINS and ARRIVAL ENDS. Section 5.3.2 pointed out that arrival processes may easily be modelled by a bootstrapping process and this means that two events will always coincide (i.e., the ARRIVAL ENDS event for enquirer N occurs at the same time as ARRIVAL BEGINS for enquirer $N + 1$). Hence, the two can be combined into a single ARRIVAL event. Identical logic allows CALL BEGINS and CALL ENDS to be combined into CALL. In this way, the list of events is reduced from eight to six.

In a discrete event simulation, the simulated time (simulation clock) is moved forward from event to event. At each event, state changes occur and these constitute the behaviour of the model. In the example of the harassed booking clerk, enquirers arrive at irregular intervals, the telephone rings, service begins and ends, phone conversations begin and end and so on. As this happens, queues of phone calls and enquirers build up and run down, the clerk is sometimes busy and sometimes idle, and money is taken for seat tickets. The problem that faces anyone trying to simulate such a system from scratch is to find some way of controlling the state changes.

A particular problem is that, on some occasions, several operations may be due at the same simulation clock time (i.e., there are parallel operations to be simulated). An unfortunate characteristic of most digital computers is that they execute instructions serially and not in parallel (i.e., parallel simulation events cannot be made to occur at the same real time). This problem is handled by making the simulation program perform a two-stage process as follows:

(1) The program moves the simulation to the time of the next state change(s). The simulation clock is then held at that time.
(2) Any operations now due at that time are performed in some sort of priority order. For example, the harassed booking clerk must serve personal enquirers in preference to answering the phone. Once all the possible operations are complete, the program returns to the first stage.

Thus, serial operations in the program are used to simulate parallel processes.

Various different ways of modelling the operations of the system exist and the four main methods are described in Chapters 6 and 7. All have in common the fact that the operations are broken down into a set of basic building blocks. The nature of the blocks varies between the four methods, but in all cases each block becomes a segment of computer program. The job of sorting out priorities and of sequencing the operations therefore becomes one of ensuring that the segments of program are executed in the right order. In this way, the question of "who" does "what" and "when" is easily managed.

5.4 ACTIVITY CYCLE DIAGRAMS: A CAVEAT

Activity cycle diagrams are most useful for systems that can be easily regarded as having a queuing structure. In fact this includes a surprisingly large number of systems which need to be simulated. The dead states are used to represent the queues and entities are assumed to pass from queue to queue via active states. Some older commercial software made use of this structure and notation (e.g., the HOCUS package and the CAPS program generator of Clementson; both appeared in the 1960s). Since such software was commercially successful it indicates the utility of the activity cycle concept. However, activity cycle diagrams are not used in most contemporary software of the type discussed in Chapters 8 and 9. Instead, Visual Interactive Modelling Systems (VIMS) use their own icons so that models can be built onscreen in the usual point and click way.

Also, there are systems that do not easily fit the activity cycle notation—although enthusiasts would argue that they can be made to fit. One such type of system is where the interruption of an active state may occur before it reaches its scheduled termination. As a rather brutal instance of this, consider the simulation of a battle tank that is hit whilst the missile launcher is being targeted. The interrupted active state "targeting" is shortened by a hit from some other entity—a missile in flight.

Another type of system not conveniently represented by activity cycle diagrams is one in which the important entities are not the temporary ones which pass around the system. Consider, for example, a T-junction on a road system. Vehicles arrive and form queues, but the main resources are the various sections of the road junction over which the vehicles pass, and it is the state of these road sections which is important—as well as whether particular queues exist at the junction. Attempts to draw activity cycle diagrams of such road junctions usually succeed, but at the cost of a hideously over-complicated view of the system. Systems which do not easily fit the activity cycle concept are best modelled directly as a set of possible state changes, as shown in the next two chapters. How this can be done for a T-junction, will be described in Section 6.2.5.

Activity cycle diagrams are, though, very quick to draw and form a useful stage of conceptual model development. They help identify the important dynamic objects of the system and help divide these into entities and resources. They also help the modeller to understand the conditions that govern the state changes that occur within the system being modelled.

EXERCISES

(1) Draw an activity cycle diagram for the following system. A barber's shop employs two barbers, each of which has his own barber's chair. Both barbers work between the hours of 9.00 am to 5.00 pm and both take a 60-minute lunch break at 12.00 noon. Customers arrive at random at the shop and are served by the first available barber. If neither is free then the customers sit in the waiting area in one of the five chairs provided and read the appropriate literature. There being no shortage of barbers, customers who arrive and find the waiting area full do not remain to wait for a seat. The length of time taken to cut a customer's hair varies randomly.

(2) What revisions would you need to make to the activity cycle diagram produced for Exercise (1) if each customer has a preferred barber?

(3)   Draw an activity cycle diagram for the following system. Trucks laden with feed grain for export arrive at a dock. At the entrance to the dock, each load of grain is sampled and, if the quality is unacceptable, the truck leaves immediately still laden. The time taken to sample a load varies randomly, as does the size of a load. Accepted loads are driven to one of three conveyors which transfer the grain to a suitable silo, of which five are available. The silos have a finite capacity and if no space is available, the trucks must wait. Periodically, ships arrive at the docks and receive grain from the silos. No ship takes grain from more than one silo.

(4)   Modify the diagram drawn for Exercise (3) so that no trucks are accepted into the port if all three conveyors are in use or if all of the silos are full.

(5)   What events would you need to consider if you were to simulate the system described in Exercise (3)?

(6)   Consider a T-junction at which all normal turns are permitted. What system events would you need to consider if you were to simulate this system?

(7)   The Management Board of the Lancaster People's Hospital is concerned about its accident and emergency service, which operates 24 hours a day, 7 days a week. A recent audit showed that patients were waiting a long time (over 30 minutes) before seeing any member of staff and that some patients spent over 3 hours in the clinic. These times breach Government Guidelines. A recent study of the clinic suggested a new mode of operation. There would be three grades of staff; doctors, nurses and specially trained nurse-practitioners. Patients, who arrive at random, would be seen as quickly as possible by a specially trained nurse-practitioner who would classify the patient into one of three groups:

- Needs to see a doctor.
- Needs only to see a nurse.
- No treatment needed.

Once classified, the patients would wait for a doctor or nurse, as appropriate, or would leave the clinic.

Patients who see a doctor will then need dressings to be applied to wounds and these will be applied by the first available nurse. Having seen a doctor, they rejoin the nurse queue for this purpose. After the application of a dressing, they leave the clinic. Patients who are sent by the specially trained nurse-practitioner to see a nurse wait for the first available nurse. The nurse may decide that the patient needs to see a doctor or needs no further treatment. Patients sent by a nurse to see a doctor must wait for the first free doctor and are then treated as if sent to the doctor by the specially trained nurse-practitioner. The Board are thinking of employing two doctors, two nurses and a single specially trained nurse-practitioner on each shift. Meal breaks are covered by staff from elsewhere in the hospital but the Board would like to know if these would be sensible manning levels. They would like to meet the following service targets:

- Arriving patients should expect to wait less than 5 minutes to see a specially trained nurse-practitioner.
- Patients whom the specially trained nurse-practitioner decides needs treatment by a doctor or a nurse should expect to spend no more than 30 minutes in the clinic after arriving.

They also believe that, of the patients who arrive at the clinic:

- 30% will be sent by a specially trained nurse-practitioner to see a nurse, 40% to see a doctor, and the rest will need no treatment.
- 10% will be sent by a nurse to see a doctor.

There is plenty of space for patients to wait for a doctor or nurse and enough consultation rooms can be made available for up to 10 staff, whether specially trained nurse-practitioners, nurses or doctors.

Develop an activity cycle diagram that may be used as the basis of a discrete simulation model of this accident and emergency department.

REFERENCES

Hills P.R. (1971) *HOCUS*. P-E Group, Egham, UK.

Mathewson S.C. (1974) Simulation program generators. *Simulation*, **23**(6), 181–9.

6

How Discrete Simulation Software Works

6.1 INTRODUCTION

6.1.1 Why understand how simulation software is organized?

Chapter 5 showed how dynamic systems of interacting entities can be modelled using simulation concepts. The key is to identify the important classes of entity and to map out the ways in which they interact and change state through time. These interactions and state changes can be captured on activity cycle diagrams so as to understand the rules that govern this behaviour. Chapters 8 and 9 discuss software packages that can be used to develop a working discrete event simulation, but it is important to understand the principles on which such software operates. As is made clear in Chapters 8 and 9, different software packages have their pros and cons and unless we understand the principles on which they operate, we are at the mercy of their foibles.

This chapter looks as what are known as "simulation worldviews" since an understanding of these is the basis for understanding how most simulation software operates. Leaving aside the question of user interfaces and links to other computer programs, it is helpful to regard discrete event programs as having two main sets of components as shown in Figure 6.1.

- *The simulation engine*. Sometimes known as the control program or engine, which ensures that the entities change state correctly. This component is general (i.e., it does not need to be changed for particular applications). It is provided by the software vendor and controls the workings of the application specific components.
- *Application specific components*. These define how the entities are to change state (i.e., the logic of the system being simulated). Each simulation worldview expects the application specific logic to be organized in particular ways, because the operation of these components is controlled by the simulation engine. The simulation modeller must provide these—either by using a Visual Interactive Modelling System (VIMS) (Chapter 8) or writing code (Chapters 7 and 9).

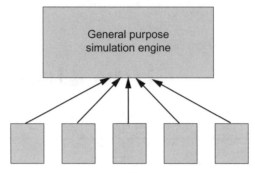

Application specific components

Figure 6.1   Two-part structure of discrete simulation programs

6.1.2   Simulation executives in more detail

A simulation executive controls the activities and events in which the entities and resources engage. It does this by maintaining, at the very least, a *simulation clock* and a *calendar*. The simulation clock denotes the time within the simulation, which will not be related to real time unless this is a real time simulation. As time within the simulation proceeds, so the clock variable increases in value. The calendar is rather like a diary into which future commitments are entered. As with a diary, once the simulation clock reaches a time for which the calendar contains an entry, then the simulation executive must do something. The executive is, thus, a form of automaton whose job is to maintain control of the entities and resources.

This control can be considered under two headings. First, the executive must see to the correct scheduling of activities and events. This means that it must ensure that they happen at the right time. Thus, for example, if a shop is due to open at 9.00 am, the executive must make sure that this happens. The executive must also ensure that any conditional activity happens at the right time. Conditional activity is not so much dependent on the passage of time as on the availability of resources. Thus, for example, the service of a customer cannot begin unless the customer is waiting to be served and there is a server ready to serve.

Second, the executive must make sure that activity occurs in the correct sequence within the simulation. Some of this sequencing is a mirror of the world that is being simulated. For example, engineering parts must be ground before they are polished. Other aspects of sequencing are slightly more subtle and are related to the nature of digital computers. Although most computers are capable of some parallel operations, they are at heart sequential machines. Hence, most computer programs consist of a sequence of steps. For example, in Visual Basic, we can write something like the following:

$$x = 10$$
$$y = 2^*x$$
$$z = x^*y$$

and we would expect the computer to put the variable x to 10, then to put the variable y to 20 and then to put the variable z to 200. If we got any other behaviour we would be very puzzled because we expect the lines of the program to be executed in the order in which they are listed. In a discrete event simulation, we often must simulate systems with activities that occur simultaneously and in parallel.

For example, in the harassed booking clerk example introduced in Section 5.3.2, if there were more than a single clerk, then it is perfectly possible for one clerk to be serving a personal enquirer and another to be answering the phone. If one of these activities has a higher priority (say, talking to personal customers since they may spend money) then the executive might need to ensure that a phone conversation only begins if there are no personal enquirers waiting to be served. Thus, the executive must be able to cope with simulating parallelism on computer systems that are essentially sequential, and must do so in the correct sequence. In many ways, this is similar to the need for a multitasking computer operating system to control several computer programs at the same time.

6.1.3   Application logic

The way in which the application logic is expressed depends on the way in which the simulation executive is implemented. This chapter discusses how application logic must be expressed for the main simulation worldviews. Any application that is suited to discrete event simulation can be expressed in any of the worldviews, although it will become clear later that some are more convenient than others. This book takes the view that a three-phase approach is, on balance, the preferred option. Hence more space is devoted to a three-phase approach.

6.2   THE THREE-PHASE APPROACH

The three-phase approach, proposed first by Tocher (1963) rests on the realization that there are two ways in which activity may start within a discrete simulation.

6.2.1   Bs

Some operations have a starting or finishing time that can be predicted in advance. These can therefore be scheduled as if they were appointments being entered into a diary. These are known as Bs. Originally they were known as B activities, which was an abbreviation for Bookkeeping activities or Bound activities, the term "bound" indicating that they were bound to happen at some specified time, and the term "bookkeeping" that they might used for keeping regular records (e.g., of queue lengths). Some people refer to B events instead, but to avoid confusion they are called Bs here.

Because these Bs can be directly scheduled, the simulation executive can precisely control when they will occur by ensuring that they are executed when the simulation clock reaches the correct time. Hence, each B must have an entry in the event calendar which serves as a reminder to the executive to take some action. A suitable analogy for this would be a central heating controller in which the start time for the heating is set at, say, 6.30 am. When the clock of the controller reaches 6.30 am, it triggers the central heating system into life.

As a general rule, to which there are some exceptions, any state which is represented by an active state on an activity cycle diagram ends with a B. For example, consider the activity cycle diagram for the harassed booking clerk in Figure 5.9. The active state SERVICE, once started, must come to an end. If we know the time at which it started then we can schedule when it will end. If the duration of this state is deterministic (e.g., it always takes 10 minutes) then the known duration can be used to make an entry in the event calendar. If the duration is stochastic, then a sample from a probability distribution (as in Section 2.3.2) can be used to find its duration and this may then be used to create an entry in the event calendar. Hence, we can consider *EndOfService* to be a B. Similarly, *EndOfTalk* will also be a B.

The usual effect of a B is to release resources and entities. Hence, when the *EndOfService* B is executed, the activity cycle diagram shows that the clerk who had been carrying out the SERVICE is released back into an IDLE state. The customer is released back into the OUTSIDE world. The *EndOfTalk* B operates similarly. Thus, when either of these Bs is executed, it frees a clerk to engage in another task, should there be customers waiting.

6.2.2   Cs

Operations that are not Bs are regarded as Cs. This was originally an abbreviation for Conditional activity or Cooperative activity, the idea being that such activity is not dependent on the simulation clock but must wait until the conditions are right or until some other entity is ready to cooperate in the task. As with Bs, some people refer to C events instead, but the term C will be used here. The simulation executive has no direct say in when these Cs will occur, for this will depend on the states of the entities and resources in the simulation. Obviously the executive has some indirect control, since the main effect of the Bs (which it does control) is to release entities and resources. This means that, as a general rule, states which are depicted as active states on an activity cycle diagram begin with a C. Thus, in general, active states begin with a C and end with a B, as shown in Figure 6.2. There is one important exception to this rule and this will be discussed in Section 6.2.3.

As with Bs, this rule can be illustrated by the active states for SERVICE and TALK in the harassed booking clerk activity cycle diagram in Figure 5.9. From the diagram it is clear that two conditions must be met before a personal service can begin. That is, there must a clerk in an IDLE state and there must be a personal enquirer waiting for service in the QUEUE. Only if both of these conditions are met can the SERVICE begin. This means that

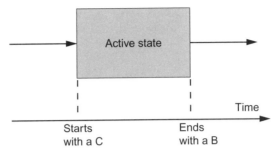

Figure 6.2 Bs and Cs in active states

BeginService is both cooperative (it involves a personal enquirer and a clerk) and conditional (the clerk must be IDLE and the enquirer must be in the QUEUE). Hence, *BeginService* is a C. The effect of this C is to engage resources and entities, unlike Bs, which release them. Thus, the clerk is no longer in an IDLE state and the enquirer is taken from the QUEUE. The two remain together for some period, which, as discussed in Section 6.2.1, may be computed. At the end of this period, the active state SERVE is over. Hence when a C is executed, it must ensure that the executive is informed that a B must be executed at some time in the future. One effect of the C *BeginService* is to tell the executive to schedule an *EndOfService* at some definite time in the future. By a similar argument, the active state TALK begins with a C, which could be given the name *BeginTalk*.

The section of computer program that represents a C has a two-part structure. First there is a test-head, which indicates the conditions that must be satisfied if the actions that follow are to be executed. This is followed by actions that will only be executed if the conditions are satisfied. For example, the *BeginServe* C might look as in Table 6.1. If the tests fail, then the actions are not executed.

6.2.3   The exception to the general rule

The rule shown in Figure 6.2 does not hold in one special case. This is for those active states that generate new entities into the system. The most common of these are ARRIVAL states, of which there are two, ARRIVE and CALL in Figure 5.9. This can be a little confusing and it arises because such states are really inter-arrival states (i.e., when an entity is in this state it is on its way to

Table 6.1 The *BeginServe* C

Test-head	If (there is a *Clerk* in IDLE) and (a *PersonalEnquirer* in the QUEUE) then
Actions	Take a *PersonalEnquirer* from QUEUE Take *Clerk* from IDLE Compute service time Schedule *EndOfService* after service time

Figure 6.3   Bootstrapping arrivals

arriving in the system). Some people find it helpful, in this context, to imagine a machine of some type that produces these entities one at a time. Thus, it takes the machine a finite gestation period to produce the next entity. The entity sits in this state until its gestation is over and it can enter the system.

These arrival-type processes are often known as bootstrapping processes, since another way to imagine them is to consider arrivals fastened to one another by variable length bootlaces. As one entity arrives, it falls into the system and jerks the next one to its feet by pulling on its bootlaces and dragging it into life. Thus, new entities are bootstrapped into the system.

This means that these states need not be represented by a C at the start and by a B at the end. If they were to be so represented, then the effect would be as shown in Figure 6.3. This is a one-dimensional graph with time as the axis. It shows that for the arrival of customer n, the start of this state (its C) coincides with the end of the same state (a B) for customer $n - 1$. Similarly, the end of arrival for customer n (its B) coincides with the start of arrival (the C) for customer $n + 1$, and so on. Instead of using C–B pairs, these inter-arrival states may be represented by just a single B, since the actual arrival of one customer causes the next one to begin its journey into the system.

6.2.4   Bs and Cs in the harassed booking clerk problem

How would the harassed booking clerk problem of Figure 5.9 be presented as Bs and Cs for a three-phase simulation? Figure 5.9 shows four active states: ARRIVE, SERVE, CALL and TALK. These can be decomposed into 4 Bs and 2 Cs as follows:

- *B1: Arrive*—in which the next personal enquirer arrives at the booking office and joins the queue.
- *B2: EndOfService*—in which a personal SERVICE is complete, releasing the personal enquirer back into the world OUTSIDE and putting the clerk back into an IDLE state.
- *B3: Call*—in which the next phone call ARRIVES, causing the phone to ring or being added to the CALLS waiting.
- *B4: EndOfTalk*—in which a phone conversation is complete, releasing the caller and putting the clerk back into an IDLE state.
- *C1: BeginService*—which will begin if a clerk is IDLE and there is a personal enquirer in the QUEUE. The effect of this C is to engage the server and the personal enquirer and to tell the executive to schedule the *EndOfService* (B2) after some known time.

- *C2: BeginTalk*—which will begin if a clerk is IDLE and there is a phone CALL waiting. The effect of this C is to engage the server and the phone caller and to tell the executive to schedule the *EndOfTalk* (B4) after some known time.

If this problem were to be simulated in a simulation package that requires the modeller to write a computer program, it is best to ensure that each B and each C is a separate module of code. That is, in C and its variants, each B or C should be a separate function and in languages such as Visual Basic should be a separate sub. This approach is used in Chapter 7.

6.2.5   Another example: a T-junction

Although activity cycle diagrams are a useful step on the way to modelling a discrete event system as a set of Bs and Cs, they are not essential. Indeed, there are systems in which their use actually makes things more complicated. As indicated at the end of Chapter 5, one such case is a simple road junction, for example the T-junction shown in Figure 6.4. This shows a road junction in a country (such as the UK, Japan or Australia) in which vehicles drive on the left-hand side of the road. If this is an unsignalled junction in which U-turns are banned, then there are six possible routes through the junction and the usual priorities would be as follows:

(1)   Routes A to B, B to A and B to C.
(2)   Route C to A.
(3)   Route A to C.
(4)   Route C to B.

To keep things simple, assume that all drivers obey the traffic regulations. This means that queues may form at the junction from any of the three arrival points. If the vehicle is not controlled by traffic lights, then the vehicle at the head of each queue is waiting for particular sections of the road to become free. These are shown in Figure 6.4 as sections I, II, III and IV. They need not all be the same size, but are safe zones (i.e., a car is safe to move out

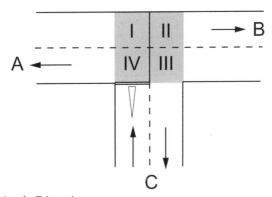

Figure 6.4   A simple T-junction

Table 6.2   The Bs and Cs for the T-junction

The Bs	The Cs
B1: Arrive from A	C1: Start move A to B
B2: Arrive from B	C2: Start move B to A
B3: Arrive from C	C3: Start move B to C
B4: End A to B	C4: Start move C to A
B5: End B to A	C5: Start move A to C
B6: End B to C	C6: Start move C to B
B7: End C to A	
B8: End A to C	
B9: End C to B	

if no other vehicle is currently passing through those zones). The sections are resources and the vehicles are entities that compete for the scarce resources.

Vehicles can arrive from points A, B or C. Thus, if we are interested only in this single junction, these are entity generation processes that may be modelled as straightforward Bs. For example, the inter-arrival times may be governed by probability distributions and a vehicle, on arrival, joins a notional queue. The queue is notional because, in the case of priority 1 routes (A to B, B to A and B to C), the way through should never be blocked and therefore the vehicle should spend zero time in the queue.

Moving through the junction is also an active state, but this time is one that should be modelled by a C–B pair. Hence, each move should include a C, which starts the move if the required road sections are free. For example, moving safely from C to B may require all four sections I, II, III and IV to be free. The end of each move is thus a B, and its effect is to free the road sections that are occupied in the C that started the move.

Thus, the legal movement of the traffic through this junction could be modelled as the nine Bs and six Cs shown in Table 6.2. There is no need to draw an activity cycle diagram to model this junction as Bs and Cs. Indeed, to do so would make the task harder.

It is important to notice that the priority of routes through the junction can be preserved by the sequence in which the Cs are attempted by the simulation executive. As will become clear in the next section, a three-phase executive attempts each of the Cs in turn. If, for example, route C to B is attempted last, then it cannot be executed if any other vehicle is using any of the road sections that it needs. It will therefore have the lowest priority. If route A to B were to have the highest priority, then it should be attempted first amongst the Cs.

6.3   HOW THE THREE-PHASE APPROACH WORKS

Although it is not necessary to know the detailed inner workings of a simulation executive in order to write a working simulation program, some

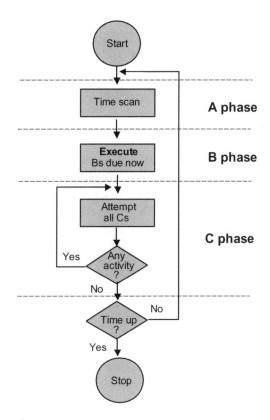

Figure 6.5   A three-phase executive

understanding may help to improve that program. This section takes a look at the inner workings of three-phase simulations, showing how the executive manages its scheduling and sequencing tasks. Figure 6.5 is a flowchart that shows how a three-phase executive operates. As might be expected, this executes a repeated cycle of three phases, known as A, B and C to make them memorable.

Section 5.2 explained that the objects of a system may be modelled as entities or as resources, the difference being that the behaviour of entities is individually tracked. In a three-phase simulation, this may be achieved by keeping at least three pieces of information about each entity as follows:

- *The time cell.* This is the time when it is next due to change state, if this is known. It is only meaningful if the entity is committed to some B in the future.
- *The availability.* This is a Boolean field that shows whether the entity is committed to some future B. If this is TRUE then the entity is uncommitted and its time cell is meaningless. If it is FALSE, then the time cell indicates when the entity will next change state.
- *The next activity.* Like the time cell, this is only meaningful if the availability is FALSE, and it indicates the B in which the entity is due to engage at the time shown by the time cell. It is meaningless if the availability is TRUE.

Thus, at the core of a three-phase simulation is a set of records, one to each entity. The executive manages the entities and their involvement in Bs and Cs by controlling the information held in these records. The records may have many more than three fields if necessary, and certainly the use of entity attributes would add extra fields to each record.

6.3.1   The A phase

The A phase is also known as the *time scan* and is analogous to someone checking his diary to see when his next appointment is due. In this time scan, the executive examines its event calendar to see when the next event is due and it moves the clock to that point. The clock is now held constant until the next A phase. Using the three-part entity record described above, the executive searches for any entity record with the minimum time cell and which has an availability field set to FALSE. This search can be accomplished in a variety of ways and a simple example will be shown in Section 6.5.

Because there may be several Bs due at this new clock time, the executive must also make a note of which of the non-available entities have this new clock time as their time cell. These form the *DueNow* list.

6.3.2   The B phase

Once the *DueNow* list has been formed, the executive must ensure that the correct Bs are executed. This is done by working systematically through the *DueNow* list and examining the record for each entity that is on that list. For each such entity, in turn, the executive does the following:

- Remove the entity from the *DueNow* list.
- Put its availability field to TRUE.
- Execute the B that is shown in the next activity field.

Note that executing the B may cause this same entity or another entity to be committed to this or some other B in the future.

6.3.3   The C phase

For the C phase, the executive maintains a light touch. It merely causes the Cs to be attempted one after the other. It does this by looking at each C in turn to see if the conditions in its test-head (see Section 6.2.2) can be satisfied. If they can, then the actions are executed. As was explained at the end of Section 6.2, the order in which these are attempted determines their priority. If there are two Cs that require the same entities or resources (e.g., in the harassed booking clerk problem, both Cs need an idle clerk) then the first to be tested gets the first pick. Thus, a later C will be pre-empted by one that is higher up the list.

In most cases, the effect of a C is to engage resources and entities, but there are exceptions to this rule and it is possible that a C later in the list may free resources and entities needed by a higher priority C. This could cause deadlock. To avoid this, the Cs are repeatedly scanned, whilst holding the clock constant, until all test-heads are failed. The executive then returns to the A phase.

6.4 THE HARASSED BOOKING CLERK—A MANUAL THREE-PHASE SIMULATION

As introduced earlier, the harassed booking clerk problem has four Bs and two Cs, described in Section 6.2.4 as follows:

- B1: Arrive
- B2: EndOfService
- B3: Call
- B4: EndOfTalk
- C1: BeginService
- C2: BeginTalk

There are three classes of object in the simulation (personal enquirers, phone callers and the clerk) and, although the obvious structure is to use entities to model each, this will not be done here. Instead, the personal enquirers and phone callers will be modelled as resources and another concept, the arrival machine, will be used to generate new arrivals into the system. As there are two such resources (personal enquirers and phone calls), two arrival machines are needed, and each such machine will become an entity in the simulation. There are, therefore, three entities in the simulation:

(1) Personal enquirer arrival machine.
(2) Phone call arrival machine.
(3) Clerk.

Clearly, if we wished to simulate a system which has more than a single clerk, each would need to be represented by an entity.

The records of each entity can be maintained as in Table 6.3, below which are some important status variables. This shows that the initial conditions for the simulation are as follows:

- The single clerk is idle (therefore its availability is TRUE).
- The first personal enquirer is due to arrive at time 4 and the first phone call is due at time 6 (suppose that these were set as the result of samples from suitable probability distributions).
- The time is zero and thus the simulation clock is zero.
- No personal enquirers or phone calls have arrived.
- All queues (QUEUE and WAIT) are empty.

Table 6.3 Harassed booking clerk simulation: initial conditions

Entity	Name	Time cell	Availability	Next Activity
1	Personal enquirer arrival machine	4	FALSE	Personal arrival
2	Phone call arrival machine	6	FALSE	Phone call
3	Clerk	0	TRUE	

Status variables: *Clock = 0; Queue = 0; Wait = 0; PersIn = 0; PhoneIn = 0; DueNow* is empty

Table 6.4 Harassed booking clerk simulation: time 4, end of A phase

Entity	Name	Time cell	Availability	Next Activity
1	Personal enquirer arrival machine	4	FALSE	Personal arrival
2	Phone call arrival machine	6	FALSE	Phone call
3	Clerk	0	TRUE	

Status variables: *Clock = 4; Queue = 0; Wait = 0; PersIn = 0; PhoneIn = 0; DueNow* contains 1

6.4.1 The first A phase

During the A phase, the executive must find when the next event is due, must move the simulation clock to that time and must add to the *DueList* all entities due to engage in a B at that time. After the first A phase, therefore, the situation is as in Table 6.4. This shows that the next event is due at time 4. Thus the *Clock* value is now 4. The only entity due to engage in a B at this stage is entity 1, the personal enquirer arrival machine. Thus the *DueNow* list contains only entity 1.

6.4.2 The first B phase

During the B phase the executive must execute the Next Activity of those entities that are on the *DueNow* list. In this case, there is just one such entity, the personal enquirer arrival machine. This is due to engage in the B that represents a personal arrival. In this case it brings the first personal enquirer into the system and schedules the next such arrival to occur after 5 minutes (i.e., at time 9). The first personal enquirer is placed in the *Queue* and *PersIn*, the counter for personal arrivals, is incremented as shown in Table 6.5. Note that the method maintains a very strict separation between Cs and Bs. Even

Table 6.5 Harassed booking clerk simulation: time 4, end of B phase

Entity	Name	Time cell	Availability	Next activity
1	Personal enquirer arrival machine	9	FALSE	Personal arrival
2	Phone call arrival machine	6	FALSE	Phone call
3	Clerk	0	TRUE	

Status variables: *Clock = 4; Queue = 1; Wait = 0; PersIn = 1; PhoneIn = 0; DueNow* is empty

Table 6.6 Harassed booking clerk simulation: time 4, end of C phase

Entity	Name	Time cell	Availability	Next Activity
1	Personal enquirer arrival machine	9	FALSE	Personal arrival
2	Phone call arrival machine	6	FALSE	Phone call
3	Clerk	9	FALSE	EndService

Status variables: *Clock = 4; Queue = 0; Wait = 0; PersIn = 1; PhoneIn = 0; DueNow* is empty

though we (and therefore the executive) know that the clerk is idle, the service does not start in the B phase, instead, the first arrival is placed in the queue.

6.4.3 The first C phase

During the C phase, the executive must attempt each C in turn by checking if the conditions in the test-heads are satisfied. In this simulation, there are two Cs, both of which have two conditions. *BeginService* requires the clerk to be idle and a personal enquirer to be in the queue. *BeginTalk* requires the clerk to be idle and a phone call to be waiting. If the agreed priority is that *BeginService* is preferred to *BeginTalk*, then it must be attempted first. Since the clerk is idle and there is a single personal enquirer in the queue, the test-head of *BeginService* is satisfied and the actions can be executed. The result of that is shown in Table 6.6. This shows that some sampling process led to a duration for the personal service of 5 minutes, therefore it is due to end at time 9. Thus, the availability field of the clerk is now FALSE, the time cell is now 9 and the next activity is *EndService*. As the personal enquirer has been taken from the queue, the variable *Queue* is now reduced to zero. The second C, *BeginTalk*, cannot succeed since the clerk is no longer idle. Repeating the C scan leads to no further activity.

6.4.4 The second A phase

The second A phase results in the situation shown in Table 6.7. It shows that the next event is found to be due at time 6, and that it will involve entity 2, the phone call arrival machine. Hence, the *DueNow* list contains the number 2 and *Clock* is moved to 6.

Table 6.7 Harassed booking clerk simulation: time 6, end of A phase

Entity	Name	Time cell	Availability	Next Activity
1	Personal enquirer arrival machine	9	FALSE	Personal arrival
2	Phone call arrival machine	6	FALSE	Phone call
3	Clerk	9	FALSE	EndService

Status variables: *Clock = 6; Queue = 0; Wait = 0; PersIn = 1; PhoneIn = 0; DueNow* contains 2

Table 6.8 Harassed booking clerk simulation: time 6, end of B phase

Entity	Name	Time cell	Availability	Next Activity
1	Personal enquirer arrival machine	9	FALSE	Personal arrival
2	Phone call arrival machine	9	FALSE	Phone call
3	Clerk	9	FALSE	EndService

Status variables: $Clock = 6$; $Queue = 0$; $Wait = 1$; $PersIn = 1$; $PhoneIn = 1$; $DueNow$ is empty

6.4.5 The next B and C phases

The next B phase involves the phone call arrival machine whose next activity is to schedule the arrival of the second phone call. Suppose that the sample taken for this interval is 3 minutes, meaning that the second phone call is due at time 9. Hence, after the B phase, the situation is as shown in Table 6.8. Notice that the phone call that arrives at time 6 is placed into the queue *Wait* and the counter for the number of arrivals so far, *PhoneIn*, is incremented.

The C phase at time 6 results in no change to the table, since both *BeginService* and *BeginTalk* fail because the clerk is not idle at this time.

6.4.6 The third A phase

The third A phase finds that the next event is due at time 9 and that there are 3 entities due to engage in Bs at that time. Thus, it moves the clock to 9 and adds entities 1, 2 and 3 to the *DueNow* list. This results in the situation shown in Table 6.9.

6.4.7 The third B phase

The third B phase involves all three entities. Suppose that this results in the next personal enquirer being due at time 12 and the next phone call at time 15. The result of the *EndService* B is to release the clerk, whose availability field is now TRUE. Hence the situation is as shown in Table 6.10. Note that there are now two phone calls and one personal enquirer waiting. Changing that situation must wait until the C phase. The simulation may be continued in this manner until it has run long enough for the experiments for which it is

Table 6.9 Harassed booking clerk simulation: time 9, end of A phase

Entity	Name	Time cell	Availability	Next Activity
1	Personal enquirer arrival machine	9	FALSE	Personal arrival
2	Phone call arrival machine	9	FALSE	Phone call
3	Clerk	9	FALSE	EndService

Status variables: $Clock = 9$; $Queue = 0$; $Wait = 0$; $PersIn = 0$; $PhoneIn = 0$; $DueNow$ contains 1, 2, 3

Table 6.10   Harassed booking clerk simulation: time 9, end of B phase

Entity	Name	Time cell	Availability	Next Activity
1	Personal enquirer arrival machine	12	FALSE	Personal arrival
2	Phone call arrival machine	15	FALSE	Phone call
3	Clerk	9	TRUE	

Status variables: *Clock = 9; Queue = 1; Wait = 2; PersIn = 2; PhoneIn = 1; DueNow* is empty

being used. Chapter 7 shows how the approach can be implemented in any general purpose computer programming language.

6.5   THE EVENT-BASED WORLDVIEW

As is shown in Figure 6.1, the core of a discrete event simulation is a simulation executive that controls the operation of the components that capture the logical operations of the system being simulated. Sections 6.2 to 6.4 describe how these components are structured into Bs and Cs for a three-phase simulation and how a three-phase executive uses these Bs and Cs. Three other worldviews have been widely proposed for discrete simulation and the first of these is usually described as event-based.

An event-based approach was popular during the early years of discrete event simulation and was implemented in the early version of SIMSCRIPT. This originated in the work of Markowitz *et al.* (1963) at the RAND Corporation and has since been developed by CACI into SIMSCRIPT II.5 (Russell, 1987). Later versions of SIMSCRIPT encourage modellers to use the process-based approach, described later in this chapter, rather than an event-based approach. For this and other reasons, event-based approaches have fallen from favour since 1980. Whereas the basic building blocks of a three-phase model are Bs and Cs, in an event-based model the atomic parts are known as event routines. An event routine is a set of statements, in some programming language, which capture the entire set of logical consequences that can flow from an event. An event, as in three-phase approaches, is a state change that occurs at an instant of time.

6.5.1   Events in the harassed booking clerk problem

To illustrate what this means, consider the harassed booking clerk problem depicted in Figure 5.9. This activity cycle diagram has four active states: *Arrival* (of personal enquirers), *Call* (arrival of a new phone call), *Service* (of a personal enquirer by the clerk) and *Talk* (a phone conversation by the clerk). In event-based terms, this system may be reduced to four events as follows:

(1)   *Arrival.* The arrival of a personal enquirer.
(2)   *Call.* The arrival of a new phone call.

(3)   *EndServe*. The end of a service.
(4)   *EndTalk*. The end of a phone call.

This contrasts with the need for four Bs and two Cs in the three-phase approach: why should this be?

The reduction is possible because each of the event routines should capture *all possible* consequences of a state change. Hence it may include a B and one or more Cs. As an example, consider the event *EndServe*. In Section 6.2.4, using a three-phase approach, this was modelled by a B (*EndOfService*) in which the clerk was returned to an idle state and the personal enquirer was released into the world outside. The fact that another service might start immediately or that the clerk might straightway answer the phone was ignored. Instead there were two Cs, *BeginService* and *BeginTalk*. As a three-phase simulation proceeds, the simulation executive determines whether either or none of these will immediately follow from the occurrence of the *EndOfService* B. That is, the links between the Bs and Cs are dynamic in a three-phase simulation.

In an event-based approach, the equivalent of the B and the Cs should be combined into a single *EndServe* event routine. In this, the clerk must check to see if there are any other personal enquirers waiting in the queue, if so, then the next personal enquirer $(n + 1)$ is taken from the queue and the next service begins. If the queue is empty, the clerk must then check to see if any phone calls are waiting. If there are, then a phone call must be taken from the phone queue and a phone conversation started. If there are no personal enquirers waiting and no phone calls waiting, then the clerk can be released into idle.

Using a form of pseudo-code, the *EndServe* event routine could be expressed as follows:

Release *PersonalEnquirer n* into the world
If *(Queue* > 0) then
   Take *PersonalEnquirer n* + 1 from the queue
   Compute the *ServiceTime*
   Schedule the *EndServe n* + 1 to occur after *ServiceTime*
Else If *(PhoneQueue* > 0) then
   Take next *PhoneCall* from *PhoneQueue*
   Compute the *TalkTime*
   Schedule the *EndTalk* for this call to occur after *TalkTime*
Else Release *Clerk* to *Idle*.

A similar logic must be applied to the other event routines. Clearly the *EndTalk* routine will be very similar to *EndServe*. The *Arrive* and *Call* event routines will also be very similar and, in the case of the *Arrive* routine might be expressed in the following pseudo-code.

Compute *InterArrival* time
Schedule *Arrival* of *PersonalEnquirer n* + 1 after *InterArrival*
If *(Queue* = 0) and *(Clerk* is *Idle)* then

Take *Clerk* from *Idle*
Engage *PersonalEnquirer n*
Compute the *ServiceTime*
Schedule the *EndServe n* to occur after *ServiceTime*
Else add *PersonalEnquirer n* to the *Queue*.

That is, the new arrival is only added to the *Queue* if the *Clerk* is currently unavailable. Thus, the *Arrival* event routine combines the logic of the three-phase *Arrive* B and the three-phase *BeginService* C.

6.5.2   Event-based executives

An event-based executive can be rather more simple than the one needed for a three-phase simulation, because it only needs to schedule the event routines and has no sequencing tasks to perform. The sequencing is managed explicitly by each event routine. For example, in the case of the *EndServe* event routine described in the previous section, the priority of personal service over phone conversations is handled directly within the logic of the event routine. This means, inevitably, that should we wish to change this logic—to see, for example, what the effect would be of different priorities—then we must dig into the program code of the event routine to do so. In a three-phase simulation, we need only swap the order in which the executive attempts the Cs in the C phase.

An event-based executive has just two phases, in contrast to the three needed by a three-phase approach. The executive maintains an event calendar into which event notices are entered. These specify what events are currently scheduled and when they are due. Thus, the executive knows which events are due to occur next. The processing of an event-based simulation is managed as follows:

(1)   Examine the event calendar to find when the next event is due and move the simulation clock to this time. Move all event notices that are scheduled for this new clock time onto a current events list.
(2)   Holding the clock constant, perform each of the event routines whose notices are in the current events list. Empty the current events list.

This cycle is repeated until the simulation is over.

An event-based simulation of the harassed booking clerk should run rather faster than the three-phase version. This is because there is no need to attempt a full scan of all the Cs at every event time. Instead, all of the logical consequences are held in the appropriate event routine. The snag, of course, is that for complicated systems it can be very difficult to ensure that all possible consequences are accounted for within the event routine. This problem is particularly acute when a model is enhanced in some way. Thus, the event-based approach is not really in accord with the "principle of parsimony" advocated throughout this book. This principle suggests that simulation models, and their computer programs, should be developed and enhanced gradually. An approach that makes this difficult can hardly be recommended.

6.6 THE ACTIVITY-SCANNING APPROACH

The three-phase approach grew out of what became known as activity scanning, an approach used in the early simulation language CSL (Buxton and Laski, 1962). It is very simple, but rather inefficient. Many writers based in the USA wrongly equate activity scanning with the three-phase approach.

6.6.1 Activities

The basic building block of the approach is an *activity*, which has exactly the same structure as a C in a three-phase approach. That is, a C has a test-head followed by a set of actions. In the harassed booking clerk simulation of Figure 5.9, there would be six such activities, as follows:

- Arrive
- EndOfService
- Call
- EndOfTalk
- BeginService
- BeginTalk

That is, the Bs and the Cs all become activities. The three-phase Cs, *BeginServe* and *BeginTalk*, remain unchanged as activities in an activity-based approach. Thus, *BeginServe* is exactly as in Figure 6.1. However, the Bs are changed since they must have test-heads.

The only conditions that govern the start of these previous Bs are whether the simulation clock has reached the time for which these activities are scheduled. Hence, the three-phase Bs need test-heads that check whether the simulation clock has advanced far enough to cause these former Bs to be executed. As an example, the *Arrive* activity would look as shown in Table 6.11. The other activities that would be represented as Bs in a three-phase simulation would have a similar structure. Hence, the activities are very simple, but do not take advantage of the fact that the executive can know when some activities are due to happen. Instead, the executive is, as in the event-based approach, a rather crude two-phase control program.

Table 6.11 The personal enquirer *Arrival* activity for activity scanning

Test-head	If *Clock* has reached the time of the next scheduled arrival then
Actions	Add *PersonalEnquirer n* to the Queue Compute *InterArrivalTime* Schedule arrival *of PersonalEnquirer n* + 1 after *InterArrival Time*

6.6.2 Activity-scanning executives

An activity-based executive can be simpler than that needed in a three-phase simulation. It has only to ensure that it detects the time at which the next activity is due to happen and it uses a repeated scan of the activities to decide what will happen at that time. An activity-based executive need not even maintain an event calendar; all it needs to do is check the time cells of each entity record and find the minimum time cell. It is, of course, perfectly possible to implement such an executive with an event calendar. Such a calendar would consist only of the times at which events are due and would not contain information about what those events are. The executive operates in a two-phase sweep:

(1) Check the time cells (or event calendar) to find the time of the next event. Move the simulation clock to this time.
(2) Repeatedly scan through the activities, trying each test-head to see if that activity is now due or able to occur. Continue the scan until no more activities are executable at that time.

This cycle is repeated until the simulation is over.

The original attraction of an activity-based approach was its simplicity, and it certainly supports the parsimonious modelling advocated in this book. However, there is a price to pay—the simulations will run much slower than their event-based counterparts. This is because, at each event time, the executive must conduct a repeated scan of all the activities even though it could know that not all of them are due at that clock time. This was the reason for the development of the three-phase approach, in which the activities are separated into Bs and Cs and then only the Cs (of which there will be fewer) are scanned. In a three-phase approach, the Bs are handled rather as if they were event routines, but with no need to follow through all the possible logical consequences.

6.7 PROCESS-BASED APPROACHES

Process-based approaches are, perhaps, the ones in most frequent use around the world, although this may not be obvious to the user of simulation software. This section of the chapter refers to process-based approaches, in the plural, since there are a number of variations on this theme.

To model a system using activity or event-based approaches, the analyst must consider the process (or life cycle) of each entity class and must then break this down into more fundamental parts. For an event-based simulation, the process is divided into independent event routines, each of which defines all the possible logical consequences of an event. For an activity-based simulation, the analyst must define the list of unique activities and the executive sorts out the dynamic linkages between activities. Process-based simulations differ from this atomization in that they take the whole process of an entity as the basic logical building block of a simulation model.

A process is defined as a sequence of operations through which an entity must pass. Tracing through all the loops of an activity cycle diagram will define the processes of the various entity classes that make up the simulation. Each class of entity has one or more of its own processes and each entity created as a member of that class will inherit these processor processes. The life of an entity is traced by checking its progress through its process. Thus a process-based executive needs to know the whereabouts of each entity in its process and needs some way of stopping and starting the entity's movement through its process.

Thus a process-based simulation model consists of a set of processes, at least one for each active entity class in the simulation. During the simulation, entities will be created as members of these classes. When an entity is created, it takes the process of its class as a template for its future life and the system then keeps track of how far the entity has moved through its process. A process-based executive has the job, at each time point in the simulation, of moving each existing entity as far through its process template as possible, the progress of an entity being halted temporarily by one of two conditions:

- *Unconditional delays.* These occur when the progress of an entity is halted for a time period that can, in principle, be determined in advance. Thus, the delay is conditional only on the passage of simulated time. Once the appropriate simulated time has elapsed, then the entity can be re-started in its progress through its process. When two entities cooperate to perform a task whose duration can be determined (e.g., by sampling), then this might be modelled as an unconditional delay for these two entities.
- *Conditional delays.* These occur when an entity's movement through its process is halted until specific conditions in the simulation are satisfied. Thus, the entity must remain at this conditional delay point in its process until told to move on. For example, a customer may remain in a queue until reaching the head of the queue and until the server is free.

6.7.1 Processes in the harassed booking clerk problem

When defining a process for an entity class, the analyst must give some thought to the points at which an entity may be delayed. These are usually known as reactivation points. As an example, consider a possible process for personal enquirers in the harassed booking clerk problem. One approach might be to define this process as follows, allowing the process for customer n to begin with its actual arrival at the booking office:

> *PersonalEnquirer n arrives;*
> Compute time of arrival of *PersonalEnquirer n + 1*;
> Instantiate process for *PersonalEnquirer n + 1*;
> ***Delay** *PersonalEnquirer n + 1* until due to arrive;
> *PersonalEnquirer n*, <u>waituntil</u> (at head of *Queue*) and (*Clerk* free);

Engage *Clerk*;
Take *PersonalEnquirer n* from *Queue*;
Compute *ServiceTime n*;
***Delay** PersonalEnquirer n* until *ServiceTime* has elapsed;
Release *Clerk* to *Idle*;
Release *PersonalEnquirer n*.

This process contains two unconditional delays and one conditional delay. The unconditional delays are indicated by the emboldened asterisked word ***Delay*** in which the progress of the entity through its process pauses until some simulated time interval has elapsed. This is equivalent to scheduling a B or an event routine for some time in the future. The conditional delay is marked by the underlined term waituntil, which indicates that the entity's progress is blocked until certain conditions are met—in this case, that the enquirer has reached the front of the queue and the clerk is free to serve them.

A similar process description could be formulated for phone calls, and their interaction could be managed by their competition for the clerk—a scarce resource. Writing down such processes is straightforward for simple problems but can get complicated when several processes need to interact.

6.7.2   Process interaction

It is also possible, though not recommended in this case, to write a process template for the clerk which would operate alongside the templates for the two types of customer. Then, instead of managing the interaction of the processes by their competition for a scarce resource, the interaction would have to be explicitly managed. This would mean that one process might create and operate upon the conditional and unconditional delays of another. Such simulations create what are known as process interaction models, which are more complicated than the simple process-based approach described here. It would be equivalent to insisting that all objects in the system are treated as entities, rather than treating some as entities and some as resources. The problem of which entity class is dominant is often managed by treating one as the active class and the others as passive as discussed in Section 5.2.1. The active class process dominates the others.

The first proper process-based simulation system was SIMULA (Hills, 1973; Dahl and Nygaard, 1966), which originated in Scandinavia as an extension to the Algol family of languages. SIMULA never achieved widespread acceptance within the simulation community, possibly because of its base in Algol, but it had an enormous effect in the wider world of computer software. SIMULA promoted the idea that a system could be divided into classes, each of which had its own process. It also promoted the idea that classes could inherit properties from previously defined classes. Thus SIMULA was the precursor of object-oriented programming, as found in languages such as Java and C++. The GPSS family of computer software (Gordon, 1979) uses a much less flexible transaction flow approach which has some similarities to the process interaction approach of SIMULA. Rather than being concerned with processes that interact with one another, GPSS considers transaction flows which may have limited interaction.

6.7.3   Process-based executives

Although, in theory, a process is simply a list of chronologically ordered operations, it should be clear from the preceding description that things are not so simple. The executive needs to know at what points an entity may be halted in its process for either a conditional or an unconditional delay. Thus each process must contain reactivation points at which they hand control of an entity back to the executive. A simple process-based executive might maintain a record for each entity which contains two fields as follows:

- Its re-activation time (if known).
- Its next re-activation point (i.e., where it is in its process).

The executive might then maintain two lists of these records.

(1)   *Future events list*. This is a chronologically sequenced list of the records of those entities whose progress is unconditionally delayed. Thus, this list is sequenced by the reactivation time of the entities whose records are in the list. Only entities whose reactivation time is ahead of the current simulation clock time would appear in this list.

(2)   *Current events list*. At any time in the simulation, this list contains the records of two types of entity. First there are those that have been unconditionally delayed and whose reactivation is due at the current simulation clock time. For example, a personal service may be due to end now. Second, the list includes the records of all those entities that are subject to conditional delays.

These two lists permit a process-based executive to operate with a three-phase cycle at each simulation clock time as follows:

(1)   *Future events scan*. The future events list is used to determine the time of the next event. This is easily found if the future events list is sequenced chronologically. The simulation clock is advanced to this new time.

(2)   *Move between lists*. Those entities on the future events list whose reactivation time equals the new clock time are moved from the future events list to the current events list.

(3)   *Current events scan*. The executive must now make repeated events to move each entity on the current events list further through its process. Thus, each entity on the list will be moved on if conditions permit (e.g., if the server is now free and the entity is at the head of the queue). Those entities that have been moved will either complete their process or will be halted due to a conditional or unconditional delay. If the delay is unconditional, then their records are moved to the future events list.

The executive notes their next reactivation points in the records of these entities.

6.8   WHICH APPROACH IS BEST?

It is safe to dismiss activity scanning and event-based approaches as serious contenders. Activity scanning is simple, but very inefficient and has been superseded by three-phase approaches. Event-based approaches are appealing until the simulation starts to get complicated and needs to be modified to allow different entity interactions. It is simply easier to allow a three-phase executive to sort this out dynamically than to hard-code it, and there is little lost in the way of execution efficiency.

6.8.1   Three-phase versus process-based approaches

Given that a process-based executive distinguishes, in effect, between two types of event (unconditional and conditional) and given that a three-phase approach uses Bs and Cs for this purpose, does this mean that the two approaches are, at heart, the same? Certainly it means that they share two common advantages. First, they avoid programs that are slow to run (as in a strict activity-based approach due to the need to scan all activities). Second, they avoid the need to think through all the possible logical consequences of an event (as in the event-based approach), which should make at least initial program construction somewhat simpler.

However, there is one very important difference that may not be obvious. In a three-phase simulation, the B phase is completed for all due-now entities before the C phase is attempted for any entity. This is to avoid possible deadlock in which an entity needs a resource or other entity that must be free before it can proceed. In general, Bs release these entities and resources, although occasionally this may happen in a C and therefore the C scan is repeated as in Figure 6.5. There is therefore, in a three-phase approach, an explicit separation of the two phases. In this way, the simultaneous and parallel activity of the real world is translated into the sequential procedures of a digital computer.

By contrast, in a process-based approach, each entity in turn is taken as far through its process as possible (i.e., until it reaches an unconditional delay, or until it reaches a conditional delay whose conditions are not met). Hence, an entity may complete some activity (equivalent to a B) and may move immediately to attempt to start something else (equivalent to a C) without waiting for any other entity to complete its B. Thus, there is no explicit separation of B and C phases in a process-based approach. In essence, the process-based executive lies dormant until asked to do something by an entity, whereas a three-phased executive maintains a much more active control over each entity.

Any discrete simulation model containing parallel and simultaneous activities that are to be run on a computer which is essentially serial in operation must have some strategy to avoid deadlock. In a three-phase approach, this is managed by repeated C scans in the C phase. In a process-based approach, the modeller must ensure that any possible deadlock is explicitly managed in the development of each process template. This is straightforward for simple models, such as that of the harassed booking clerk, but can be very tricky with models in which there is much interaction across many processes. This problem is particularly acute when a complex model is developed in a parsimonious way as advocated here. As each enhancement is made to the model, the process-based modeller must think about possible deadlocks. The three-phase modeller is freed from such worries.

What then is the attraction of process-based approaches? The first is that they are closest to the approaches that might be taken by novice modellers. Many people, faced with the need to consider how entities interact within a simulation model, will imagine themselves acting as one of those entities. "Now let me see, first I arrive, then I wait until it's my turn to be served, and, oh yes, until the clerk is free. Then I suppose I talk to the clerk for a while, who might need to phone someone for information. Then, I suppose, the clerk can serve someone else, or might even answer the phone, when I'm finished." This is clearly a very helpful way to think about these things and it provides a good starting point for modelling. However, it can be helpful to atomize a model somewhat further into its Bs and Cs, because this finer fragmentation makes things rather easier when the model grows complicated.

The second attraction of process-based approaches is that the first software to embody these ideas was SIMULA (Dahl and Nygaard, 1966), which was also the precursor to modern object-oriented approaches. As discussed by Pidd (1995), object-oriented approaches have many advantages for simulation modelling and also serve as the basis for recent component-based simulation approaches. However, as Pidd (1995) argues, it is a mistake to assume that object-oriented approaches must be implemented via process-based simulation. Implementing a three-phase approach on object-oriented principles is straightforward once a modeller has mastered those principles.

For all of these reasons, the author takes the view that a three-phase approach is preferable when dealing with simulations of some complexity, although for simple systems, it matters little which approach is chosen. In many cases, the approach that must be taken is determined by the computer software being used. If it relies on a process-based executive, then the modeller must use such an approach. If it relies on a three-phase executive, then that approach must be used.

EXERCISES

(1) Write down the logic of the Bs and Cs that would be necessary for a three-phase simulation model of the T-junction as described in Section 6.2.5.

(2) Write down the logic of the Bs and Cs that would be necessary for a

three-phase simulation model of the delivery depot described in Section 5.3.3.

(3)   Write down the logic of the Bs and Cs which would be needed for a three-phase simulation model of the following system. Trucks arrive randomly at a weighbridge in a port, having travelled by ferry from another country laden with various goods. The weighbridge is used to check whether the vehicles are overloaded before they are allowed to travel on the roads. Trucks queue for the weighbridge after leaving the ferry. If they are found to be overloaded then they are moved to another area in the port where the surplus load is removed and the drivers are interviewed by the police. They may then leave the port where they rejoin those trucks whose loads were within the regulations.

(4)   Write down the logic of the Bs and Cs which would be needed for a three-phase simulation model of the following system. The Morecambe Bay Hovercraft Company (MBHC) is anxious to make its new service more efficient before the Cross-Bay Tunnel opens. They wish you to study the operation of their Hest Bank Shore terminal. Hovercraft land at the Shore terminal after their flight from Humphrey Head at intervals which are more or less according to a timetable, the variation in landing times being due to obvious factors such as weather and problems at the Humphrey Head terminal. If the slipway is free then the craft floats onto it and lands. Any vehicles and passengers then disembark and, in the meantime, the passenger cabin is cleaned. When all vehicles and passengers have disembarked, and when the cabin is clean, the vehicles and passengers who wish to travel to Humphrey Head are loaded. High vehicles are loaded first, followed by all other vehicles of less than 1.6 metres in height. Foot passengers board the craft whilst the vehicles are being loaded. When all vehicles and passengers are loaded, the doors are closed and the flight to Humphrey Head can begin.

At the moment, MBHC operates only a single slipway at Hest Bank and is wondering whether to double its capacity by adding an extra slipway. The extra capacity would be used to add extra flights on this route. They might be able to add extra flights without doubling the capacity—but there is a risk that customers might sometimes face long delays and also that an incoming flight may not be able to land. There is plenty of spare capacity at Humphrey Head.

(5)   Write down the Bs and Cs that would be needed to simulate the accident and emergency department described in Exercise 7 of Chapter 5.

(6)   Using an event-based, activity-based or process-based approach, develop a description of the modules needed to simulate a modified version of the harassed booking clerk problem in which clerks have dedicated tasks—some answer the phone, whilst others attend to personal callers.

(7)   Using an event-based, activity-based or process-based approach, develop a description of the modules needed to simulate the barber's shop described in Exercise 1 of Chapter 5.

(8) Using an event-based, activity-based or process-based approach, develop a description of the modules needed to simulate the grain dock described in Exercise 3 of Chapter 5.

(9) Using an event-based, activity-based or process-based approach, develop a description of the modules needed to simulate the T-junction described in Exercise 6 of Chapter 5.

(10) Using an event-based, activity-based or process-based approach, develop a description of the modules needed to simulate the MBHC described in Exercise 4 of Chapter 5.

(11) Using an event-based, activity-based or process-based approach, develop a description of the modules needed to simulate the accident and emergency department described in Exercise 7 of Chapter 5.

(12) A common problem in computer simulation is deadlock, which occurs when more than one entity is waiting for the same resource to be released. In this regard, consider how the three-phase approach compares with the approaches discussed in this chapter.

REFERENCES

Buxton J.N. and Laski J.G. (1962) Control and simulation language. *Computer J.*, **5**, 194–9.

Dahl O. and Nygaard K. (1966) SIMULA—an Algol-based simulation language. *Comm ACM*, **9**, 671–8.

Gordon G. (1979) The design of the GPSS language. In: N.R. Adam and A. Dogramaci (eds), *Current Issues in Computer Simulation*. Academic Press, New York.

Hills P.R. (1973) *An Introduction to Simulation Using SIMULA* (NCC Publication No. 5-s). Norwegian Computing Centre, Oslo.

Markowitz H.M., Hausner B. and Karr H.W. (1963) *SIMSCRIPT: A Simulation Programming Language* (RAND Corporation No. RM-3310-pr). Prentice-Hall, Englewood Cliffs, NJ.

Pidd M. (1995) Object orientation, discrete simulation and the three-phase approach. *Journal of Operational Research Society*, **46**, 362–74.

Russell E.C. (1987) *SIMSCRIPT II.5 Programming Language*. CACI, La Jolla, CA.

Tocher K.D. (1963) *The Art of Simulation*. English Universities Press, London.

Writing A Three-Phase Simulation Program

7.1 INTRODUCTION

Chapter 6 introduced the main simulation worldviews, devoting most space to the three-phase approach. In this, the activity within a model is divided into Bs, which can be controlled by the executive; and Cs, which depend upon the entity states within the model. This chapter takes these ideas further and shows how they can be used to develop a three-phase simulation in almost any general purpose programming language. Most of these principles apply to the development of a simulation program using one of the other worldviews.

For the sake of illustration, the program code in this chapter will be shown in Microsoft Visual Basic™, but the same ideas have been used by the author to develop similar three-phase libraries in BASIC, C, C++, Pascal and Java. With the exception of the original versions of BASIC, all of these languages allow a programmer to split the overall program into independent units or modules. This makes it much easier to test programs as they are developed and also eases the task of developing libraries for other people to use. Apart from the original BASIC program, full copies of all of these libraries, in a range of programming languages, are available on the Internet. To find them, use an appropriate search engine and look for my personal web page. At the time of printing, this is located at `http://www.lancs.ac.uk/ staff/smamp/`. The libraries are stored in a compressed format using the ZIP system and therefore, once downloaded, they need to be unzipped using software that is compatible with the UNZIP system. Readers are welcome to use this software with no restriction other than some form of acknowledgement. The author accepts no liability whatsoever in any country for any uses to which these three-phase libraries are put.

The chapter begins by explaining the basic structure of such a three-phase library and then develops each part gradually, using Visual Basic as the exemplar. Visual Basic is not the ideal language for simulation and some of the problems will be introduced at appropriate places in the chapter. Languages such as C++, Java and Pascal are much better, but are known by fewer management scientists. Whatever language is used, developing a straightforward three-phase simulation library is well within the capability

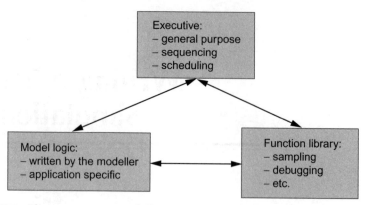

Figure 7.1   Three-part structure of discrete event simulation programs

of anyone with average programming skills. There is no need to be a qualified rocket scientist to do this.

7.1.1   The basic structure of the library

Fishman (1973) was perhaps the first person to point out that a basic discrete event simulation program has a three-part structure as shown in Figure 7.1. Even commercial simulation software, which may be sold at high prices, has a similar organization. The elements are as follows:

(1)   *Simulation executive.* The nature of these executives is discussed in Chapter 6. Their main task is to ensure that the entities and resources of the model engage in appropriate activity at the correct simulation time. The executive acts like a puppeteer, pulling the strings that make the entities and resources cooperate so as to display the behaviour that characterizes the system being simulated. Without the executive to pull the strings, nothing would happen. The executive is, therefore, in complete control over what happens within the simulation and is sometimes known as the control program. The executive developed in this chapter is for three-phase simulation, but the basic design of other executives is very similar.

(2)   *Model logic.* This is not a part of the library, since this is the simulation model as written by the modeller, whereas the executive is written by the system provider. The model logic describes how the entities and resources are used to mimic the dynamic activity within the system being simulated. It must be expressed in such a way that it can be controlled by the executive and can communicate with it. In this chapter, the model logic will be expressed in three-phase terms, using Bs and Cs to represent the activities.

(3)   *General tools.* The third component, which is the second part provided by the system provider, is a set of general tools that may be used by the executive and by the model logic. This covers obvious aspects such as input/output, plus features such as debugging aids, random sampling

functions, graphical displays and other desirable features. In many cases, this library will be much larger than either the executive or the model logic. Its size and features will be wholly dependent on the facilities that form part of the language in which the library is to be written and on the computer operating system being used.

Things get a little more complicated when developing software to run in a windowing environment, as is the case with Visual Basic. In such languages, much effort must go into producing forms and screens that are used for parameterizing the simulation, for user interaction and to display the results. The detail of these is not covered in this chapter, but appropriate files are provided on the website.

The library developed here is clearly not a commercial system, but it has many of the same features, albeit in a rudimentary form. The general tools component of most commercial systems is much better than that provided here, although there is no particular reason why readers should not extend this library to meet their own needs. Over the years, quite a number of simulation projects have used this library as the simulation engine for the work. These have included applications in the motor industry, food manufacturing, emergency planning and retailing. Versions used were written in Visual Basic, C, C++ and BASIC.

7.2   INSIDE THE EXECUTIVE

Section 6.3 shows how a three-phase simulation could be controlled by creating a record, with three fields, for each entity within the simulation. As far as the executive is concerned, this record is the entity. The executive must continually monitor and interact with these entity records and thus they must be linked into some form of data structure. The simplest way to do this is to link them into an array, the control array. They could, of course, be linked in some dynamic form such as a linked list, tree or heap, but Visual Basic does not provide the pointers that are needed to create proper versions of these dynamic data structures. There are ways of mimicking these dynamic data structures in Visual Basic, but they are messy. Hence, this chapter will use a control array, with the name *Details*, as shown in Figure 7.2.

	Name	Avail	TimeCell	NextAct	Util
1					
2					
3					
4					
n					

Figure 7.2   The *Details* control array

Readers using the other libraries should note that:

- The C++ version of this library, available on the website, uses a linked list of entity records rather than a simple array.
- The Java version uses the dynamic *Vector* type of the *java.util* class for this purpose.

Since both of these libraries support object orientation, entities are instances of a *GEntity* (general entity) class. Visual Basic programmers who are lost at this point should not despair, but should read on.

7.2.1   The control array

Each row of the *Details* array is devoted to an entity and each entity that is active in the simulation must occupy one row. The array has five columns, meaning that each row has five fields—two more than those in Section 6.3. The fields are shown in Figure 7.2 and are as follows:

(1) *Name.* A String variable that is used to give a name to each entity. This is the first extra field and is useful for debugging and report generation.
(2) *Avail.* A Boolean field, which indicates whether the entity is available.
(3) *TimeCell.* An integer or long integer that holds the time at which the entity is next due to change state, if the *Avail* field is false.
(4) *NextAct.* Data that points to the activity in which the entity is next scheduled to engage, if the *Avail* field is false. How this field is implemented is entirely dependent on the programming language being used.
(5) *Util.* An integer or long integer field that holds the total utilization of the entity within the simulation, up to and including its next state change. This is the second extra field, which is also useful for report generation.

The control array shows the status of all entities that are currently active in the simulation. The row number of the array that contains the entity details is used to identify the entity during the simulation. The modeller must decide which entity occupies which row. If the *Avail* field is *false*, this means that the entity is currently committed and is in an active state. In this case, the *TimeCell* shows when this state will end and the *NextAct* field shows which B will terminate that state. If *Avail* is *true*, this means that the entity is available and can be committed to a new active state.

7.2.2   Using the control array to operate a three-phase simulation

As described in Section 6.3 the three phases, repeated at each event time, are:

- *A phase* (time scan). Determine the time of the next event and move the simulation clock to this time. This is done by examining the array for those entities whose *Avail* field is currently *false*. From these entities, the

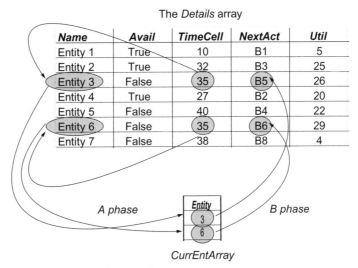

Figure 7.3   Using the *Details* control array

algorithm must select those with the smallest *TimeCell*, which is the time of the next event and will become the value taken by the simulation clock at the end of the *A phase*. The row number of these entities due at this time are moved into a one-dimensional array, *CurrEntArray*, as shown in Figure 7.3.

- *B phase*. Execute any Bs now due at this time. To do this, the executive uses the *CurrEntArray* and works down this array, using the numbers that it stores. These are the row numbers of the *Details* array that hold the records of the entities now due to engage in a B. The executive returns to the *Details* array, finds the correct row, takes the data from the *NextAct* field and executes the B that it indicates (see Figure 7.3). When it has worked through the entire *CurrEntArray*, the executive empties it, ready for the next *A phase*.

- *C phase*. Attempt all Cs until none are executed. This is done in the order in which the Cs are numbered. That is, it tries C1, then C2, then C3 and so on. The order in which the Cs are processed should reflect their priority. Thus, the C with the highest priority should be labelled C1, the next as C2 and so on. To carry out a simulation experiment with different priorities, the names of the Cs must be changed appropriately.

7.3   THE VISUAL BASIC IMPLEMENTATION

7.3.1   Some comments on Visual Basic

The executive and model described here were developed in Visual Basic 6. Later versions of Visual Basic are likely to use the same keywords and syntax, though the way a program communicates with the Windows graphical user interface (GUI) and other programs may change. This should not affect the code fragments shown in this chapter.

Visual Basic programs are usually developed in Microsoft Visual Studio, an environment that includes a dedicated text editor, debugging tools, standard add-ins, objects and tools. The programs should be written as a set of modules that form a project and this can be compiled to produce an executable application program. The modules are relatively independent and can be separately debugged before being linked into a project. The project should also be debugged because there may be unexpected dependencies. A Visual Basic project normally includes at least two types of module.

- *Program code*. Usually has the .bas suffix and will instruct the computer to do the computations required for, in this case, the simulation. This chapter only discusses the code modules.
- *Forms*. Usually has the .frm suffix and will specify how the user will interact with the program through the Windows interface. This chapter does not discuss the forms used by the program, though these are included in the files on the website.

In Visual Basic there is no need to define the type of a variable, however, this can lead to unexpected behaviour and it is good practice to include the "Option Explicit" line at the start of every code module. This tells the compiler to flag an error if a variable is used before it has been given a defined type. This practice is followed in the Visual Basic code discussed here.

It is important that each B or C should be based on its own program module (whether this be a function, procedure, method or whatever term is used by the language). Doing so may seem tedious, unintelligent even, but it does make debugging easier and greatly simplifies any later enhancement to the program. In Visual Basic, each B and C occupies its own SUB and, to use the executive, must carry defined names. The SUB of the first B should be called B1, the SUB of the second B should be called B2 and so on. Likewise, the SUB of the first C should be given the name C1, the SUB of the second C should be called C2 and so on. The *NextAct* field of the entity record, which points to the next B in which the entity should engage, is an INTEGER field that will contain the index number of the B. Thus, if the field contains n, then this means that this entity is next due to engage in the B contained by the SUB with the name Bn. (Note that, in Figure 7.3, the *NextAct* fields contain B1, B2, etc. for clarity. In the implemented software this is an integer field that will contain only the integer value of the B; 1, 2, etc.)

In the implementation discussed here, the three-phase executive occupies the file code module vbexec.bas and the model, in this case the modified harassed booking clerk, occupies the code module model.bas.

7.3.2   The variables and their types

Figure 7.4 shows the Declarations section of the vbexec.bas file. This is general and will work with any three-phase simulation that has no more than 30 active entities. Increasing the size of the entity list merely requires a different

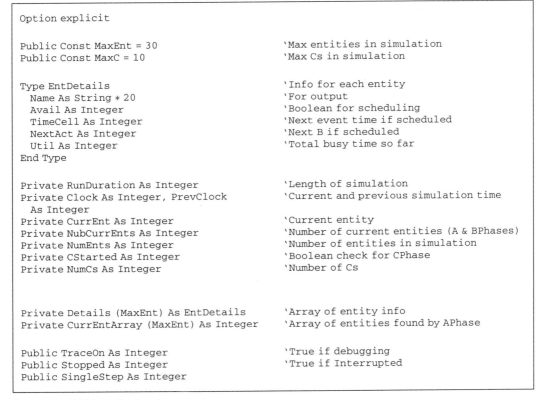

```
Option explicit

Public Const MaxEnt = 30                'Max entities in simulation
Public Const MaxC = 10                  'Max Cs in simulation

Type EntDetails                         'Info for each entity
   Name As String * 20                  'For output
   Avail As Integer                     'Boolean for scheduling
   TimeCell As Integer                  'Next event time if scheduled
   NextAct As Integer                   'Next B if scheduled
   Util As Integer                      'Total busy time so far
End Type

Private RunDuration As Integer          'Length of simulation
Private Clock As Integer, PrevClock     'Current and previous simulation time
   As Integer
Private CurrEnt As Integer              'Current entity
Private NubCurrEnts As Integer          'Number of current entities (A & BPhases)
Private NumEnts As Integer              'Number of entities in simulation
Private CStarted As Integer             'Boolean check for CPhase
Private NumCs As Integer                'Number of Cs


Private Details (MaxEnt) As EntDetails  'Array of entity info
Private CurrEntArray (MaxEnt) As Integer 'Array of entities found by APhase

Public TraceOn As Integer               'True if debugging
Public Stopped As Integer               'True if Interrupted
Public SingleStep As Integer
```

Figure 7.4 VBExec Declarations section

value to be given to the *MaxEnt* constant. Setting this constant as low as possible can be very useful in debugging.

The Visual Basic comments on the program in Figure 7.4 provide reasonable documentation about the role of each variable and type. These are briefly discussed here, section by section.

- The EntDetails type. Visual Basic allows users to define their own types and *EntDetails* is one such type. It enables the record of any entity to be treated as if it were a single variable, even though it is a composite of several fundamental types. As defined here, this has 5 fields; 4 of these are integers and the other is a String used to store the *Name* of the entity.
- *Private* variables. Visual Basic allows variables to be declared as *Private*, which means that they cannot be accessed outside the module in which they are defined. This is a useful safeguard against accidental changes to their values. Hence, all the important variables for the simulation executive are *Private*. Most of the variables are self-explanatory.
  ○ *Details* is an array of size 0 ... *MaxEnt* in which each row is a variable of *EntDetails*, and forms the control array.
  ○ *CurrEnt* is an integer that is used to hold the number of the entity that has a B selected for execution during the current B phase.

○ *NumCurrEnts* holds the number of entities with Bs that are due at the current simulation time. It is only meaningful once the A phase is complete and is set to zero at the start of an A phase.

○ *NumEnts* holds the number of entities currently in the simulation. This is updated as entities are created.

○ *Clock and PrevClock* are used to control the flow of time in the simulation. The executive must keep track of simulation time and the library uses the integer or long integer variable *Clock* for this purpose. Why is an integer variable used, when time in the real world is continuous? The main reason is that all models are approximations (see Pidd, 2003, for a discussion of such approximations in models) and sensible modellers use these approximations to their advantage. Using integer time will make a model run quicker than one based on floating point (real valued) time. There are two reasons for this. The first is that the computer arithmetic is faster. The second is that most data collections on which simulations are based stem from a sample of values. Thus the integer approximation is perfectly adequate, given the ways in which the data will be aggregated. In addition to *Clock*, it can be useful (although not essential) to use an extra global integer (*PrevClock*) to store the previous event time.

○ The *RunDuration* variable is used by the executive to store the planned length of the simulation run. Thus, at the end of each C phase, it compares the current *Clock* value with *RunDuration* to see if the simulation run is complete or whether it should work through a further sequence of A, B and C phases.

○ The *TraceOn*, *Stopped* and *SingleStep* variables are used to control the operation of the simulation in the Visual Basic environment. If *TraceOn* is set to *true*, the simulation writes text output to the standard output window of Visual Studio. If *Stopped* is *true*, this tells the executive that a user has interrupted a running simulation for some reason or other and this allows it to take safe action. If *SingleStep* is *true*, the simulation will run from event time to event time, rather than running continuously until the planned run-time is over or until a user interruption occurs. Single-step execution can be useful when debugging. The values of *TraceOn*, *Stopped* and *SingleStep* are set in the *InitForm* shown in Figure 7.15.

7.3.3   The A phase

During the A phase, the executive must examine the records of all entities and, from those which are not currently available, must find the ones with the smallest time cells. This time cell value is used to update the simulation clock to the time of the next event, this clock being held constant until the next A phase. The identities of those entities that are due to engage in Bs at this new event time are held in a temporary list, *CurrEntArray*, which is emptied at the start of each A phase. Figure 7.3 shows how this is implemented in the approach described here.

THE VISUAL BASIC IMPLEMENTATION   117

```
Public Sub APhase ()
'Performs time scan by examining the Details array
'Checks all entities for which Avail is false, looks for smallest time cells in these
'Min time cell entity numbers stored in CurrEntArray

  Dim Entity As Integer                          'Number of entity being inspected
  Dim Minm As Integer                            'Initial value for minimum search

  NumCurrEnts = 0                                'Set CurrEnt counter
  Minm = 32767                                   'Set Minm value

  For Entity = 1 To NumEnts                      'Go through Details Array
    If Details(Entity) .Avail = False Then       'Skip if Avail
      If Details(Entity) .TimeCell ⇐ Minm Then   'Find if Minm > Time Cell
        If Details(Entity) .TimeCell < Minm Then
          NumCurrEnts = 1                        'Reset NumCurrEnts
          Else: NumCurrEnts = NumCurrEnts + 1    'or increment NumCurrEnts
        End If
        Minm = Detail(Entity).TimeCell           'Reset Minm
        CurrEntArray (NumCurrEnts) = Entity      'Add Entity number to Array
      End If
    End If
  Next

  If Minm = 32767 Then
    Debug.Print "Error in A Phase, no entities
      scheduled"
    Stop

  ElseIf Minm < 0 Then
    Debug.Print "Error in A Phase, Minm gone -ve"
    Stop

  Else: Clock = Minm                             'Found next Clock value

  End If
End Sub
```

Figure 7.5   VBExec A phase

The Visual Basic code for the A phase is shown in Figure 7.5. It should be possible for anyone familiar with a standard programming language to follow what is happening. The first steps are to put *NumCurrEnts* to zero and to put *Minm*, which will be used to search for a minimum time cell, to some very large value. The A phase procedure then works down the *Details* array, entity by entity, *NumEnts* being the number defined in this simulation. During this scan it checks whether the *Avail* field of the entity is *false* and, if so, it compares the value of its *TimeCell* with the current value of *Minm*. If *TimeCell < Minm*, it puts *NumCurrEnts* to 1, or if *TimeCell = Minm*, *NumCurrents* is incremented by 1, otherwise the entity is ignored. The value of *Minm* is then updated and the number of the entity involved is placed in the appropriate cell of the *CurrEntArray*.

The A phase ends with some sensible checks to make sure that nothing strange is happening—which could be the case if the modeller has, foolishly, altered one of the global control variables in another module. Finally, it resets the values of *Clock* and *PrevClock* ready for the B phase.

7.3.4 The B phase

This is similarly straightforward and is shown as a Visual Basic listing in Figure 7.6. The aim of the B phase is to complete all the Bs that have been scheduled for the current clock time, before moving on to work with the Cs at this clock time. This reduces the possibility for deadlock, since most Bs release resources and entities, if only temporarily.

The first section of the *BPhase* sub in the Visual Basic listing of Figure 7.6 is used when debugging a simulation. It writes the current simulation *Clock* time to a specified output file for later interrogation. It then uses another

```
Public Sub BPhase ()
'Works through the CurrEnt Array.
'For each entity stored therein it executes the correct B Activity
'Executed after APhase and before CPhase
'Uses clumsy Select Case because of inadequacies of Visual BASIC

  Dim Entity as Integer
  If (TraceOn = True) Then
    Debug.Print "Time now ", Str(Clock)
  End If
  ShowEntDetails                        'If debugging, show Details array
  For Entity = 1 To NumCurrEnts         'Work through CurrEntArray
    CurrEnt = CurrEntArray(Entity)      'Take CurrEnt number
    Details(CurrEnt) .Avail = True      'Set CurrEnt as Avail
    Select Case Details (CurrEnt) .NextAct  'Now do the correct B activity
      Case 1
        B1
      Case 2
        B2
      Case 3
        B3
      Case 4
        B4
      Case 5
        B5
      Case 6
        B6
      Case 7
        B7
      Case 8
        B8
      Case 9
        B9
      Case 10
        B10
      Case Else
        Debug.Print "B number out of range in BPhase"
    End Select
  Next
End Sub
```

Figure 7.6 VBExec B phase

```
Public Sub CPhase ()
'Just tries each C activity in turn until no more activity
'C's need to be defined by the user

  CStarted = True

  Do Until CStarted = False
    CStarted = False
    C1
    C2
    C3
    C4
    C5
    C6
    C7
    C8
    C9
    C10
  Loop

End Sub
```

Figure 7.7 VBExec C phase

Visual Basic sub, *ShowEntDetails*, to write a copy of the *Details* array to this same trace file. It does this writing to the trace file if a Boolean variable, *TraceOn*, is currently true. This part of the procedure is not essential, but it can save a lot of heartache when debugging a simulation program.

The main section of the Visual Basic sub then follows. As might be expected, it works down the *CurrEntArray*, line by line. It uses the value stored in the appropriate cell of this array to go to the correct row of the *Details* array and from this to call the appropriate procedure for whatever B is scheduled for the entity in question. It also sets the entity in question free, by putting its Boolean *Avail* field to *true*. This means that the entity is now available for committal to some other B, should that be required, and it means that the entity will not be picked up in the next A phase, should that happen before the entity is recommitted.

7.3.5 The C phase

Figure 7.7 shows the Visual Basic code for the C phase. The *CPhase* sub simply works its way down the list of Cs created for the particular application. It does so, by default, in the order in which they have been created. It involves a repeated scan of the Cs, attempting each C in turn and continuing until there is no more successful C activity at this clock time. The *CStarted* flag is used for this purpose.

7.3.6 Running the simulation

The simulation itself is run by the *Simulate* sub of vbexec.bas, which is shown in Figure 7.8. This is the loop that works through the 3 phases; A, B and C

```
Public Sub Simulate()
' Calls A, B & C phases after initialisation
' Requires a public Initialisation sub in the model being run
' Would need to be edited if no UpDateScreen() in RunTime form
' There is probably a better way to update the screen via OLE
' Performs no Initialisation - should be done elsewhere

  Do While Clock < RunDuration
    APhase
    BPhase
    CPhase
    RunTime.UpDateScreen
    DoEvents
  Loop

End Sub
```

Figure 7.8   VBExec main simulation loop

and then updates the screen so that the user can, in the case of Visual Basic, see dynamic simulation output. The duration of the simulation is controlled by *RunDuration*, which is compared with the simulation *Clock* at the start of each loop. Once the simulation is complete, the user may display the results.

7.4   USING VBSIM TO SIMULATE THE HARASSED BOOKING CLERK PROBLEM

7.4.1   Entities, Bs and Cs

To illustrate the use of this library, a slightly enhanced version of the harassed booking clerk problem of Section 5.3.2 will be used. The enhanced version has seven entities:

(1)   *PersEnq* (the personal enquirer arrival machine).
(2)   *PhoneEnq* (the phone call arrival machine).
(3)   *Observer* (an imaginary entity whose job is to note performance statistics at regular intervals).
(4)   and *Clerk 1*.
(5)   *Clerk 2*.
(6)   *Clerk 3*.
(7)   *Clerk 4*.

That is, the booking office has space for up to four clerks, each of which has a phone. Adding an imaginary entity, the *Observer*, is a very useful way of collecting statistics about the simulation as it runs.

This enhanced version has five Bs and two Cs and this will be linked to the entities as follows:

B1: Arrival of a personal enquirer (*PersEnq*).
B2: End of personal service (*Clerks*).

B3: Arrival of a phone call (*PhoneEnq*).
B4: End of a phone conversation (*Clerks*).
B5: Observation of queue lengths (*Observer*).

C1: Begin personal service (*Clerks*).
C2: Begin phone conversation (*Clerks*).

As presented, the executive copes with up to 10 Bs, thus B6 to B10 are empty Visual Basic subs. For same reason, C3 to C10 are empty Visual Basic subs.

Each of these Bs and Cs will be a separate block of code that communicates with the general tools and the executive, but not directly with other Bs or Cs. As the problem is a simple one, each B and C can be contained within a single Visual Basic sub. It makes sense to put the Bs and Cs in a separate program module, here called model.bas.

7.4.2 Personal enquirers and phone calls arrive

As shown above, each of these is modelled with a separate B, and the Visual Basic listing for these is given in Figure 7.9. Given that the problem is, at heart, a simple queuing system with two types of customer who have many similarities, it should not be surprising that their procedures are very similar. The B for personal enquirer arrival will be discussed here and the comments made apply also to the B for the arrival of phone calls.

```
'Arrival of a personal enquirer
'
Sub B1 ()

  PersIn = PersIn + 1
  PersQ = PersQ + 1
  If TraceOn Then
    Debug.Print "PersEnq "; Str$ (PersIn); " arrives"
  End If
  Schedule PersEnq, 1, -PersArrTime * Log(Rnd(PhoneEnq))
End Sub


'Arrival of a phone call
'
Sub B3 ()

  PhoneIn = PhoneIn + 1
  PhoneQ = PhoneQ + 1
  If TraceOn Then
    Debug.Print "PhoneCall "; Str$(PhoneIn); " arrives"
  End If
  Schedule PhoneEnq, 3, -PhoneArrTime * Log(Rnd'PhoneEnq))

End Sub
```

Figure 7.9 Harassed booking clerk: the arrival Bs

```
Public Sub Schedule(ByVal ThisEnt As Integer, ByVal NextB As Integer,
ByVal ThisDuration As Integer)
'Schedules an entity for a B activity after This Duration has elapsed
'Checks to see that the entity is already free

  With Details(ThisEnt)
    If .Avail = False Then
      Debug.Print "Tried to schedule an already Scheduled entity"
      Stop
    End If

    .Avail = False
    .NextAct = NextB
    If GetClock + ThisDuration > GetRunDuration Then
      ThisDuration = GetRunDuration - GetClock
    End If
    .TimeCell = GetClock + ThisDuration
    .Util = Details(ThisEnt).Util + This Duration
  End With

End Sub
```

Figure 7.10   VBExec scheduling on entity for a B

The first step in the B is to keep track of the number of arrivals so far by incrementing a variable *PersIn*, which is set to zero at the start of the simulation. The next line notes that the arrival is added to the queue by incrementing the variable *PersQ*. Note that this version of the program makes no attempt to distinguish between individual customers: were it to do so, then it might be necessary to represent the customers as proper entities. If *TraceOn* is *true*, the sub then writes a message to Visual Basic's debug window—this can be useful to debug a program.

Finally, the B must schedule its next occurrence. The Visual Basic library includes a sub, *Schedule*, for this purpose—shown in Figure 7.10. This has 3 parameters whose values are taken and used to modify the *Details* array, and so ensure that the B is scheduled to occur at the correct simulation time. This works as follows.

First, it checks that the entity is not already committed. If it is, something has gone awry in the simulation and so an error is thrown, which writes a message on Visual Basic's debug window and terminates execution of the program. If the entity is available, then it can be committed to some future B by updating the appropriate fields of the *Details* array. Thus, the *Avail* field of the entity is set to *false*, the *NextAct* field is set to the correct B and the *Util* field is updated. The method used to terminate the simulation by comparing *RunDuration* with the current *Clock* value can lead to an over-estimate of *Util* and this is adjusted accordingly.

The call of the *Schedule* sub shown in the *B1* sub of Figure 7.9 includes the following Visual Basic code as its third parameter:

```
PersArrTime * Log(Rnd(PhoneEnq)
```

This generates a sample from a negative exponential distribution using the method discussed in Section 10.4.1. `PersArrTime` is the mean inter-arrival time for personal enquirers and `PhoneEnq` is a positive constant that controls the random number generator, `Rnd`. The negative exponential distribution is often appropriate in queuing systems.

7.4.3 The end of personal service and phone calls

These two activities are also modelled by Bs and the Visual Basic code for these is shown in Figure 7.11. As in the case of the Bs in Figure 7.9, the two shown in Figure 7.11 are very similar and the one relevant to personal enquirers, *B3*, will be discussed here. The procedure is simple, doing only two things. The first line increments the number of personal enquirers who will leave, *PersOut*, by one—so as to keep track of the number of satisfied customers. The next line will, if appropriate, generate a debug print as discussed in Section 7.4.2.

It is important to understand that, when the B phase of the executive calls a B, it does some of the work. Specifically, it sets the *Avail* field of an entity to *true*, which allows it to be rescheduled, should that be necessary. Looking back at Figure 7.6, the *BPhase* sub works its way down the *CurrEntArray* for each entity stored therein. The *CurrEnt* variable is given the integer value of the entity and the *Avail* field of the entity is set to *true*. Hence there is no need to free the entity in this, or any other, B.

```
'End of a personal service
'
Sub B2()

  PersOut = PersOut + 1
  If TraceOn Then
    Debug.Print "End of personal service "; Str$(PersOut); "with clerk ";
    Str$(GetCurrent - FirstClerk + 1)
  End If

End Sub

'End of a phone conversation
'
Sub B4()
  PhoneOut = PhoneOut + 1
  If TraceOn Then
    Debug.Print "End of phone conversation "; Str$(PhoneOut); " with clerk ";
    Str$(GetCurrent - FirstClerk + 1)
  End If

End Sub
```

Figure 7.11 Harassed booking clerk: the end of service/call Bs

```
'Observation of queue lengths
Sub B5()

  PersRec(Obs) = PersQ
  PhoneRec(Obs) = PhoneQ
  Obs = Obs + 1

  Schedule Observer, 5, ObsInterval

  If TraceOn Then
    Debug.Print "Observation no: "; Str$(Obs); Str(PersQ)
  End If

End Sub
```

Figure 7.12 Harassed booking clerk: the *Observe* B

7.4.4 Observations

As mentioned earlier, this version of the harassed booking clerk includes an extra entity, the *Observer*, which is used to take regular observations of the queue lengths as the simulation proceeds. The observation interval is specified by the user at the start of the simulation in the *Initialisation* procedure of the simulation (see Section 7.4.6). The Visual Basic code for the *Observe* B is shown in Figure 7.12. It uses two arrays, *PersRec*() and *PhoneRec*() in which to store the queue lengths that are current at the simulation clock time of which the B is executed. The meaning of the program code should be self-evident.

7.4.5 The Cs

There are two Cs and they are very similar. Figure 7.13 shows the code for C1: Begin personal service. The code for the phone conversations, C2: Begin phone conversation, is very similar, with references to personal enquirers being replaced by references to phone calls.

Since there are several clerks all of whom are available to answer the phones and to speak to people who arrive in person, the Cs must allow for several services to begin at the same time and thus the test-head is formed, in Visual Basic, by a Do ... While loop. Thus, the code inside the loop will only be executed whilst the queue exists ($PersQ > 0$) and whilst some of the clerks have yet to be tried. If this test is successful then the clerk is examined to see if it is available. If both conditions are met, the service can begin. As with the Bs that control arrivals, the service time is taken from a negative exponential distribution and the *Schedule*() function is used to commit the relevant clerk to B2 at the appropriate time.

The C phase must be repeated until there is no more activity possible at the current clock time, since successfully executing a C may change the resources available to other Cs. To achieve this repeat scanning, the global

```
'Begin personal service
'
Sub C1()

  Dim ThisClerk As Integer

  ThisClerk = FirstClerk - 1

  Do While (PersQ > 0) And (ThisClerk < LastClerk)
    ThisClerk = ThisClerk + 1
    If CheckAvail (ThisClerk) Then
      SetCStarted
      PersQ = PersQ - 1
      Schedule ThisClerk, 2, -PersServeTime * Log(Rnd(ThisClerk))
      If TraceOn Then
        Debug.Print "Start personal service with "; Str$(ThisClerk - FirstClerk + 1)
      End If
    End If
  Loop

End Sub
```

Figure 7.13 Harassed booking clerk: the *BeginServe* C

variable *CStarted* is used. If a C is successfully executed, this is set to *true*. Repeated scanning of the Cs continues in *CPhase* (see Figure 7.7) until *CStarted* is set to *false*.

7.4.6 Initialization and finalization

To allow for experimentation and analysis, the simulation must be controlled and parameterized. This is done by two procedures: *Initialisation*, which is called before the first A phase, and *Finalisation*, which is called when the run is complete.

In the *Initialisation*, all variables used in the model must be explicitly set to whatever initial values are required. Thus, all counters (such as *PersIn*) must be set to zero and any activity which is in progress at the start of the simulation must be set in train. All entities and Cs required by the simulation need to be declared in the *Initialisation*, which means ensuring that the *Details* array has the correct number of rows and that each row contains the correct information. The *Finalisation* is used to collect the results of the simulation and to put them in some suitable state for analysis. This might mean writing them to the screen or to a file that could be analysed, say, with a common spreadsheet such as Microsoft Excel.

The Visual Basic implementation of the *Initialisation* and *Finalisation* relies on several subs that ensure safe operation of the private variables of vbexec.bas. For the detail of these subs, download the files from the website and follow their logic by starting from the *Initialisation*.

```
Sub Main()

  InitValues
  InitForm.SetPars
  InitForm.Show

End Sub
```

Figure 7.14 The VB *Main*( ) procedure for VBExec

7.5 PUTTING IT ALL TOGETHER

To run this simulation under Visual Basic, another sub is needed within model.bas; *Main*, which is shown in Figure 7.14. The simulation starts with the *Main* sub, which is part of the model.bas module. First, this initializes the variables used in the model, such as *PersIn* and *PersOut*, using the *InitValues* sub of model.bas to do so. It then uses *InitForm*, which presents the window shown in Figure 7.15 that allows the user to specify the parameters of the simulation.

Once the user starts the simulation, the *InitForm* disappears and is replaced by *RunTimeForm* (shown in Figure 7.16), which allows the user to interrupt and restart the simulation. Once the simulation is complete, the user may display the results.

By far the best way to understand the workings of this and the other libraries is to use them. The full libraries can be downloaded from my personal website at http://www.lancs.ac.uk/staff/smamp/

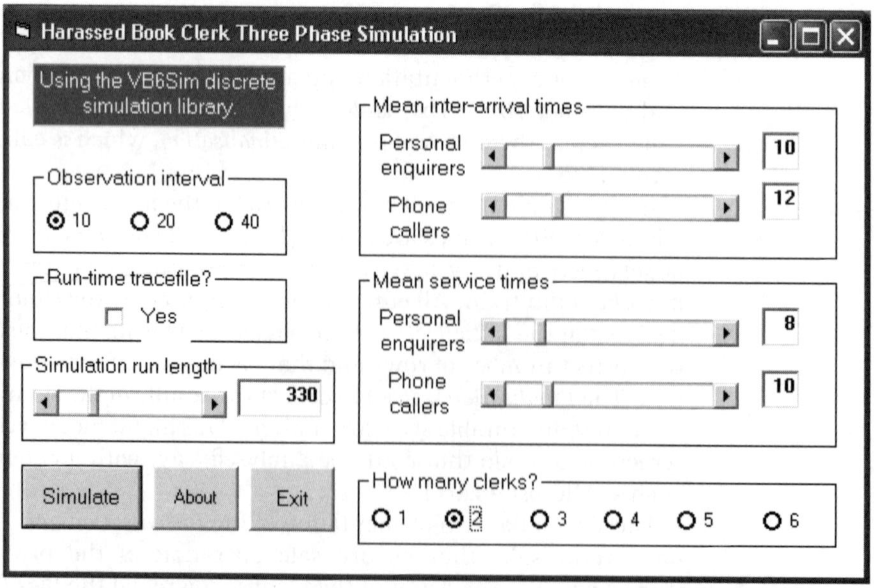

Figure 7.15 The *InitForm* for the VB harassed booking clerk simulation

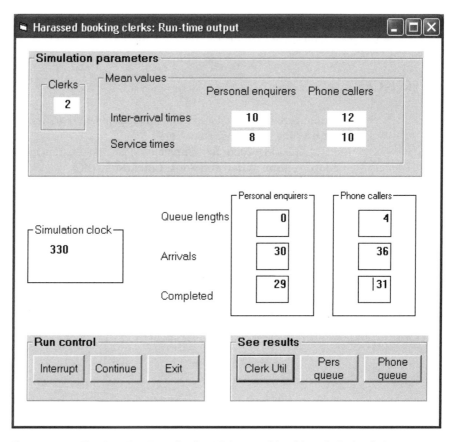

Figure 7.16   The *RunTimeForm* for the VB harassed booking clerk simulation

EXERCISES

(1) Modify the harassed booking clerk program so as to give priorities to phone callers rather than to personal enquirers.

(2) Modify the harassed booking clerk problem so as to have dedicated clerks—some to serve personal enquirers and some to answer the phones. Use this simulation model to decide which system is best, dual-purpose or single-purpose clerks.

(3) Modify the harassed booking clerk problem so as to have phone callers waiting for a limited period of time only. (Hint: when a call arrives, keep track of when it will ring off and create a new B which will remove it from the queue if it is not answered by the time the caller becomes frustrated.)

(4) Develop a three-phase simulation program of the T-junction discussed in Section 6.2.5.

(5) Develop a three-phase simulation program of the Morecambe Bay Hovercraft Company described in Exercise 4 of Chapter 6.

(6) Develop a three-phase simulation program of the accident and emergency room described in Exercise 7 of Chapter 5.

REFERENCES

Fishman G.S. (1973) *Concepts and Methods of Discrete Event Digital Simulation.* John Wiley and Sons, New York.

Pidd M. (2003) *Tools for Thinking: Modelling in Management Science* (2nd edition). John Wiley and Sons, Chichester, UK.

8

Visual Interactive Modelling and Simulation

8.1 BASIC IDEAS

When discrete simulation methods were first developed, the process of programming a computer and of getting the results from the program was a laborious and highly skilled task. Until the mid-1970s, most computers were large and expensive and were operated mainly in batch mode. Thus, someone writing a simulation program would have to develop the program on coding forms, have the program punched on to cards, have someone else feed the cards to the computer and then wait for the results. Often as not it was impossible to achieve more than one or two runs each day on most commercial computers. The results, when they appeared, were usually printed by a line printer onto wide computer paper by a line printer.

Nowadays, most simulations are developed in a very different computing environment. Users take for granted that programs and data can be directly entered into the computer from a keyboard or with help of a device such as a mouse. They also assume that they will have direct control over their own computing via networked workstations or a personal computer. They are also accustomed to seeing the results of computer programs reported and manipulated on a display screen rather than handed over as a pile of printout. Inevitably, these technological changes have altered the methods of discrete simulations and they affect the analyst as well as the user.

Computer users assume that they have high-quality graphics screens available and that they will interact with the computer via a graphical user interface (GUI). Much business analysis is done using spreadsheets such as Microsoft Excel, which also provide good graphical output. Well designed displays can be used to convey complicated ideas in a way that would require many words.

8.1.1 Visual interactive modelling (VIM)

Strictly speaking, visual interactive simulation is a subset of VIM. The latter covers other management science techniques such as multi-criteria analysis and heuristic search and really refers to a general approach (Elder, 1992). The VIM approach relies on a GUI for the development, enhancement and running of the model—of whatever type. That is, the visual interaction is intended to support the analyst and the client as they cooperate through a project, more or less as shown in Figure 3.2.

In any management science project, the analyst must inhabit two worlds. The first is the abstract world of analysis in which symbols and mathematics are used to develop models. The second is the real world of day-to-day life in which customer needs must be met and goods and services must be produced. The idea is that the model world can be used to shed light on the real world as part of a process of improvement or design. These two worlds are shown interacting in Figure 3.2.

From the analyst's point of view, the abstract work is shown as having, for simplicity, three phases and a VIM approach is intended to be of value in all three. Thus, the ability to develop rough and ready models in which major factors can be investigated is part of problem structuring. Also, the ability to show what will happen, through interactive computer graphics, is helpful in implementation. From the client's point of view, the organization of a project is shown as having four or five phases, all of which are also supported by a VIM approach.

Nevertheless, it has been common to use the abbreviation VIMS (Visual Interactive Modelling System) to refer to simulation software that fully embodies the VIM approach. Hence, this is what the VIMS abbreviation will mean here.

8.1.2 Visual simulation output

Most discrete computer simulations are written on personal computers and workstations. Most often they are intended for use by the client directly rather than by the analyst on the client's behalf. That is, the modeller may deliver the model rather than an analysis based on the model, and the client may take his/her own control over the analysis. It is thus very sensible to use the graphical displays that are available.

Virtually all commercial discrete simulation software packages allow the modeller to set up visual interactive simulations, although it can be rather time consuming to do so. Some software can also be linked with graphics post-processors. In these cases, the simulation runs with no graphical output: instead, the simulation outputs values to a file as it runs. This file is then read later by the graphics post-processor, which produces an animated display of the simulation. Clearly it is not feasible to interact with a post-processed display, but it does allow a user to stop the run, to rewind it as if it were a video recording or even to fast-forward to interesting aspects. An example of a graphics post-processor is Proof Animation (Henriksen, 1996), provided by Wolverine Corporation, originally developed for use with GPSS-H, but able to be linked to other simulation languages.

Three benefits come from using dynamic graphical display in simulations, the first two of which accrue to the client of the study. First, when properly designed, a graphical display can give a very good idea of the logical behaviour of the simulation program. Thus, in a simulation of a flexible manufacturing system, the display may clearly show automatic guided vehicles moving from cell to cell. It may also show the cells changing state as jobs are completed. In this way, the client—who may be the owner or designer of the system being simulated—may quickly gain an idea of whether the model logic is correct. There is less need for the user to take on trust that the simulation is a valid representation of the system. This logical clarity also makes it possible to think of developing simulation programs in cooperation with the client. The developing display will give the client some idea of whether the developing model is sensible.

The second advantage will also benefit the user of the simulation, for even with no ability to interact with the program the graphics are an aid to effective experimentation on the model. It is often easy to spot that a particular experiment is fruitless by watching a dynamic graphical display. For example, a simulation of a warehouse may display, amongst other things, the queue of vehicles waiting to be unloaded. If this queue is seen to grow too large, then it is clear that more resources must be supplied if the queue is to be kept to acceptable lengths. There may be no need to complete a full run of the simulation once such undesirable behaviour is noted. Instead, the run can be aborted and other possibilities may then be simulated. This is much quicker than having to wait for a finished printout before learning that the experiment is unprofitable.

There is, of course, the danger that this may lead to ill-considered experimentation. It could be argued that, because batch computing was slow, the analyst was likely to be careful about which experiments were likely to be worthwhile. This risk of lazy experimentation must be faced; however, the solution to the problem lies in better analysis and not in abandoning the use of graphics. As can be seen, there are clear benefits from the use of graphics. The use of graphics does not remove the need for carefully planned experimentation using the type of statistical methods described in Chapter 11. However, graphics may be of use to reduce the potential set of sensible experiments.

The third advantage accrues to the programmer. Unlike many types of computer program, the main concerns in debugging a simulation program are often logical variables rather than numeric variables. That is, in a discrete event simulation, the state of the system results from the states of the individual entities, therefore, the important variables are the ones that represent and link these logical states. If the analyst is to be confident that the system is being modelled correctly, then he/she must carefully follow through all the logical consequences of state changes in the system. This can be done by following a trail of text printed out from each activity—as is provided by the trace file in the harassed booking clerk program of Chapter 7. However, dynamic interactions are best seen dynamically. That is, it is easier to spot errors of logic when entities are seen to change state wrongly on a properly designed graphical display.

8.1.3 Interaction

In effect, a visual interactive simulation is a form of computer game in which an artificial world is created as the simulation runs. The user can interact with the model, as if it were a computer game, to carry out experiments, albeit informal ones. As the user watches the progress of the simulation it may become obvious that performance could be improved by a small change to one of the variables. For example, in a simulation of a warehouse it might become clear from the screen that too many vehicles are waiting to be unloaded outside the building. It might be thought that adding an extra forklift truck could have a dramatic effect on this queue of waiting trucks. With an interactive simulation of such a warehouse, the user might be permitted to interrupt the running program and add an extra forklift truck. Continuing the simulation with the new truck would show the effect of the addition. Interrupting the running program, modifying the appropriate variables and restarting the simulation from its previous state, is equivalent to using the program in a gaming mode. Thus the user may quickly home in on suitable operating policies by dynamically interacting with the program.

This type of interactive gaming with a discrete simulation program was suggested by Greenberger and Jones (1968) and became popular through the work of Hurrion (1976), who suggested the addition of animated graphics. Commercial simulation packages virtually all allow sensible interaction, following the trail set by See-Why (described by Fiddy *et al.*, 1981). Nowadays it is hard, if not impossible, to find a discrete event simulation package that does not offer visual interaction.

8.1.4 A caveat

It should though, be noted that visual simulation is no panacea and is no substitute for sensible thought and analysis. It is tempting to develop a simulation model quickly with very little thought, with the result that the model grows like Topsy and is soon out of control. Like spreadsheets, visual simulations are a great boon if properly conceived and used, but can become a disaster area when carelessly used.

There is a further point to note about graphical displays. Though the ones available on personal computers are very powerful, it is still true that many simulations run much slower when employing interactive graphical output. This is because the visible screen must be kept up to date as the simulation proceeds and this adds a computing overhead to the simulation program. Hence, many users turn off the graphics once they are happy that the model is valid. They do this so they can run multiple replications or make long runs: both for statistical purposes (see Chapter 11).

8.2   DESIGNING A VISUAL SIMULATION DISPLAY

Broadly speaking, there are three types of display employed in a visual interactive simulation. The idea of the display is to convey information in a way that the user, whether an analyst or client, can quickly comprehend. This does not mean that the displays must be works of art, nor that they must always be hyper-realistic. They should simply support the analyst and client in

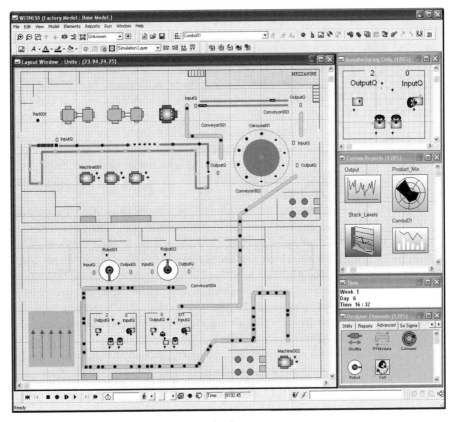

Figure 8.1   A Witness (mainly) iconic display

developing and running a simulation so as to bring about some improvement. Needless to say, the three types of display can be combined, as in Figure 8.1.

8.2.1 Iconic displays

Perhaps the most obvious way to display the simulation graphically is to use a set of icons to represent the entities. The resulting display forms a mimic diagram that gives some schematic representation of the system being simulated. The effect is like watching a video of the system as the simulation proceeds. For example, in a simulation of a warehouse, the display might aim to show a floor plan of the building on which are seen the trucks and pallet loads moving about and the cranes moving to storage locations. A small picture of a truck might be used to represent a truck in the simulation and, as the truck changes state, the truck icon is seen to move around the screen in some appropriate way. The idea of an iconic display is that the screen should resemble the simulated system in some recognizable way. An iconic display of a manufacturing system, produced by the Witness simulation system (Lanner Systems, 2003), is shown in Figure 8.1.

In designing an iconic display there are several considerations to be borne in mind:

(1) *Choice of entities*. It is not necessary to display all the entities of the simulation. Too much complexity may make the display hard to understand and difficult to follow. The final display should only show those entities which are of concern to the user and important for experimentation. This suggests that the programmer may require a different display from the user, for the programmer may wish to check on all the entities at some time or another. To the naive user, the display and the simulation may seem identical, but things are much more complicated for the analyst.

(2) *Choice of icons*. Ideally the icons should be easily recognizable by the intended user of the simulation, this being the point of using an iconic display. However, this simple rule is not always easy to follow, especially when there are several similar entities to be displayed. The resolution of the graphic device will be another constraint to be borne in mind when designing appropriate icons. How the icons are constructed and stored will depend on the computer, the terminal and whatever graphics software is available. Graphic images can be heavy users of memory, but this is increasingly less of a constraint.

(3) *Displaying states*. The icons are used to show how and when the various entities are changing state in the simulation. Thus, these state changes need to be displayed in some sensible manner. This is not always straightforward, especially in complicated systems—as the designers of analogue displays have found when attempting to plan monitoring and control stations for process control equipment. The screen designer should use the colour, scale, orientation and position of the icon on the screen to represent state changes. All can be effectively used to display the system state in an easily understandable way.

8.2.2   Logical displays

A logical display is not intended to mimic the appearance of the system being simulated, but instead focuses directly on the logical interactions of the system. Consider, for example, a food manufacturing plant in which the raw materials are mixed, cooked, shaped, cooled and packed. Simulations can be useful in designing such plant, particularly where the various plant sections are known to be unreliable and therefore require in-process buffer stocks. Rather than attempting to develop icons which resemble the plant, it can be entirely satisfactory to use on-screen block diagrams which show the state of the plant sections. A simple logical block display from such a simulation is shown in Figure 8.2.

These block diagrams need not resemble the analogue displays used to control and manage the physical plant, but need only show how the total plant behaves as a system when particular events occur during the simulation. For example, the display of Figure 8.2 could at some stage show the

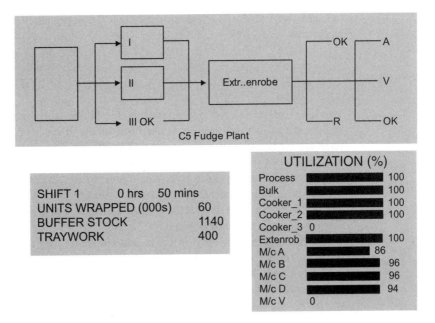

Figure 8.2   A logical display

plant oscillating if particular plant sections are going online and offline due to failures. The plant sections need only to be shown as named rectangles or other shapes in order to achieve this effect. Various colours and types of line may then be employed to show the different states. Changes in colour and line type show the interaction of the various state changes.

For this type of display, there is no need for the blocks themselves to correspond directly with the entities whose behaviour is driving the simulation model. That is, the blocks need not represent entities, unlike with iconic diagrams, but may represent more aggregate system components. For example, a single aggregate block might be used to represent the state of all the early processes on a production line, the later processes being shown in detail.

8.2.3   Chart displays

This third type of display is seen in its purest form in simulations of financial and economic systems. The chart display takes the form of histograms, line graphs and bar charts to show the performance of the model as measured by specified variables. For example, the display might show the order backlog and cumulative profit when simulating an inventory system. Whereas an iconic display directly attempts to mimic the physical appearance of the system and a logical display concentrates on discrete system state, a chart display focuses on continuous system performance. As before, the aim is to produce a display that is meaningful to the user of the simulation model (i.e., a display which allows the user to monitor the performance of the model easily as it runs).

8.3   VIMS

The use of VIMS is so widespread that it is likely that, apart from the defence sector, most simulation models are built using them. Many of the simulation packages listed in the regular *OR/MS Today* software survey (Swain, 2003) are VIMS. All such packages are capable of simulating simple systems with ease, though some run out of power when simulating problems of some complexity and scale. The remainder of this chapter shows how two simulation VIMS, Micro Saint (Micro Analysis and Design, 2003) and SIMUL8 (Simul8 Corporation, 2003) can be used.

A well-designed simulation VIMS will allow the user to interact graphically with the model as it is built, as it is run, as its results are analysed and whilst it is modified. Not all of this is necessarily done within the VIMS itself, however. For example, most VIMS provide some analysis and graphing tools to enable the user to analyse and interpret the simulation output. However, there are much more powerful analysis tools available, including statistical packages such as SPSS (SPSS Inc, 2003) and SAS (SAS Institute Inc, 2003), plus the analysis routines with spreadsheets such as Microsoft Excel. Hence, a VIMS may provide a direct link to these packages or may allow the user to write simulation results in compatible file formats.

There is insufficient space to explore the full features of either package, and so they will be used to show how most VIMS work. Given that software vendors regularly update their products, there may be some differences between the versions used here and those available later. However, the examples should still work.

8.3.1   Joe's exhaust parlour

Joe owns and runs an exhaust replacement business on an industrial estate. This exhaust parlour provides a service to private motorists who are concerned about the state of their car exhaust systems. Joe has run the business successfully for a number of years but is concerned at the competition from a national franchise which has opened up nearby. He knows that most potential customers will visit his parlour as well as that of the national competitor and he ensures that his prices are competitive. Given this, he believes that the other keys to winning an order are surroundings which are clean and business-like, but not too plush; and also in keeping a customer waiting for the shortest possible time.

Joe's parlour is open from 9.00 am to 7.00 pm and he and his fitters work throughout that period if there is work to be done. Meals and rest breaks are taken whenever the activity is slack. The mode of operation is as follows:

Motorists arrive unannounced and wait for Joe himself to inspect their car's exhaust system. To do this, the car is driven by Joe onto any free hydraulic ramp so that the car's exhaust system may be checked from below. Joe then advises the customer on the necessary work and 70% of customers elect to stay at Joe's parlour to have the work done. The other 30% go elsewhere.

Those drivers who choose to have the work done at Joe's sit in the lounge from which they can watch one of Joe's fitters work on their car on the ramp. When the fitter is finished, Joe inspects the work and, if it is satisfactory, he prints out the bill for the driver, who then pays and leaves. If Joe decides that the work is not satisfactory (which seems to happen in 10% of the jobs) then the fitter must rework the job—and this may take as long as the original work. Rework, too, is inspected in the same way as the original job.

Joe would like some advice from you. He needs to know how many fitters and ramps he should employ in the parlour. He is very secretive about his finances and will not give you this information, preferring to carry out a financial analysis himself after you have advised him about fitters and ramps. Ideally, he would like to keep his customers waiting for rather less than 10 minutes before he inspects their vehicle after their arrival; he would also like to ensure that customers spend less than 60 minutes in total at the parlour.

Whatever software is used, the starting point is to think through the sequence of tasks and activities that characterize the system. Also, it is important to consider the main entities and resources. Joe's exhaust parlour has cars, drivers, fitters, Joe himself and ramps that are used to carry out the work. Of these, only cars are involved in most of the activities of the system, which suggests that they should be the focus of the model. We have no information about what happens to the drivers—except that they make the decision whether to have the work done and that they pay Joe afterwards. For the time being, there is no need to worry about the drivers.

The main active states in the system are as follows:

- Cars *Arrive*. They then wait for inspection if Joe is busy or no ramp is free.
- *Inspect*. In which cars are driven onto a ramp and are inspected by Joe. This therefore requires a waiting car, a free ramp and Joe. At the end of this state, the driver decides whether to leave or to stay and have the exhaust replaced. If the driver leaves with the car, this releases the ramp and Joe. Otherwise, the car continues to occupy the ramp.
- *Replace*. This is carried out by the first available fitter and uses the ramp occupied during *Inspect*.
- *Check*. Joe does this as soon as he is free. Meanwhile, the fitter and ramp are still engaged. If the work is unsatisfactory, the work must be redone by the fitter; otherwise the fitter and ramp are freed at the end the *Check*.
- *PayJoe*. This requires Joe.
- *Leave*. The cars leave, driven by their drivers; either after the driver decides not to replace an exhaust, or because they have paid Joe.

This leads to the activity cycle diagram (see Chapter 5) shown in Figure 8.3. Note that, since *Leave* takes no time, it is not shown on the diagram but, instead, the cars go directly into the *Outside* dead state.

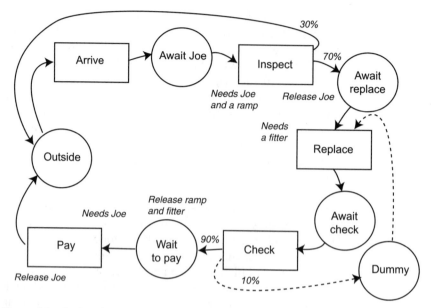

Figure 8.3 Joe's exhaust parlour: activity cycle diagram

8.3.2 Joe's exhaust parlour in Micro Saint: model building

As with all simulation VIMS, Micro Saint allows the user to develop a model by selecting icons and linking them into a network. Micro Saint is *task-based*, which means that each node of the network represents a task that may require resources for its completion. The main entity class, cars in this example, flow through the network from task to task as shown by the arrows that link the tasks. Given the above description and analysis of Joe's way of operating, this leads to the Micro Saint task network shown in Figure 8.4. This uses just 3 icons;

(1) *Ovals*. Represent the tasks: *Arrive, Inspect, Replace, Check, Pay* and *Leave*.
(2) *Diamonds*. These are shown at the right-hand end of those tasks from which there is more than one exit link.
   - Icons with marked with a letter "M" are multiple nodes, which are used when the end of the task triggers more than one subsequent task. Thus, the arrival of a car may trigger both an *Inspect* task (if Joe and a ramp are free) and the scheduling of the arrival of the next car.
   - Icons marked with a letter "D" are decision nodes, which are used when the end of one task will trigger one or more others, depending on the value of some attribute. These occur at the end of the *Inspect* task (since 30% of drivers choose to *Leave*) and at the end of the *Check* task (since 10% require rework).
   - Though not shown in Figure 8.4, the diamond icons can also carry at letter "T", which signifies a tactical node. This means that the task

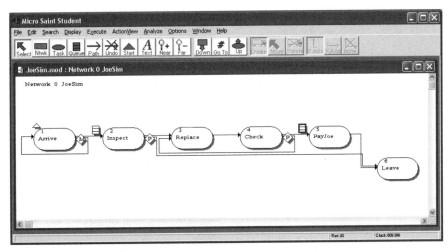

Figure 8.4 Joe's exhaust parlour: a Micro Saint task network

next triggered for the main entity will depend on some conditions in the model—which the modeller must specify.
(3) Icons shown as a small rectangle with two horizontal lines represent queues that are allowed to form before a task. Two are used in Figure 8.4 and both are placed before Joe is needed for his two specific tasks.

The tasks on the network must now be parameterized, so as to specify how long they take and any conditions that govern their execution. Since this cannot be easily done on the diagram itself, Micro Saint, like other VIMS, provides fill-in forms through which the user may specify the detail of the model. Some VIMS provide sensible default values for parameters, but others do not. Micro Saint assume zeroes.
Specifically, the user may define the following for each task:

- *Release conditions*. These are used to specify the conditions under which a task may begin. Thus, for *Inspect*, these would be that Joe is free and that at least one ramp is available. Micro Saint will automatically check that there is a car in the queue, as the queue is linked by the system itself to the correct task.
- *Beginning effect*. This defines the logic of what happens when the task starts. In the case of *Inspect*, this would be that Joe is no longer free and that there is one less ramp available.
- *Ending effect*. This defines what happens at the end of the task. In the case of *Inspect*, this would be that Joe is now free again. As with incoming queue logic, Micro Saint links the probabilistic node after *Inspect* to this task and automatically deposits the car into this node. From there they will proceed either to the *Check* queue or to *Leave*.
- *Launch effect*. This permits the user to carry out tasks after the task duration has been computed, but before the beginning effect is executed. This

might, for example, allow action to be taken if the task duration would otherwise take the task completion time to beyond the end of the working day.

Thus, Micro Saint and other simulation VIMS allow the user to specify the detailed event logic of the system. One problem with these VIMS is that each one seems to use its own programming language for this purpose. In the case of Micro Saint, the language uses a syntax that is rather like a cross between C and Pascal. It might be better if the VIMS vendors could cooperate to define a language standard or adopt an existing syntax (such as C). However, this seems unlikely to happen.

8.3.3   Joe's exhaust parlour in Micro Saint: running and analysing the simulation

Micro Saint allows the user to watch a number of different windows as the simulation proceeds, including:

- *The network diagram.* As drawn on-screen to develop the model, so as to allow the user to check the task logic as the simulation runs. This also gives some idea of the build-up of queues, if appropriate icons are selected.
- *The variable catalog.* Which contains all variables defined by the user. Any of these can be displayed in a window as the simulation runs. This might include queue lengths, for example.
- *An action view.* Which is an iconic representation of the model designed to resemble the physical system. Thus icons may be developed for Joe, the fitters, ramps and cars. Cars may be shown arriving, waiting for service, moving onto and off ramps and the fitters and Joe may be seen attending to them (see Figure 8.5). This can be useful for demonstrating the simulation to a client and convincing them of its acceptability.
- *The event queue.* Which is another name for the event list or calendar (see Chapter 6). This is the heart of the Micro Saint control program onto which events are entered and from which they are executed at the correct simulation time. Viewing this can be very useful when debugging a model.

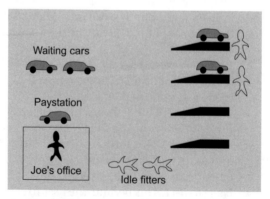

Figure 8.5   Joe's exhaust parlour: an action view

It is not always necessary to view all such displays, but if a large display screen is available, doing so can greatly ease the debugging task. However, even with today's powerful PCs, the execution speed of a program is greatly reduced if dynamic graphics are used. Hence, once a program has been thoroughly debugged and its users are confident in its validity, then it is common practice to turn off the dynamic graphics as the simulation runs. Micro Saint, like most simulation VIMS, provides a menu option to enable this.

Simulation exercises are conducted with some purpose in mind and this usually requires the analysis of simulation runs. This is discussed in detail in Chapter 11, which in turn builds on the sampling theory discussed in Chapter 10. Hence, simulation VIMS allow the user to manage multiple simulation runs and to store the results in a file for later analysis. As mentioned earlier, this analysis may be done within the VIMS itself or by exporting the data to another analysis package. In Micro Saint, some analyses are provided as standard, though may be over-ridden, and others are set up by the user. User-determined data collection is set up by the use of snapshots, which are parameterized through a Snapshot Description window. This allows several different types of snapshot to be written to a file:

- *At the beginning or end of a specified task.* Thus, for example, we might record the time at which each car arrives at Joe's exhaust parlour and write this to a file as it happens.
- *At specific clock times.* Thus, every 30 minutes we might record the number of cars that are waiting for their initial inspection by Joe. This is the same as the concept of an *Observer* introduced in the three-phase simulation at the start of Section 7.4.
- *As entities enter or leave a queue.* This is slightly different from a snapshot at the end of a task, since not all entities will enter a queue.
- At the end of a simulation run.

For example, Table 8.1 shows an extract from a snapshot file with information about each car as it finally leaves the system. It has 6 columns, all user-defined:

Table 8.1   Extract from a Micro Saint snapshot file for Joe's exhaust parlour

Clock	Tag	TR	ID	TinS	Trigger
77.99559	1	1	0	49.28581	end 6
104.764	4	1	5.100517	53.23449	end 6
106.3503	7	0	36.23718	37.8235	end 6
112.3402	5	1	0.150967	52.69222	end 6
117.7862	9	0	27.76746	33.21346	end 6
120.8142	3	1	3.725739	72.23117	end 6
129.818	6	1	13.66789	65.49033	end 6
139.4028	2	2	0	92.78466	end 6
145.0816	12	0	4.58223	10.26099	end 6
597.7792	48	0	5.162231	9.543884	end 6

(1) *Clock.* The simulation time at which this car left the exhaust parlour.
(2) *Tag.* The car number in arrival order.
(3) *TR.* The number of times that the car went through the *Replace* task. Some require rework and some never go through this task as the car owner decides not to proceed with the replacement of the exhaust system.
(4) *ID.* The initial delay (i.e., the time after its arrival that a car is kept waiting before Joe can carry out his initial inspection).
(5) *TinS.* The total time that elapses after a car arrives until it finally leaves Joe's exhaust parlour.
(6) *Trigger.* The task triggering the snapshot. In this case this is Task 6, *Leave.*

Micro Saint provides a basic set of built-in analysis tools, which include the ability to plot different types of graph and to check for the statistical properties of the results. For example, the summary statistics of the whole of Table 8.1 are as shown in Table 8.2. This shows, very clearly, that Joe is nowhere near reaching his performance targets—at least as far as this single simulation run is concerned. Some unfortunate drivers are waiting as long as 36 minutes for the initial inspection and others spend over 90 minutes in the parlour. This is with five ramps and five fitters, but this is not good enough. Perhaps Joe is the bottleneck?

The use of these built-in analysis tools is fundamental to the underlying philosophy of VIM. The idea is to allow the user to conduct quick, albeit crude, analysis to guide rapid experimentation on the model. Table 8.2 shows that even with five fitters and five ramps Joe cannot meet his targets. Running the model many more times will produce similar results, and so other policies must be tried to see which ones work. This requires the user to edit the model or its parameters and then to rerun the simulation. Doing so, in this case, leads us to a view that we need two Joes—which is impossible without cloning! Hence, Joe will have to trust someone else with some of the inspecting, checking and receipt of money. It is easy to modify the model and its parameters to find a policy that will meet his performance targets.

Once we have found what seems to be a sensible policy, we can export performance data to a spreadsheet or statistics package to confirm the results in more detail. Persuading Joe to trust someone else may be much harder.

Table 8.2 Summary results from a Micro Saint simulation of Joe's exhaust parlour

	Minimum	Maximum	Mean	Standard deviation
Clock	78.00	597.78	333.30	161.34
Tag	1.00	48.00	24.04	13.78
TR	0.00	2.00	0.74	0.57
ID	0.00	36.24	8.29	10.15
TInS	3.77	92.78	48.86	26.85

8.3.4   Joe's exhaust parlour in SIMUL8: model building

SIMUL8 (Simul8 Corporation, 2003) is another easy to use simulation VIMS. As with Micro Saint, model building is done on-screen by placing icons and linking them into a network. Whereas Micro Saint starts with an abstract task network, a SIMUL8 visual model is an iconic representation that more closely resembles the appearance of the system being simulated. Thus, to simulate Joe's exhaust parlour, each ramp is shown separately. For simulating larger systems, such as call centres, the screen would be too crowded and so a mixed display would be used. To illustrate this, albeit for a small system, Figure 8.6 shows a SIMUL8 task display for the harassed booking clerk problem discussed in Section 5.3. Figure 8.7 shows a SIMUL8 model of Joe's exhaust parlour.

SIMUL8 provides a palette of basic, generic objects that are used to build a model:

- *Work entry points*. Where work, effectively the main entity class flowing through the system, enters the simulation model. In the case of Joe's exhaust parlour, a work entry point represents the arrival of cars. As with Micro Saint and other VIMS, SIMUL8 allows the user to double click on the icon to bring up a properties window, which is used to parameterize the arrivals.
- *Storage bins (or queues)*. Where work, in this case cars, wait for processing. To simulate Joe's exhaust parlour, two are needed: one for new customers waiting for inspection and the other for customers waiting to pay.

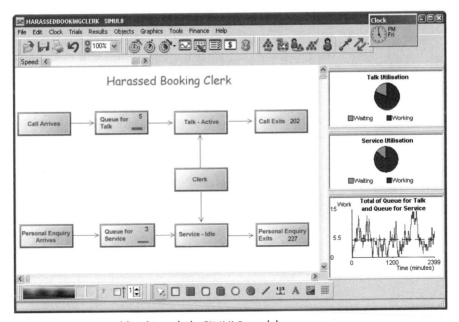

Figure 8.6   Harassed booking clerk: SIMUL8 model

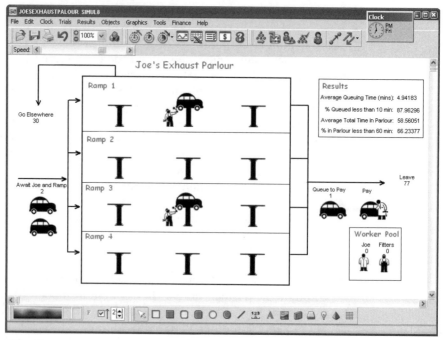

Figure 8.7   Joe's exhaust parlour: a SIMUL8 model

- *Work centers.* Where the processing occurs in the system. That is, where the productive (we hope) activity is modelled, as distinct from time wasted sitting in queues. Since each ramp is modelled separately, three work centres are needed for each ramp to represent the initial inspection, fitting a new exhaust and the final quality check. In addition, a work centre is used to represent the time taken to pay Joe for the work.
- *Work exit points.* Where work leaves the model. Though Joe's exhaust parlour could be modelled with a single exit point, it is a little clearer if two are used—one for customers who decide not to have their exhaust systems replaced and the other for customers who do.
- *Resources.* These are not part of the flow of work, but are typically shared tools or people who are shared by the tasks (work centres). To model Joe's exhaust parlour, two resource types are needed: Joe and the fitters.

The generic objects are used to represent system objects by parameterizing them by double clicking on the icon as described earlier for work entry points. The properties define the detailed behaviour of those objects and include the iconic image that will represent the object on-screen. In the case of work centres, the resource properties are used to define what resources are needed for each task. Thus, fitting an exhaust requires a fitter. The usual windows-style cut and paste operations can be used to clone icons and their parameters—this might, for example, be used to clone ramps after completing the properties of ramp 1.

In SIMUL8's case there is no need to use any programming language to create and run this model. But SIMUL8 has its own programming language that can be used to create complex entry and exit rules when the rules required are not available in simple check boxes. (As with Micro Saint, this language has been invented by the vendor of the software rather than conforming to any useful standard.)

8.3.5   Joe's exhaust parlour in SIMUL8: running and analysing the simulation

As with other simulation VIMS, a SIMUL8 model is run interactively by clicking the Run button and its speed is controlled by setting the position of a "speed" slider. Simulation results are available as the simulation proceeds and at its completion. Three types of results display are commonly used.

In the first, shown in Figure 8.6, performance measures are placed on the iconic model screen and can be seen at the same time as the moving and changing icons as the simulation runs. These results come from standard statistical performance measures that are automatically collected by SIMUL8 for each icon used in the model. The second form of results display uses a standard results window that is available from an icon's property box. This is available whenever execution of the model is stopped—either when temporarily paused or when permanently halted at the end of the simulation run.

The third option is to use a SIMUL8 Results Summary Window to combine a number of performance measures for several icons in the model. Figure 8.8 shows such a window that has the performance measures for the final exit point and for the queue of new arrivals.

This ready access to results and performance measures is fundamental to visual interactive simulation. It makes the behaviour of the model as open as possible so that the decision maker can be fully involved in the modelling process. All simulation VIMS have features to allow the display of this type of information, as well as the types of charts and graphs that we are used to seeing in software like Microsoft Excel.

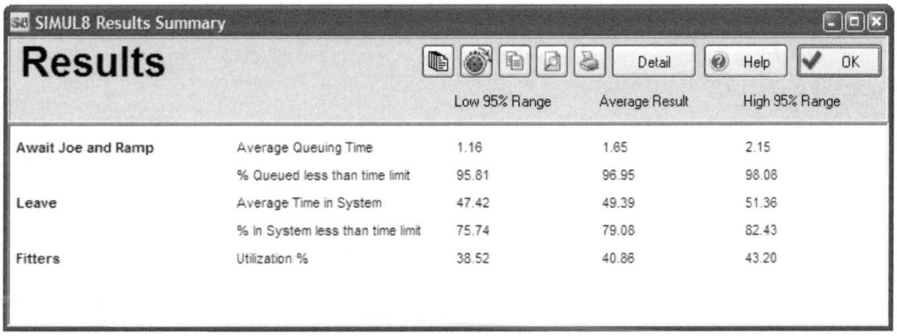

SIMUL8 Results Summary				
Results		Detail	Help	OK
		Low 95% Range	Average Result	High 95% Range
Await Joe and Ramp	Average Queuing Time	1.16	1.65	2.15
	% Queued less than time limit	95.81	96.95	98.08
Leave	Average Time in System	47.42	49.39	51.36
	% In System less than time limit	75.74	79.08	82.43
Fitters	Utilization %	38.52	40.86	43.20

Figure 8.8   Joe's exhaust parlour: a Results Summary Window

8.4   VISUAL INTERACTIVE SIMULATION: A REPRISE

Though developing and running a computer simulation in a management science project involves much more than computing ability, it is certainly true that developments in simulation technology have depended on developments in computing. Visual interactive modelling and simulation is only possible because powerful computers are cheap and widely available and because they provide excellent graphical output. This enables a modeller to develop and run a simulation model in an interactive way in close cooperation with a client. Simulation software vendors have developed VIMS that harness this technology and are excellent tools for the rapid development and running of simulations. In essence they support the "principle of parsimony" discussed elsewhere in this book. They do this by allowing graphical modelling and interactive running, supported by built-in analysis tools that allow a rapid appraisal of simulation model performance.

The challenge facing simulation modellers is to ensure that their styles of working are also parsimonious by making full use of these powerful tools.

EXERCISES

(1) Using a language with which you are familiar and one of the libraries, modify the harassed booking clerk program of Chapter 7 so as to allow the user to interrupt the program while it is running and, at that stage, to see preliminary results. Allow the user to restart the program.

(2) Investigate how the built-in controls of programming languages such as Visual Basic and Java may be used to support visual interactive simulation.

(3) Using a VIMS develop a model of the harassed booking clerk problem introduced in Chapter 5.

(4) Using a VIMS, develop a simulation of the T-junction described in Exercise 1 of Chapter 6.

(5) Using a VIMS, develop a simulation of the Morecambe Bay Hovercraft Company described in Exercise 4 of Chapter 6.

(6) Using a VIMS, develop a simulation of the accident and emergency department described in Exercise 7 of Chapter 5.

REFERENCES

Elder M. (1992) Visual Interactive modelling: Some guidelines for its implementation and some aspects of its potential impact on Operational Research. Unpublished PhD thesis, Department of Management Science, University of Strathclyde.

Fiddy E., Bright J.G. and Hurrion R.D. (1981) See-Why: Interactive simulation on the screen. *Proceedings of the Institution of Mechanical Engineers*, **C293**(81), 167–72.

Greenberger M. and Jones M. (1968) On-line, incremental simulation. In: J. N. Buxton (ed.) *Simulation Programming Languages*. North-Holland, Amsterdam.

Henriksen J.O. (1996) The power of Proof animation. *Proceedings of the 1996 Winter Simulation Conference, December, Coronada, CA*. The Society for Computer Simulation, San Diego, CA.

Hurrion R. (1976) The design, use and requirements of an interactive visual computer simulation language to explore production planning problems. PhD thesis, University of London.

Lanner Systems (2003) www.lanner.com

Micro Analysis and Design (2003) www.maad.com

SAS Institute Inc (2003) www.sas.com

Simul8 Corporation (2003) www.simul8.com

SPSS Inc (2003) www.spss.com

Swain J. (2003) Simulation software survey. *OR/MS Today*, August 2003. Also available at http://www.lionhrtpub.com/orms/surveys/Simulation/Simulation.html

9

Discrete Simulation Software

9.1 GENERAL PRINCIPLES

In an ideal world it would be possible to produce a list of all available options for implementing a simulation on a computer. It might even resemble those found in consumer magazines in which each option is given a relative score telling the reader which is the "best buy". However, trying to do this for computer simulation is unlikely to be profitable for a number of reasons. First, the products available on the market are constantly changing. Completely new products appear and existing software is updated as enhancements are made and bugs are corrected. Thus any attempt at a proper survey would be out of date before this book is printed. Instead, this chapter discusses the trends that have driven simulation software since the early days, and it places products and options in product families and categories.

The second reason why a full survey is pointless is that most computer users are idiosyncratic in their choice of software. Most programmers have their own preferred language, whether C, C++, Java, Visual Basic, FORTRAN or whatever, and can be very evangelistic in their zeal. Similarly, there are arguments that rage over object orientation, functional programming, symbolic programming and the rest. Within the world of computer simulation, few people have much experience of more than a couple of software packages or simulation languages, which make comparison very difficult. Hence, this chapter can only take a general view, though the preferences of the author are bound to come through.

It seems obvious that some software will be better suited to particular applications than others. Perhaps this calls for "best buys" in each category? However, if this is attempted, some software vendor somewhere is bound to feel aggrieved. Hence, this chapter spells out some of the general principles that ought to be borne in mind when selecting simulation software. The idea is to permit readers to think through their own preferences in the light of the work they have to do and the resources available to them.

Two good sources of up-to-date information on available discrete simulation software are the annual Winter Simulation Conference and the INFORMS publication *OR/MS Today*. The Winter Simulation Conference (http://www.wintersim.org), held each December in the USA includes a stream of sessions under the heading "Modelware" in which vendors show their products. For those unable to attend the conference, the Simulation College of INFORMS places the Conference Proceedings on the Internet (`http://www.informs-cs.org/`). *OR/MS* Today is a monthly publication sent to all members of INFORMS and it includes a simulation software survey about every two years. Online copies can be found at the *OR/MS Today* website (`http://www.lionhrtpub.com/ORMS.shtml`). A less comprehensive, but more detailed review is provided by Valentin (2003).

9.2   A QUICK OVERVIEW OF DISCRETE SIMULATION SOFTWARE

There are many different ways in which discrete simulation software may be provided and later sections of this chapter will describe these. It is important to realize that, like an iceberg, much of a discrete simulation software package is hidden below the surface. Chapter 6 discusses the different discrete event simulation worldviews, with particular emphasis on the three-phase approach. It points out that the simulation engine is general and is used by the components that represent the logic of particular applications. Discrete event simulation software must provide an executive that is independent of the application and there are many ways of doing this. The operation of the executive will determine the ways in which it communicates with the activities, events and processes that represent the logic of a particular application. It should be noted that there are several ways in which an executive can be implemented. For small applications this may not matter, but an efficient simulation with many thousands of entities requires an executive that is designed for this purpose. A discussion of the main issues can be found in Davey and Vaucher (1980). Schriber and Brunner (2002) discuss the ways in which different executives operate in commonly used simulation software including AutoMod (Brooks Automation, 2003), SLX (Wolverine Software, 2003), Extend (Imagine That, 2003), SIMAN/Arena (Rockwell Software, 2003), ProModel (ProModel Solutions) and GPSS/H (Wolverine Software).

Most contemporary simulation applications run on PCs and workstations within a graphical user interface (GUI) such as Microsoft Windows™, X-Windows or Apple Mac OS. Hence, in addition to the simulation specific tools provided by software, the developer must also supply tools that enable the simulation modeller to use and exploit the GUI. This is taken to its extreme in Visual Interactive Modelling Systems (VIMS) of which two, Micro Saint and SIMUL8, were introduced in Chapter 8. In a VIMS, the GUI is used to build, debug and monitor the model as well as to analyse its results and to display its performance as it runs. Recent years have seen an increasing interest in high-quality graphics displays in simulation, leading some vendors to provide virtual reality. Examples include the Witness VR suite that extends the widely used Witness package (Lanner Group, 2003). Other software systems such as QUEST (Delmia Systems, 2003) were fully developed around virtual reality concepts from the start.

Finally, discrete event simulation software usually includes a library of functions to ease common tasks. These commonly include functions for random sampling (see Chapter 10), for list processing and for the collection of statistics as a simulation model runs. Hence, Figure 9.1 shows the outline

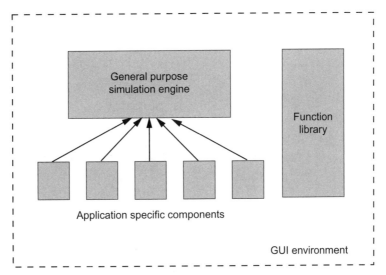

Figure 9.1   Organization of discrete event software

organization of much contemporary discrete event simulation. The user must develop the activities, events and processes required for a particular application. This may be done by directly coding (writing a computer program) or by making use of tools such as VIMS that reduce or remove the need for programming.

As stated above, there are many different ways in which the modeller may develop a working simulation program, but the two extremes are as follows:

(1)   Develop a proper computer program by writing code. This might be in a general purpose language such as Pascal, C or Java; or it might be in a simulation language such as SIMSCRIPT II.5 (CACI, 2003).

(2)   Employ a GUI-based VIMS that allows the logic to be developed by selecting icons from an on-screen palette, thus building the model by pointing and clicking with a mouse. Examples of this approach are Micro Saint (Micro Analysis and Design, 2003), SIMUL8 (Simul8 Corporation, 2003) and Witness (Lanner, 2003).

Figure 9.2 is a taxonomy of types of simulation software, showing the links between different approaches. This will be used to discuss the different types of software available.

9.3   VIMS AND THEIR RELATIVES

9.3.1   VIMS—a reprise

VIMS were introduced in Chapter 8 and will not be discussed in detail here. Instead this section will examine the right-hand side of the family tree shown in Figure 9.2. When using a VIMS, models are created using a

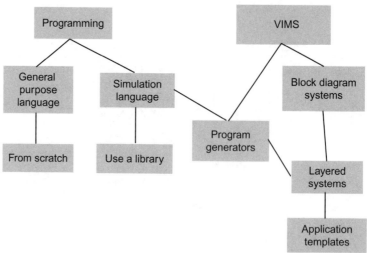

Figure 9.2   A taxonomy of simulation software

point-and-click approach with a mouse to select predefined simulation objects and place them on-screen. In a manufacturing application, the icons most commonly represent machines and workstations, between which parts flow as they are manufactured. In a business process application, the icons might represent people, computers or other processing stations between which paperwork and messages pass. The paths taken by the parts, paperwork or messages are created on-screen by drawing lines that link the workstation icons together into a logical network. In most such software, the user may click on any icon and open a window which provides fill-in forms by which the object in question may be parameterized (e.g., this may be used to specify the size and speed of a machine). Also, similar fill-in forms are used to specify complicated event logic that cannot be shown directly on the diagram, usually via some form of macro language.

Hence, most VIMS employ a network as their underlying generic model. Thus, entities are assumed to flow through a network from node to node, at which they may be delayed as they engage in activity with other entities and resources. The entities placed at the nodes may also have their own private lives. For example, in a manufacturing application, they may be machines that occasionally fail or stop for maintenance. The underlying generic model of any VIMS is a general purpose simulation program that takes information from the diagram and from the fill-in forms, checks it for consistency and then runs a simulation if all appears to be in order. In most cases, the user must be satisfied with the predefined objects provided by the system developer of the VIMS as it is rarely possible to extend these in any useful way. Hence, although VIMS are quick and easy to use, they do have their limitations.

9.3.2   Block diagram systems

To develop a simulation program using a general purpose language or a simulation language requires the modeller to be a competent computer programmer. Because of this, a number of block-structured systems were developed. The original idea of these systems, the first of which appeared in the early 1960s, was to enable non-programmers to develop discrete simulations. This was done by defining a set of flow-charting symbols that are suitable for discrete simulation. The modeller would then develop a flow diagram on paper to represent the system to be modelled. In the early days, each such symbol had an associated punched card on which parameters (e.g., the number of entities) would be punched. The "program" was a deck of these cards that were fed into the computer. The two earliest such systems were the General Purpose System Simulator (GPSS; developed in a cooperative effort by IBM and Bell Laboratories in the late 1950s) and HOCUS (originally developed by Robin Hills, 1971). GPSS used its own special flow diagram symbols and HOCUS used simple activity cycle diagrams. A later block diagram system was SIMAN, developed by Dennis Pegden. This section will discuss GPSS and SIMAN.

GPSS

The original idea of GPSS was to produce a system for simulating telecommunications networks that would be simple enough to use by engineers who were not expert computer programmers. That this design goal was sensible is demonstrated by the fact that versions of GPSS are still in use 40 years after its appearance. GPSS has spawned a family of products based on its ideas, and a good description of the GPSS approach is to be found in Gordon (1969), Greenberg (1972), and Schriber (1974).

GPSS does not use the concept of activity cycle diagrams introduced in Chapter 5. Instead, the user needs to envisage a simulation as consisting of transactions which flow around a network. These transactions are equivalent to entities and the nodes of the network are equivalent to points at which the progress of the entities may be delayed in their life cycles. Note that, as would be expected from its origins, the terminology of GPSS is rooted in the telecommunications world of the early 1960s.

Although GPSS is classified here as a block-structured system, according to Greenberg (1972) there is rarely any need to actually draw the GPSS diagram. Instead, GPSS is often described as a simulation language—but this is something of a misnomer. What is commonly referred to as a GPSS program is in fact a sequence of commands, each of which corresponds to a block type which can be shown via a GPSS template. Hence, a perusal of a GPSS program shows blocks such as GENERATE, SEIZE, ADVANCE, etc., and with each of these blocks is a set of numerical attributes which define how a block is to be used.

Rather than using the conventional terminology of entities, activities, events and processes, GPSS uses the following:

- *Transactions*. The temporary entities of the system which are created and may be destroyed as the simulation proceeds. These transactions move through the various blocks which are permitted in GPSS. A generate block

```
GPSSR/PC V2.1D    26-Apr-1989    9:25              PAGE 1
   mm1.LST=mm1.gps


LINE BLOCK

   1         *            M/M/1 QUEUE MEAN ARRIVAL TIME=20, MEAN SERVICE TIME =16
   2                      RMULT       ,31415
   3         SERVER   EQU       2,F
   4         LINE     EQU       1,Q           SYMBOLS EQUATED TO
   5         SYST     EQU       3,Q           NUMERICAL VALUES
   6         EXPON    EQU       1
   7         EXPON    FUNCTION  RN$2,C24
   8         0,0/.1,.104/.2.222/.3,.355/.4,.509/.5,.69/.6,.915/.7,1.2
   9         .75,1.38/.8,1.6/.84,1.83/.88,2.12/.9,2.3/.92,2.52/.94,2.81
  10         .95,2.99/.96,3.2/.97,3.5/.98,3.9/.99,4.6/.995,5.3/.998,6.2
  11         .999,7/.9998,8
  12       1        QTABLE    1,1,4,50      TIMES SPENT IN QUEUE
  13       2        TABLE     Q$3,1,1,50    NUMBER IN SYSTEM
  14       3        QTABLE    3,4,4,50      TIMES SPENT IN SYSTEM
  15                SIMULATE                RUN SIMULATION
  16   1            GENERATE  20,FN$EXPON   CUSTOMER ENTERS SYSTEM
  17   2            QUEUE     SYST          COLLECTS STATS FOR SYSTEM
  18   3            QUEUE     LINE          COLLECTS STATS FOR QUEUE
  19   4            SEIZE     SERVER        CUSTOMER GETS SERVER
  20   5            DEPART    LINE          FINISH STATS OF QUEUE TIME
  21   6            ADVANCE   16,FN$EXPON   SERVICE TIME
  22   7            RELEASE   SERVER        CUSTOMER LEAVES SERVER
  23   8            DEPART    SYST          FINISH STATS OF SYSTEM TIME
  24   9            TABULATE  2             COUNT SYSTEM QUEUE
  25  10            TERMINATE 1             CUSTOMER DESTROYED
  26                START     100,NP        WARM-UP RUN WITH NO PRINT
  27                RESET                   ;CLEAR STATISTISTICS
  28                START     999           RUN FOR 1000 TERMINATIONS
```

Figure 9.3   GPSS M/M/1 queue model

is used to create a transaction and a terminate block ends its life. The sequence of blocks make up the processes of these temporary entities.

• *Facilities*. The permanent entities of the system which may be used to represent the resources needed by the transactions at the nodes of the network. These can be regarded as countable resources.

GPSS uses other terminology as well, but the above is all that is needed to gain a basic understanding of its operation.

As with all such systems, the best way to gain some understanding of GPSS is to consider a simple example and one such is shown in Figure 9.3. This is a GPSS listing of a single-server queuing system with exponential service and inter-arrival times. This queue type is known as M/M/1 to queuing theorists. The example shown in Figure 9.3 was produced using a PC version of GPSS. To make things easier to follow, the example is shown with line numbers. The listing shows the following:

• *Lines 1–11*. These set up the variables and functions which are needed to model this simple system in GPSS. Note that this version of GPSS has no built-in negative exponential function and that this had to be provided as a histogram as shown in lines 7–11. Lines 2–6 tell the GPSS system that SERVER is entity number 2 (a FACILITY), LINE is entity number 1 (a QUEUE), SYST is entity number 3 (a QUEUE) and that EXPON is the defined function.

- *Lines 12–14*. These define three tables for data collection as the simulation proceeds. Thus, Table 1 is a histogram of time spent by customers queuing in the system. This histogram will have 50 cells, the cell interval will be 4 and the maximum of the first cell will be 1. Histograms are also defined for the time within the system and the imaginary system queue length.
- *Lines 15–25*. These are the simulation itself.
  - ○ *Line 16*. Generates customers at random intervals sampled from the negative exponential function with mean of 20.
  - ○ *Line 17*. Notes the time that the customer enters the system (an imaginary queue).
  - ○ *Line 18*. Notes the time that the customer enters the queue for the server—as in line 17, this is the creation time of the customer.
  - ○ *Line 19*. When the customer is at the head of the queue, it seizes the server.
  - ○ *Line 20*. At this same time it departs the queue, which allows the GPSS system to compute its time in the queue.
  - ○ *Line 21*. This line computes the service time from the negative exponential function with a mean of 16. The server and customer stay together for that time.
  - ○ *Line 22*. The server is released.
  - ○ *Line 23*. The customer departs the imaginary system queue. This allows the GPSS system to compute the time that the customer has spent within the entire queuing system.
  - ○ *Line 24*. The GPSS system adds the current imaginary system queue length to its histogram.
  - ○ *Line 25*. The customer is now of no interest and so its record is destroyed.
  - ○ *Lines 26–29*. Control the running of the simulation.

Figure 9.3 and the discussion above should make it clear that GPSS employs a version of the process-based approach, described in Chapter 6. Thus, the analyst must produce a chronological sequence of operations that are modelled as the blocks through which the entity must pass. In the M/M/1 queue, the customers are created as transactions and two "physical" queues are updated. The first is the customers waiting to be served (queue 1) and the second is the customers waiting to enter the system (queue 3). These queues are held in first in first out (FIFO) order and customers leave queue 1 to be linked to the server until the service is complete. When the service is complete, the customer record in the system queue (queue 3) is removed, the server is freed and the customer is destroyed.

It should be clear that the GPSS approach provides a fast and powerful way to develop certain types of simulation model. It is ideal for certain types of queuing network in which there is relatively limited interaction between classes of transaction. If the system being simulated does contain complicated interactions (e.g., those in which there are operations which involve several classes of entity and for which the operation may be interrupted by exogenous events, then GPSS does not offer the best way forward). Gordon (1969) makes it clear that such complex interactions can cause problems for some versions of GPSS. Thus, the main virtue of GPSS is its appealing simplicity, but this simplicity comes at a price—a loss of flexibility for some types of application.

As was mentioned earlier, there are many versions of GPSS available on the market and it would be almost impossible to give a complete list that would be regarded as accurate for more than a short time. Versions exist for most mainframes, super-minis such as the DEC Vaxes, PCs and MacIntosh platforms. Perhaps the most commonly used version nowadays is GPSS/H (Wolverine Software, 2003).

SIMAN/Arena

SIMAN, developed by Dennis Pegden, is a fundamental part of the Arena package (Rockwell Software, 2003). An introduction to SIMAN is given in Pegden *et al.* (1990) and a thorough discussion of its major features is given in Banks *et al.* (1995). Like the GPSS family, SIMAN is a block-structured language. Thus, a SIMAN program is actually a listing of blocks which have parameters associated with them. For example, the customer process in a queuing system might be represented in something like the following sequence of block commands, shown together with the actions they cause.

CREATE	Create a new customer instance (this implies a time interval).
QUEUE	Place the customer in the queue where it might have to wait.
SEIZE	When at the head of the queue, seize the server.
DELAY	Hold onto the server until the service is complete.
RELEASE	Release the server back into an idle state.
DISPOSE	Lose interest in the customer and destroy its record.

If the above were a proper simulation program to be represented by the sequence of block commands, then each would have attributes associated with it (e.g., the QUEUE block can have three attributes (known as operands) associated with it). These are as follows:

- *Queue ID*. An identifier for the queue. This may be an integer or a text expression.
- *Capacity*. An integer expression that indicates the maximum size of the queue or a logical expression that specifies the conditions under which it is regarded as full.
- *Balk label*. A label used to identify the block that will specify the action to be taken if an entity balks when there are capacity problems.

Hence, if a customer were to join a queue *WaitingLine*, with a capacity of five, then the block command would be written as:

```
QUEUE, WaitingLine, 5;
```

Only the Queue ID operand is mandatory.

Thus, the basic face presented by SIMAN has close affinities to that presented in GPSS. It does, however, include a great many special purpose blocks that are used to model common elements of manufacturing systems such as conveyors. SIMAN models consist of two files, known as frames:

- *The MODEL FRAME.* This is the simulation program that describes the logical interaction of the entities that make up the simulation. As should be clear from the simple example above, SIMAN is process-oriented (see Chapter 6).
- *The EXPERIMENTAL FRAME.* This file is used to control the simulation run, using an appropriate model frame. The experimental frame provides data that is used by the simulation, defines experimental parameters and generates the output of the simulation.

Thus, SIMAN is more than just a simulation programming language, for the ability to control simulation experiments is a fundamental part of its design and this explains much of its popularity. When a SIMAN simulation program is compiled, the compiler translates both the model and experimental frames and links these to provide executable files.

Early versions of SIMAN came with a separate program, known as CINEMA, which was used to generate animated graphical output. Thus, SIMAN could be used as a visual interactive simulation language (see Chapter 8). It is now available with the ARENA environment, which makes it possible to use SIMAN as part of a VIMS. As with other VIMS, the user interacts with ARENA by pointing and clicking within a GUI. In effect, icons are selected to represent the blocks, and fill-in forms are used to parameterize these. Thus, ARENA may be used to support the development of the model and experimental frames and it also supports animated graphical output. ARENA comes with different templates that are designed to support modelling in particular application areas, such as manufacturing or business process re-engineering.

9.3.3   VIMS and block diagram systems

Chapter 8 developed models in two VIMS: Micro Saint and SIMUL8 as representatives of that class of simulation software. In many ways, VIMS are block diagram systems brought up to date. GPSS and HOCUS both assume a flow chart with symbols that carry parameters that must be given values. These symbols are then strung together in a sequence to define the simulation model. There is no computer program in a conventional sense, instead a generic simulation model is parameterized using the block symbols, their parameters and the sequence. That is, the block diagram is data to the GPSS, HOCUS or SIMAN program.

The same is true of a VIMS. The diagram defines the process logic of the system being simulated and the symbols on the diagram have parameters, often known as properties, which must be given values. The sequence of parameterized symbols forms data that is read by the underlying generic simulator of the VIMS, which then produces a running simulation. The simulation languages provided by most VIMS allow some of the properties of the symbols to be modified and, in particular, allow logical dependencies that cannot be shown in a simple on-screen diagram. The languages also allow the VIMS to interface with other, suitable software.

9.4 PROGRAMMING USING A GENERAL PURPOSE LANGUAGE

In the early days of computer simulation in the late 1950s, writing in some general purpose language was the only option open to the would-be simulator. The languages available have increased and improved since those early days and so it is no longer necessary to write in a version of machine code or assembler. Many simulations are still written in the common computer languages such as FORTRAN, C or Pascal. Given the availability of simulation programming languages, block-structured systems and VIMS, why should this be?

9.4.1 Pros and cons

One reason is cost. Some organizations and many academics are unable to pay the prices asked for commercially available simulation software. As should be clear from Chapter 7, it is not very difficult to write a simulation system from scratch—given reasonable fluency in a programming language. Many people prefer to write programs in a language that they (and their colleagues) understand well and whose compiler is thought to be bug-free. The second reason is that this approach allows simulation programs which are highly specific, which can be tuned to run extremely fast and which might link into other software which may have very detailed requirements. This is why many military and defence simulations are written in general purpose languages. Bespoke software can be written to suit strange applications that cannot be modelled properly by simulation software packages.

However, anyone taking this approach should beware of a number of disadvantages. The first is the time and cost of developing the software. Writing bespoke software is always time consuming and, assuming that programmers have to be paid, can be very expensive. It may not be worth paying the price of extended development just for a slightly faster program. It may also not be worth paying this price for a marginally more detailed model. As in all simulation applications, the analyst must ask whether the effort to be expended will be worthwhile. The second snag is that detailed and developed programming skills are needed. Although a proficient programmer in C or C++ would not find it difficult to write the kernel of a simulation package, not all organizations have such people available.

Nevertheless, it is still the case that many simulations are written in general purpose languages and in such cases the analyst should at least choose a language with data structures and syntax well suited to simulation. FORTRAN lovers will not wish to read this, but their favourite suffers from many disadvantages in this regard. Specifically, until recently, it had no mixed data types (such as the records of Pascal and structs of C and C++), it still does not support built-in pointer types for dynamic variables and it has a limited set of operators. Similarly, though Visual Basic provides a good platform for rapid program development, the underlying language does not offer the facilities that are needed in discrete simulations. There are always ways round these problems, but it makes sense to use a language in which workarounds are unnecessary. Recent years have seen the growing popularity of Java as a simulation language (Pidd and Cassel, 2000) because it is fully object oriented (see Pidd, 1995 for a discussion of object orientation in discrete simulation) and because there are widely available class libraries providing many of the functions needed in a simulation. Examples of discrete simulation systems in Java include SimKit (Buss, 2002) and Silk (Kilgore, 2002b). A quick search of the World Wide Web will show that Java has become extremely popular for other types of simulation too.

9.4.2   Libraries and component-based software

Anyone who has attempted to write several discrete simulation programs soon realizes that the same tasks make up large parts of most such programs. These tasks include the time advance, event scheduling and sampling. Most general purpose programming languages allow a program to be decomposed into subroutines (FORTRAN), procedures and functions (Pascal), functions (C and C++) and methods (Java). Some allow a final executable program to be composed by linking together independently compiled files (C, C++) or units (Turbo Pascal). Others allow the linkage of packages already partially compiled into an intermediate code (Java). These features lend themselves to the reuse of program code by storing it in a library. It is possible that object-oriented approaches may increase the safety and desirability of such libraries.

To use a library of simulation routines, the analyst must write the skeleton of the program in the host language (FORTRAN, C, Java or whatever). This skeleton consists of the logic and other features that are specific to the application. To use a library properly means that the analyst must be a fluent programmer in that language. The user's program then uses the routines of the library to carry out the general simulation tasks. Note that this is slightly complicated by the fact that the executive calls the application logic blocks (activities, events and processes) and not the other way round.

Pre-written libraries appeared quite early in the history of discrete simulation, as they offered an obvious way to reduce the development time for simulation software. Examples were SIMON (Hills, 1965; 1971), which, in its original version, was a set of Algol procedures and which later appeared in a FORTRAN version. The GASP family of products (Pritsker, 1974) is written in FORTRAN. SIMON adopted a three-phase structure and GASP followed a strict event-based approach. A later version of GASP, GASP IV (Pritsker, 1974) also included routines for numerical integration so as to allow the development of programs for mixed-discrete simulation. More recent FORTRAN libraries were those offered as See-Why (Fiddy *et al.*, 1981) and

FORSSIGHT, which added routines that enable visual interactive simulation. Thus, these later packages supported animated displays and safe interaction. Neither See-Why nor FORSSIGHT are now in use.

In addition, it is of course possible for any individual or organization to develop a simulation library. Indeed, the routines developed in Chapter 7 could be used to form the basis of a (rather limited) library, as could the other routines that are available on the same World Wide Web page. Individuals or organizations that develop such libraries for their own purposes are likely to add routines to perform tasks that are specific to their own needs. This approach has much to commend it, as long as the library is efficiently written and properly tested and debugged. Documentation is also important.

Recent developments such as Microsoft's .NET™ technology allow programs to be developed from a mixed set of source languages if their data files and machine function calls are consistent. If permitted, such multi-language programming means that the analyst writing a simulation program can write in a language known to him/her rather than the language of the library. Recent attempts to exploit .NET include OpenSML (Kilgore, 2002a) and HighMast (Highpoint Software Systems, 2003).

Another recent development is the creation of component-based simulation modelling. Component-based software development has been around for some time and a good introduction can be found in Szyperski (1999). In a component-based approach, the application is broken down into smaller tasks that can be separately programmed. If the programming is done correctly, the resulting module can be used as a component and the application is developed by linking these components together. This plug and play approach is attractive and is analogous to the way in which hardware components, made by different manufacturers, fit together in a PC. This is possible because three conditions are met:

(1)   There are agreed hardware interfaces that define how the components inter-operate.
(2)   There is a defined architecture that specifies what tasks need to be done and how the interconnections will work.
(3)   The components themselves are fully tested and carry out a defined function.

Software components are independent and separate code modules that have been tested before being combined for a particular application. For some tasks there may be components available for purchase and these are also linked into the final application. Component-based approaches support the reuse of existing software, which is desirable because of the high cost of software development.

Oses *et al.* (2003) discusses the application of component-based approaches in discrete simulation and points out that components must be independent of one another and should implement a clear function. A component is independent if it requires little from the context and makes no direct references to other components. For example, a component that implements the functionality of a queue depends on other components to provide it with the objects to queue, and on others to make requests to queue objects. But this queue component must never have direct references to the components providing and requesting the objects.

It may not be important if the component makes a few assumptions about the context, it depends on the purpose for which the component is designed. For example, the common core of an application family remains the same across all the applications in that family. A component could be built to implement part of the core functionality and, even if it relies on the environment, it could still be reused in other members of the family. Having a clear functionality is also important for reuse—components must make their requirements, functionality and output absolutely explicit.

It is too soon to say whether component-based simulation will deliver all its potential benefits. There is considerable cost in developing and testing software components and success will depend on whether people are prepared to bear those early development costs to reap later benefits.

Hence, it should be clear that the attractions of pre-written libraries are that they permit bespoke programming (in the same way as writing from scratch) but offer some time saving over the do-it-all-yourself option. However, they still force the analyst to program in a language that may not be well suited to discrete simulation. Thus, program development may still be a long, drawn-out process. A further problem, which should not be overlooked, is that many analysts find that using other people's program code is very difficult. There are two reasons for this. The first is that considerable expertise is often needed if an analyst is to feel confident in using other people's programs. The second reason is that a full library needs extensive documentation that can outface even a dedicated programmer. Thus, a training course is probably essential if the analyst is to get the best from a library. This is especially true when it comes to understanding the error messages that can be produced when a program goes wrong. This usually happens in a way that the analyst believes to be impossible!

9.5 PROGRAMMING APPROACHES USING SIMULATION LANGUAGES

A digital computer is a logical machine that obeys the instructions that are sent to it. The language in which those instructions are coded must be one that the machine can obey—this being achieved by a process of translation, often known as compilation. In addition, the language should be one that is well suited to the tasks which the machine is being told to carry out. Problem-oriented languages have a syntax that is well suited to the tasks being implemented on the computer. Conventional, general purpose languages do not have a simulation-oriented syntax—hence the development of simulation programming languages.

Many such languages have been developed since the early 1960s and the most popular have passed through a series of revisions as they have been adapted to suit particular computers or as extra facilities have been added. Probably the most widely used languages over that period have been the

SIMSCRIPT, SIMULA and ECSL families and, for a time, MODSIM. This section considers the common features of simulation programming languages using SIMSCRIPT II.5 to illustrate the general ideas, with the harassed booking clerk (see Section 5.3.2) as an example.

9.5.1   Common features of simulation languages

These simulation programming languages provide a number of common features:

(1)   *A hidden executive.* To perform the sequencing and scheduling tasks which underlie any discrete event simulation. In the case of SIMULA the executive is based on a process-interaction approach. The SIMSCRIPT family was originally event-based but is usually presented as process-based nowadays. ECSL embodied a quasi three-phase approach in which those Bs which mark the end of active states are implemented in the activity body by using the AFTER keyword.

(2)   *A well-suited syntax.* The syntax of these languages is designed to ease the process of simulation modelling. Indeed, as the system developers have provided the executive, the task of the analyst/programmer is to express the application logic in the syntax of the chosen language. Implicit in the syntax is a set of data structures to support tasks that are common in discrete simulations. Hence, the SIMSCRIPT family allows a form of set membership which can be used to represent the system state as entities move from set to set. Thus, the syntax of simulation languages, seen in the context of discrete simulation modelling, is both powerful and expressive. It is powerful in that one line of program written in these languages might be equivalent to dozens of lines coded in general purpose languages such as FORTRAN. All the evidence about programming errors suggest that the number of mistakes is related to the number of lines in the program. Thus, a more powerful language is likely to lead to more rapid program development. The languages are also expressive in that, as discussed above, their syntax is well suited to simulation tasks and to the application being simulated. In simpler terms, expressive languages are easier to read and, once again, this cuts down the risk of errors.

(3)   *Variable tracing and data collection.* A simulation program is a set of operations which are conducted sequentially on data that defines the application. Thus, that data must be stored and controlled by the simulation system itself. Hence, simulation programming languages allow the analyst to trace the values taken by any variable through time. Such tracing is useful for debugging but is also valuable for analysis purposes (e.g., for collecting timeseries of relevant response variables).

(4)   *Experimentation support.* Most simulation languages also provide a control shell within which the simulation program may be run to carry out experiments. Indeed, for this reason, many systems are interpreted rather than fully compiled. Thus, the control shells allow the same

model to be run against different data sets or with different random numbers for alternative sampling (see Chapters 11 and 12). Similarly, there may be some support for data collection for the analysis of the results of the simulations.

9.5.2   An example: SIMSCRIPT II.5

The languages of the SIMSCRIPT family have been in use since the early 1960s and are now available on a wide range of computers and under most common operating systems. SIMSCRIPT originated at the RAND Corporation in the USA (Markowitz *et al.*, 1963) so as to allow non-specialists to write simulation programs.

As originally conceived, SIMSCRIPT was a pre-processor for an early version of FORTRAN. Thus, the analyst was to use the syntax of SIMSCRIPT to code the model and then the SIMSCRIPT translator would generate FORTRAN code. The idea was that the syntax of SIMSCRIPT was both more powerful and more expressive than that of FORTRAN and thus it should ease the tasks of simulation modelling and programming. To run the simulation program, the generated FORTRAN program would need to be compiled and could be run away from the SIMSCRIPT system itself.

The FORTRAN pre-processor version of SIMSCRIPT was replaced by later versions which ran within their own environment and did not need a FORTRAN compiler. The most widely used version of the system is SIMSCRIPT II.5 (CACI, 2003), which allows two alternative modelling approaches, event-based and process-based. The SIMSCRIPT II.5 literature encourages the user to take a process-based view where possible. Thus, the basic application logic is built up as a series of process blocks that define the chronological sequence of activities in which each entity class may engage.

PC users who wish to run SIMSCRIPT may do so in its Simulation Development Studio that provides a complete environment in which SIMSCRIPT II.5 programs may be developed, debugged, tested and run. It includes an editor and a debugger as well as a run-time environment. As with most software, SIMSCRIPT II.5 allows the programmer to add animated graphics to show the state of a simulation as it runs, and this can be a great boon for experimentation as well as in convincing a client that a model has some face validity. Full details of the current version of SIMSCRIPT II.5 can be found on the CACI website (http://www.cacias1/.com/).

The best way to appreciate the power of SIMSCRIPT II.5 is to consider an example such as that of the harassed booking clerk, introduced in Section 5.3.2. This has two classes of customer (personal customers and phone callers) who are served by one or more booking clerks. Using the terminology favoured by Law and Larmey (1984), this means that a SIMSCRIPT II.5 program to simulate this system could represent these as:

- *Two process entities.* Personal customers and phone callers.
- *A single resource.* The clerk(s) available to serve these two classes of process entity as the simulation proceeds.

```
PREAMBLE          ''HBC - Simscript Harassed Booking Clerk

  processes include ARRIVE, CALL, PERSCUST, PHONECALL and SHUT

  resources include CLERK

  define NUM.CLERKS as an integer variable
  define MEAN.INTERARRIVAL.TIME, MEAN.CALL.TIME, MEAN.SERVE.TIME,
    MEAN.TALK.TIME, DELAY.IN.QUEUE, DELAY.IN.WAIT and
    RUN.DURATION as real variables

  define .MINUTES to mean units

  tally MEAN.DELAY.QUEUE as the mean and NUM.CUSTS as the number
    of DELAY.IN.QUEUE

  tally MEAN.DELAY.WAIT as the mean and NUM.CALLS as the number
    of DELAY.IN.WAIT

end  ''PREAMBLE


main
  call READ.DATA
  call INITIALISE

  start SIMULATION

  call REPORT
end  ''main
```

Figure 9.4   SIMSCRIPT II.5 preamble and main section: harassed booking clerk

In SIMSCRIPT terms, processes stem from entities and require resources if they are to be executed.

Any SIMSCRIPT II.5 simulation program must have a certain minimal structure, which can be enhanced for particular applications. It must include a preamble followed by a main segment. The preamble defines the variables, parameters, processes and events that make up the model. The main segment defines the sequence in which the computation will take place. In its syntax, SIMSCRIPT II.5 has some similarities with the various versions of FORTRAN and experts in that language will, therefore, feel more at home than C or Pascal programmers.

The preamble and main segment of the harassed booking clerk model are shown in Figure 9.4. Starting with the preamble, the lines of the program are as follows:

- *processes include* . . . This line defines the processes of the simulation model in which the entities engage. In this case there are four such processes. Two generate new instances of personal customer and phone caller (Arrive and Call) and the other two follow these two entities from the time that they are deposited in their respective queues awaiting service.
- *define* . . . These three lines are used to define the important variables of the

```
routine READ.DATA
  print 3 lines thus

HARASSED BOOKING CLERK: SIMSCRIPT II.5 MODEL
- - - - - - - - - - - - - - - - - - - - - - - - -
  skip 1 line
  print 1 line thus
"Number of clerks: "
  read NUM.CLERKS
  print 1 line thus
"Simulation duration .."
  read RUN.DURATION
  print 1 line thus
"Personal customers: mean inter-arrival time, mean service time"
  read MEAN.INTERARRIVAL.TIME and MEAN.SERVE.TIME
  print 1 line thus
"Phone calls: mean inter-arrival time, mean service time"
  read MEAN.CALL.TIME and MEAN.TALK.TIME
  print 10 lines with NUM.CLERKS, MEAN.INTERARRIVAL.TIME,
    MEAN.CALL.TIME, MEAN.SERVE.TIME, MEAN.TALK.TIME
    and RUN.DURATION thus
No. of clerks: **

All times are exponentially distributed, mean values are ..
  Personal customer inter-arrival:  ***.*
  Phone call inter-arrival:         ***.*
  Personal service:                 ***.*
  Phone conversation:               ***.*

Duration: ****.* minutes.

end  ''Read.DATA
```

Figure 9.5   SIMSCRIPT II.5 read data section: harassed booking clerk

simulation. Several are defined as floating point (real) and NUM.CLERKS is defined as an integer. The time units of the simulation are defined as MINUTES.

- *tally* ... These two statements define data to be collected as the simulation proceeds. New personal customers and new calls are placed in the two queues, QUEUE and WAIT respectively, as they arrive. The SIMSCRIPT II.5 system recognizes that it must collect tally data based on the entities moving to and from the two queues.

There are other SIMSCRIPT II.5 commands that could be incorporated in a preamble, but the example of Figure 9.4 shows some of the common ones.

The main segment is also shown in Figure 9.4. This shows that the program calls a routine known as READ.DATA, which sets up the parameters of the simulation. The READ.DATA routine is shown in Figure 9.5 and is reasonably self-explanatory. The main segment then calls the INITIALIZE routine shown in Figure 9.6 and then starts the simulation, after which it calls the REPORT routine. The short INITIALIZE routine is shown in Figure 9.6. The first two lines establish that there is only a single class of CLERK entities and that the available clerks (these are resources) is initially set to be NUM.CLERKS—the

```
routine INITIALIZE
  create every CLERK(1)
  let u.CLERK(1) = NUM.CLERKS
  activate an ARRIVE now
  activate a CALL now
  activate a SHUT in RUN.DURATION   .MINUTES
end '' INITIALIZE
```

Figure 9.6   SIMSCRIPT II.5 initialize section: harassed booking clerk

```
process ARRIVE
  while TIME.V < RUN.DURATION do
    wait exponential.f(MEAN.INTERARRIVAL.TIME, 1)   .MINUTES
    activate a PERSCUST now
  loop
end ''  ARRIVE

process PERSCUST
  define ARRIVAL.TIME as a real variable
  let ARRIVAL.TIME = TIME.V
  request 1 CLERK(1)
  let DELAY.IN.QUEUE = TIME.V - ARRIVAL.TIME
  work exponential.f(MEAN.SERVE.TIME, 2)   .MINUTES
  relinquish 1 CLERK(1)
end ''PERSCUST

process CALL
  while TIME.V < RUN.DURATION do
    wait exponential.f(MEAN.INTERARRIVAL.TIME, 2)   .MINUTES
    activate a PHONECALL now
  loop
end ''  ARRIVE

process PHONECALL
  define ARRIVAL.TIME as a real variable
  let ARRIVAL.TIME = TIME.V
  request 1 CLERK(1)
  let DELAY.IN.WAIT = TIME.V - ARRIVAL.TIME
  work exponential.f(MEAN.TALK.TIME, 2)   .MINUTES
  relinquish 1 CLERK(1)
end ''PHONECALL

process SHUT
  interrupt ARRIVE
  interrupt CALL
end ''SHUT
```

Figure 9.7   SIMSCRIPT II.5 processes: harassed booking clerk

number of clerks in the simulation. The next three lines tell the SIMSCRIPT II.5 system to enter process notices on its list of processes at time zero. They will be activated in the order in which they are mentioned here. Thus, the arrival of the first personal customer and the first phone call are set up to happen immediately (NOW). Also, the booking office is set to close at the end of the simulation (after RUN.DURATION).

Figure 9.7 shows the five processes which make up the simulation model. These are as follows:

- *ARRIVE*. This causes new personal customers to be added to the simulation at intervals determined by a negative exponential distribution with a mean value of MEAN.INTERARRIVAL.TIME. As the customers are injected into the simulation, this activates their PERSCUST process.
- *PERSCUST*. This is activated as soon as a new customer is injected into the system and, at this time, the ARRIVAL.TIME variable for this entity is set equal to TIME.V (the simulation clock of SIMSCRIPT). In order to proceed in its process, the entity needs a CLERK, hence it requests 1 of the first (and only) class of CLERK. The process is then suspended until such a CLERK is available. When the service can proceed, the DELAY.IN.QUEUE can be computed from the time elapsed since the process was activated (ARRIVAL.TIME) and the current simulation clock time (TIME.V). The service time is computed from a sample from a negative exponential distribution with mean equal to MEAN.SERVICE.TIME. The process is once again suspended until this time has elapsed, at which point the CLERK is freed.
- *CALL and PHONECALL*. These are the equivalent processes for phone calls.
- *SHUT*. This process is used to close the simulation cleanly after a time equivalent to RUN.DURATION has elapsed. Thus, this was set up in INITIALIZE to occur after RUN.DURATION minutes. It interrupts any active ARRIVE or CALL processes and thus prevents any more personal customers and phone calls from being injected into the system when it is activated.

One final routine, REPORT completes the model and is shown in Figure 9.8. As should be clear it merely produces a report that summarises the results of the simulation.

Of course there is much more to SIMSCRIPT II.5 than could be presented in a short example of this type. Indeed, one of the problems with SIMSCRIPT is that it has a complicated syntax which may cause some confusion. One example is the WITH keyword which can be used in several ways in a SIMSCRIPT II.5 program. These problems apart, SIMSCRIPT II.5 provides a powerful way of developing bespoke simulation programs.

```
routine REPORT
  print 2 lines with RUN.DURATION thus

HBC run over at ****.*
  skip 2 lines

  print 2 lines thus
          Num served        Mean wait time
_ _ _ _ _ _ _ _ _ _ _ _ _ _ _ _ _ _ _ _ _ _ _ _ _ _
  print 1 line with NUM.CUSTS and MEAN.DELAY.QUEUE thus
Personal customers   ***              ***.*
  print 1 line with NUM.CALLS and MEAN.DELAY.WAIT thus
Phone calls          ***              ***.*
end ''REPORT
```

Figure 9.8 SIMSCRIPT II.5 report section: harassed booking clerk

9.6 LAYERED SYSTEMS AND APPLICATION TEMPLATES

It should be clear that the two extremes of writing a program and using a VIMS both have their pros and cons. For new application areas it may be best to write a simulation program, but for a routine application a VIMS seems the best option. What about those in between applications in which there is no suitable VIMS and yet there is likely to be several similar models required. Is there a way of enjoying the best of both worlds?

9.6.1 Layered systems

Figure 9.9 shows the basic idea of a layered simulation system, of which SLX (Wolverine Software, 2003) is an example. The top layer presents itself as a point-and-click VIMS interface within which simple models can be developed very quickly. However, beneath this top level are others, which may be needed for more complex or novel simulations. The number of layers varies between different products, but the set shown in Figure 9.9 is probably the minimum. At the bottom of the hierarchy is a general purpose programming language, probably C since this is also suitable for very low-level system programming. Whereas only some systems may be conveniently simulated via the VIMS interface, almost anything can be done in C—though only by some people.

In between these two extremes are two other layers. Beneath the VIMS interface is a simulation programming language. The data from the VIMS are taken by a program generator that writes a simulation program in the simulation language. The advantage of this approach is that the resulting program may be edited by a skilled modeller in order to make it do things that were difficult or impossible to place on the VIMS network.

The next layer, which sits above the general purpose programming

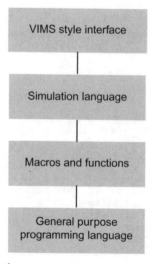

Figure 9.9 A layered simulation system

language, is a set of macros and functions written in that programming language to perform tasks that are not built into the simulation language but which are known to recur from time to time. This avoids the need to write detailed code in the base general purpose programming language.

Before a simulation model is run, it is translated into the base general purpose programming system and then compiled into some executable form. In doing so, intermediate representations are developed. Thus, a VIMS generates a simulation program in a simulation language, which in turn generates macros and functions, which in turn lead to a program written in a general purpose language. What is the point of this? The idea is to allow the same, layered system to be used for routine and non-routine applications. The former are developed through the VIMS, and the resulting program can be successively enhanced if necessary. As the analyst descends through the layers, the program becomes more detailed and more specific. Operating at the bottom layer requires very detailed programming skills.

9.6.2 Application templates

The early VIMS were aimed at manufacturing companies in which discrete parts (e.g., car engines) move from workstation to workstation in a factory, changing state as they do so. Without too much effort, other types of system can be simulated with the same software (e.g., patients moving through a clinic can be modelled analogouly to the car engines). However, there comes a point at which the metaphor is so stretched that it is in danger of breaking. That is, the modeller has to find so many workarounds that much time and effort is wasted.

Application templates provide one way of coping with this. Like VIMS, these are based on generic simulation models and allow the user to develop and run a model using a point-and-click approach. However, the objects on the VIMS template are specific to particular types of application and automated data collection is also set up to suit those applications. Thus, a template for business process modelling might differ from one for a telephone call centre, for a health clinic or for a manufacturing service centre. The idea is to support modelling by people who are familiar with the application are but who do not wish to become simulation experts. Examples of commercial software that offers templates include the ARENA family (Rockwell Software, 2003) and the SIMSCRIPT family (CACI, 2003). In the case of ARENA, it is possible for skilled modellers to develop their own templates to meet recurring simulation needs.

9.7 APPRAISING SIMULATION SOFTWARE: SOME PRINCIPLES

There are many ways of providing the required facilities and features, but is there any single best way of doing so? This chapter takes the view that there is no single best way, although there are certainly rather poor ways of doing so. A range of factors is important when appraising discrete simulation software and the balance of importance will vary between these from case to case. What are these factors?

9.7.1 The type of application

The type of application is likely to play a major part in determining the features of the software to be used to write a simulation model and run a simulation. It is not unusual for software vendors to claim that their product will cope with any type of application. It may be true that the designers of a product intended it to be truly general purpose but it is unlikely that they have achieved this end. Because any software design involves a set of compromises, there are always horses for courses. For example, some software packages are designed for the simulation of manufacturing systems. Thus they come with predefined objects such as parts, machines, conveyors, guided vehicles, etc. They may also include smart ways of simulating common operating rules such as Just-In-Time and, therefore, these packages are much better suited to manufacturing applications than, say, to simulating an airport.

However, it would be a mistake to imagine that they are always well suited to all types of manufacturing. For example, most such systems assume that parts flow through a network of machines and change their states according to the operations performed at the machines. They then occupy set states as they await in-process stores for their next operation. This is fine for discrete parts manufacturing of the type found in, say, the automotive industry, but is not well suited to continuous manufacture as in process industries.

Of course, these caveats do not mean that such dedicated packages cannot be used for applications outside their main application domain. However, it does mean that the analyst may need to think rather creatively about how to implement the actual system within the set of options provided by the software package. At one extreme this means no more than accepting that, say in a clinic, a doctor treating patients may be modelled as if he/she was a machine processing parts. At the other extreme, the analyst may find that the system simply gets in the way of proper modelling as so many ways have to be found of getting around its restrictions.

If the application being considered is entirely novel then the analyst may have no option but to write a program from scratch, either in a general purpose language or in a simulation language. Probably any system can be simulated in this way, but it may not be sensible to do so. This type of bespoke software creation is expensive and, even with good programmers, can be very time consuming. But routine simulations may be best done by using a VIMS.

9.7.2 The expectations for end use

It is also important to consider the anticipated end use of the simulation. Is it solely for the use of the analyst who has developed the model, or will it be handed over to a client who may run the simulation unaided? In the former case, it may be less important that the simulation runs neatly and attractively—that it produces results may be enough. If the software is to be run by a client, however, then ease of run and graceful, friendly operation are crucial. In either case it is also important to know whether this simulation will be run just a few times or whether it might be expected to be run many times over a lengthy time period.

Some simulation software packages require a run-time system to be present whenever a model is created or a simulation is run. This is especially true of VIMS but may also be true of programming systems that have their own dedicated development and run-time environments. There may be further complications if the software package is protected by a hardware dongle which must be present before the package can be used. What such restrictions mean is that the organization must purchase separate packages for each parallel application. If only one simulation is in use at any one time, then this is no problem—but this is rarely the case. Some software vendors provide run-time systems at a lower price than the full development and run-time systems. This allows the organization to purchase, say, one development system and the number of run-time systems needed for its applications.

9.7.3   Knowledge, computing policy and user support

Few organizations are keen to see a wide range of different computer packages appearing unannounced on their computers, however clever the software. All software products need to be supported by someone within an organization and, possibly, by the vendor. Thus some consistency and standardization is desirable when planning software purchases. There is obviously the risk that over-bureaucratic standardization may lead to the continued use of outdated and unsuitable software. Equally, though, a free-for-all can become a nightmare when things start to go wrong. Thus, software needs to be chosen in the light of an organization's software policy and bearing in mind the ability of the software vendor to offer extended support.

It would be pleasant to imagine that all simulation software packages are backed up by proper and continued support. Consideration of their market will reveal why this is not, and cannot, be so. Discrete simulation software occupies a niche in the market for software and thus sales volumes are, in total, relatively low. Thus, there may not be enough business for a large number of substantial suppliers and only the latter are able to offer proper support if this is required. Much simulation software is developed and sold by small companies who can only offer limited support. For a one-off and never to be repeated simulation exercise this may not matter, but to some organizations it is very important.

9.7.4   Price

Needless to say this is very important. Simulation software can be obtained very cheaply for a few dollars or the purchaser may need to budget tens of thousands of dollars. There is no guarantee that the most expensive products are any cleverer or have a wider application range than the cheaper ones. However, purchase price is only one element in the cost of using simulation software. If a more expensive product can dramatically reduce the time to develop and implement a valid simulation then it may well be worth paying the high price. Of course it can be difficult to assess in advance whether this will be the case, but most vendors of high-priced software should be able to demonstrate the virtues of their product—if they are asked to do so.

In considering cost, the organization must also bear in mind the support provided by the vendor. This is expensive to provide and thus can be a major element in a purchase price. Not all companies need this expensive support.

9.8   WHICH TO CHOOSE? HORSES FOR COURSES

9.8.1   VIMS

As should be clear from the brief description of Micro Saint and SIMUL8 in Chapter 8 and the comments in the previous section, VIMS are simple to use and do not require the user to be fully conversant with the internal operation of a simulation model. This greatly expands the number of people who are able to gain the undoubted benefits of simulation. However, there are a couple of drawbacks that must be stated.

The first is that it is currently impossible to use these systems for very detailed work within large simulations. For such special applications there is little escape from bespoke programming in either a simulation language or a general purpose language. VIMS are growing more powerful but just may not be suitable for some applications. As an analogy, consider the chore of painting a house with whitewashed walls and many small Georgian windows. The best way to paint the walls is to use a large roller or a paint spray. However, if these are used on the windows, they tend to obscure the view! For the detailed work on the windows, it is best to use a fine brush—it takes time, but is the only way to produce a good result. VIMS are, in their present states, best thought of as the paint rollers. They offer splendid tools for relatively standard applications. Sometimes, however, bespoke programming is needed.

The second drawback might sound like intellectual snobbery. It is sometimes rather harder to interpret the results of a simulation than to build the model with a VIMS. This is because many simulations are highly stochastic and their results need careful analysis by people who are reasonably well trained in statistics. One day there may be artificial intelligence systems that act as intelligent statistical advisors, but these are not yet on the market. If they existed, they would at least reduce the possibility for horrendous mistakes. But the solution to this problem is not to stop using these systems, it is to educate their users.

9.8.2   Simulation languages

The advantages of simulation programming languages are that they employ a syntax which is both powerful and expressive and that, therefore, they can greatly reduce the time taken to develop a working computer simulation. They make programming a simulation model simpler and more accessible.

Their disadvantages also need to be considered, however. First, the organization needs to acquire the special software needed to develop, translate and run the simulation programs. As is always the case in commercial software, some of the products available are cheap but others are rather expensive. The issue of continued support is also important for many organizations and this is seen in two considerations. First, it is important that the whole expertise does not rest in the brain of a single employee—a passing bus or the attraction of a long visit to the Pacific may remove that expertise. Second, the organization needs to be sure that the software vendor can offer long-term support and training.

REFERENCES

Banks J., Burnette B., Kozloski H. and Rose J. (1995) *Introduction to SIMAN V and CINEMA V.* John Wiley & Sons, New York.

Brooks Automation (2003) `http://www.brooks.com/`

Buss A. (2002) Component based Simulation Modeling with Simkit. In: J.M. Charnes, E. Yücesan and C.-H. Chen (eds), *Proceedings of the 2002 Winter Simulation Conference, San Diego, CA.*

CACI (2003) `http://www.cacias/.com/`

Davey D. and Vaucher J.G. (1980) Self-optimised partitioned sequencing sets for discrete event simulation. *INFOR*, **18**, 41–61.

Delmia Systems (2003) `http://www.delmia.com/`

Fiddy E., Bright J.G. and Hurrion R.D. (1981) See-Why: interactive simulation on the screen. *Proceedings of the Institution of Mechanical Engineers*, **C293**(81), 167–72.

Gordon, G. (1969) *System Simulation.* Prentice-Hall, NJ.

Greenberg, S. (1972) *GPSS Primer.* John Wiley & Sons, New York.

Highpoint Software Systems (2003) `http://www.highpointsoftware.com/`

Hills P.R. (1965) SIMON—a simulation language in Algol. In: S.M. Hollingdale (ed.), *Simulation in Operational Research.* English Universities Press, London.

Hills P.R. (1971) *HOCUS.* P-E Group, Egham, UK.

Imagine That (2003) `http://www.imaginethatinc.com/`

Kilgore R. (2002a) Multi-Language, Open-Source Modeling Using the Microsoft .Net Architecture. In: J.M. Charnes, E. Yücesan and C.-H. Chen (eds), *Proceedings of the 2002 Winter Simulation Conference, December 2002, San Diego, CA.*

Kilgore R. (2002b) Object-Oriented Simulation with Java, Silk and OpenSMLl .Net Languages. In: J.M. Charnes, E. Yücesan and C.-H. Chen (eds), *Proceedings of the 2002 Winter Simulation Conference, December 2002, San Diego, CA.*

Lanner Group (2003) `http://www.lanner.com`

Law A.M. and Larmey C.S. (1984) *Introduction to Simulation Using SIMSCRIPT II.5*. CACI, La Jolla, CA.

Markowitz H.M., Hansher B. and Karr H.W. (1963) *SIMSCRIPT: A simulation programming language* (RAND Corporation RM-3310-pr 1962). Prentice-Hall, Englewood Cliffs, NJ.

Micro Analysis and Design (2003) http://www.maad.com/

Oses N., Pidd M. and Brooks R.J. (2003) Critical issues in the development of component-based discrete simulation. *Simulation modelling: Practice and Theory* (submitted).

Pegden C.D., Shannon R.E. and Sadowski R.P. (1990) *Introduction to Simulation Using SIMAN*. McGraw-Hill, New York.

Pidd M. (1995) Object orientation, discrete simulation and the three-phase approach. *Journal of Operational Research Society*, **46**(3), 362–74.

Pidd M. and Cassel R.A. (2000) Using Java to develop discrete event simulations. *Journal of Operational Research Society*, **51**(4), 405–12.

Pritsker A.A.B. (1974) *The GASP IV Simulation Language*. John Wiley & Sons, London.

ProModel Solutions (2003) http://www.promodel.com/

Rockwell Software (2003) http://www.arenasimulation.com/

Schriber T.J. and Brunner D.T. (2002) Inside discrete-event simulation software: how it works and why it matters. In: J.M. Charnes, E. Yücesan and C.-H. Chen (eds) *Proceedings of the 2002 Winter Simulation Conference, December 2002, San Diego, CA*.

Schriber T. (1974) *Simulation Using GPSS*. Wiley-Interscience, New York.

SIMUL8 Corporation (2003) http://www.simul8.com/

Szyperski C. (1999) *Component Software: Beyond Object-oriented Programming*. Pearson Education Limited, Harlow, UK.

Valentin E. (2003) Discrete event simulation software packages. http://www.tbm.tudelft.nl/webstaf/edwinv/SimulationSoftware/

Wolverine Software (2003) http://www.wolverinesoftware.com/

10

Sampling Methods

10.1 BASIC IDEAS

It should be clear from the previous chapters that many discrete event simulations include elements that are random or stochastic. For example, in the harassed booking clerk problem we do not know how long a service will take, all that we know is that the service times follow a probability distribution. In the Visual Interactive Modelling System (VIMS) models of Joe's exhaust parlour in Chapter 8, a proportion of the car owners decide not to have their car exhausts replaced, although we do not know which ones. Such instances are common in virtually all discrete event simulations and therefore many systematic approaches have been developed to aid this sampling.

It is important to realize that the modeller must decide whether to model something within a system by a sampling procedure. It is a moot point, philosophically, whether the real world contains any randomness, for some would argue that probabilities are simply statements about our uncertain state of knowledge rather than descriptions of what is actually there. For example, consider a production process of the type often used to produce large quantities of chocolate bars. These are typically deposited on a moving conveyor that carries them through a cooling tunnel and into wrapping and packing machines. The conveyors might be a metre or two across and, were the equipment all to be working properly, each row of chocolate bars would be identical and evenly spread across the conveyor with no gaps. However, in reality there are often gaps in the rows of chocolate bars and it is not unusual to see something like Figure 10.1 when viewing these conveyors. The gaps appear for many reasons, all of which could be determined if necessary. However, it may be perfectly acceptable to model the appearance of gaps as if it were a random process if all we wish to know is the number of chocolate bars to be wrapped. In such a case, a probability distribution could be used to represent this statistic, rather than bothering to determine the cause of each and every gap.

On other occasions, it might (paradoxically) be acceptable to model something that appears to be probabilistic as if it were deterministic. For example, although the time taken for a product to appear in a warehouse after ordering it from the manufacturer may be known to vary slightly by a day or two, it may be acceptable to use the average delay when looking at the monthly operations of the warehouse and its distribution systems. The important point is to ensure that the decision of whether or not to include

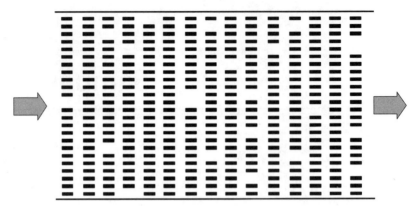

Figure 10.1   Stochastic or deterministic variation?

probability distributions is taken sensibly in the light of the variation seen in the system. All models are approximations, and the aim, as discussed in Chapter 12, is to develop a model that is appropriate for its intended purpose.

10.1.1   General principles of random sampling

Random sampling is used within a discrete simulation so as to produce, from a probability distribution, a set of samples that have two important properties. Firstly, the samples that are produced should have the same distribution as the probability distribution from which they are taken. That is, the distribution of the samples should be in the same proportions as the distributions from which they come. In statistical terms, the sample moments (the mean, the variance, etc.) should be the same as the population moments (the mean, the variance, etc.), as shown in Figure 10.2. In fact, this will never be the case, since an infinite sample size would be needed to guarantee this. Instead, the sample moments should be adequate estimates of those from the

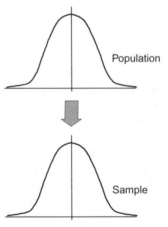

Figure 10.2   Representative samples

population. Thus, the first aim in random sampling is to produce a set of samples that are representative of the distribution from which they come.

The second aim in random sampling is to ensure that when a set of samples is placed in the sequence in which it is produced, there is no unintended pattern in that sequence. That is, random samples are required, otherwise probability theory does not apply and it is crucial, when analysing simulation output (see Chapter 11) that this theory should apply.

10.1.2   Top-hat sampling

Chapter 2 introduced the basic ideas of sampling from histograms in the disk failure example of Section 2.3.2. The approach used in Chapter 2 is often known as "top-hat sampling" and it illustrates the basic principles of most random sampling algorithms. The example was based upon the histogram shown here in Figure 10.3, and the sampling method relied upon the conversion of the histogram into the cumulative form that is also shown in Figure 10.3. Samples were taken from the probability distribution by using the vertical axis of the distribution (which runs from 0 to 1) and using a random number (distributed from 00 to 99) to select a point on that axis. Thus, a value of 45 points to a life of 4 days in Figure 10.3.

The approach is called "top-hat sampling" because it could be conducted as follows:

(1)   Take 100 counters (use poker chips or tiddlywinks) and number them in the same proportion as the life distribution of the disks. Hence, 5%

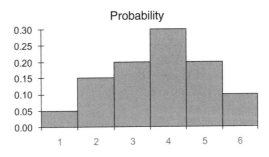

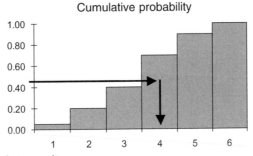

Figure 10.3   Top-hat sampling

Table 10.1 Sampling scheme using random numbers

Life	Random numbers
1	0.00 to 0.04
2	0.05 to 0.19
3	0.20 to 0.39
4	0.40 to 0.69
5	0.70 to 0.89
6	0.90 to 0.99

should be marked with the number 1, 15% with the number 2, 20% with the number 3, 30% with the number 4, 20% with the number 5 and 10% with the number 6.

(2) Place all 100 counters in a hat, preferably a top-hat, and shake it so that the counters are randomly distributed in the top-hat.

(3) Without looking into the hat, place a hand inside and select, at random, a counter and write down the number that is written on it.

(4) Replace the counter in the hat, shake the hat and repeat the sampling until enough samples have been produced.

This procedure is an example of sampling with replacement. The hope is that, if enough samples are taken, the sample histogram will be the same shape and at the same position as the histogram in Figure 10.3. The unseen selection of randomly distributed counters should guarantee that the samples occur in a random sequence.

As employed in a discrete event simulation, top-hat sampling does not rely on a top-hat and counters. Instead, the method relies on random numbers. The random numbers are usually distributed on the interval 0 to 1 (but excluding the value 1 itself), which is usually written down as (0, 1). They are converted into the correct distribution by using a look-up table. In the example of Chapter 2, for which the histogram is shown in Figure 10.3, this might be as shown in Table 10.1, if the random numbers are accurate to two decimal places. The random numbers correspond to the edges of the steps that occur on the cumulative histogram of Figure 10.3. Hence, for each random number, the look-up table can be examined to find the life of the disk unit to which it corresponds.

10.1.3   The fundamental random sampling process

In principle, the random sampling algorithms used in discrete event simulations are based on the same two-stage process that underlies top-hat sampling, which is as follows:

(1) Produce one or more random numbers.

(2) Convert these random numbers into samples from the required distribution, either by using a look-up table or by employing a suitable algorithm.

The rest of this chapter will describe the main features of random numbers as used in discrete simulation and will show some of the common algorithms used as stage two of the process.

10.1.4   Use of pre-written libraries of algorithms

In many cases, it is not necessary to write code to implement these algorithms, since there are libraries of these routines available from a number of sources, written in common programming languages such as C, C++, Pascal and FORTRAN. Examples include the NAG libraries, widely used in the UK and the ISML libraries widely used in the USA. In addition, there are sites on the Internet that include code that can be downloaded for random number generation and for generation of samples from probability distributions. A suitable search engine should find the appropriate sites.

10.2   RANDOM NUMBER GENERATION

So far, the question "What is meant by random?" has been carefully ignored, but it is important to understand that term. An obvious point is that it is not sensible to speak of any single number as "random". There is no such thing as a single random number. Generally, what is meant by randomness is that the process that produces the number is not deterministic (i.e., we cannot be sure what number will be produced next). In this sense, the idea of "randomness" is a confession of ignorance that relates to the process producing the numbers and not to the numbers themselves. Consequently, early random number generators were produced by physical processes that were believed to be inherently random in this way.

10.2.1   Truly random numbers

Streams of numbers that have been produced by a process that is believed to be random are usually described as "truly random numbers". One example might be the spinning of a roulette wheel. This is rather a slow method of producing random numbers, yet some people find these devices to be of compelling interest. Another example might be the throw of six-sided dice, with which the same group of people also seem to be fascinated.

   A discrete event simulation usually needs long streams of random numbers and this precludes the use of these manual devices for practical purposes. It is possible to devise truly random generators that are much faster by using electronic and radioactive devices. Most machines that draw lottery numbers around the world are of this type, because the truly random nature of their operation is very important and no suggestion of favouritism in their selection of numbers can be allowed. These fast physical devices rely on particle emission theories such as those from radioactive sources. In these, the number of particles emitted in a short time period is known to be random.

Hence, something like a Geiger counter can be used to count these particles in each unit time interval and these can be converted into random numbers on the unit interval. Tocher (1963) describes several such generators that are of historical interest. However, these truly random devices are not used in discrete event simulation for reasons other than their unfortunate effect on transistors and on humans.

10.2.2   Pseudo-random numbers

A discrete event simulation can be regarded as a complex sampling experiment. As the simulation proceeds, samples are taken from various distributions and are combined to produce the behaviour of the model. That is, many of the conditions within the simulation are determined by the results of the random samples and their combination. The random samples themselves are determined by the random numbers used to produce them. If a simulation is being used to compare various ways of operating a system, it is clearly important to ensure that each policy is examined under the same conditions. These conditions are at least partially determined by the samples taken, which are themselves determined by the random numbers used. Hence, to control a simulation and to ensure fair comparisons, it may be important to ensure that the same random numbers are used for each policy alternative. For this reason, it is important that the stream of random numbers be reproducible.

An obvious way round this problem would be to use a truly random device to generate a stream of random numbers and then to store these numbers in some way or other. They could then be used several times, once for each policy option. Random number tables, as found in most books of statistical tables, are examples of numbers treated in this way. One such random number table was produced by the RAND Corporation (RAND Corporation, 1955) and consists of a million random digits. In principle, such a sequence could be stored on a disk file and then read into a computer simulation as the numbers are needed. If computer memory were unlimited, they could be read from RAM instead.

However, there are other ways to proceed, once it is realized that even truly random numbers cannot really be random once they have been written down. How can they be random if we know what is coming next by looking at the list or table in which they are stored? Once held in this way, the list is determined and the sequence is deterministic. This suggests another approach, the use of methods that are deterministic, but which produce streams of numbers that look as if they are random. These pseudo-random numbers are produced by generators that are based on well-understood mathematics. The streams of numbers that they produce pass the same tests as those passed by truly-random numbers, if we were to pretend that we have no idea how the pseudo-random numbers were produced. That is, they are good enough to fool an observer who is ignorant of the method by which they are generated.

There are many websites devoted to the subject of pseudo-random number generation. Examples include Carter (2003) and Hellekalek (2003), who provide thorough surveys of available generators, with links to code in different programming languages.

10.2.3   Congruential generators

Although many methods have been used over the years to produce pseudo-random numbers, the consensus for some time has been that congruential generators are satisfactory for most discrete event simulations in management science. It should be noted, though, that L'Ecuyer (1994) and others point out that most congruential generators should not be used if very long streams of random numbers are required.

Congruential generators, sometimes known as linear recurrence generators, were first proposed by Lehmer (1951) and they have the following general form:

$$X_{i+1} + 1 = aX_i + c \pmod{m} \qquad \text{for } i = 0, 1, 2, \ldots, n$$

where $\{X_i\}$ is a stream of random integers on the interval $(0, m - 1)$; a, c and m are constants, where a is known as the multiplier, c as the increment (or additive constant) and m as the modulus; and X_0, the initial value of the stream, is known as the seed, and (mod m) means divide the right-hand side by m and use the remainder as the result.

As a trivial example, suppose that $a = 3$, $c = 0$, $m = 5$ and $X_0 = 4$. This gives a generator of the form: $X_{i+1} = 3X_i \pmod{5}$. Hence, its operation is as shown in Table 10.2. This simple example illustrates two important points about these generators: first, that their maximum value is $m - 1$; second, that they are cyclic or periodic. That is, once a value recurs, then the generator will repeat itself. In the above example, $X_4 = X_0$, $X_5 = X_1$, and in general, $X_{i+4} = X_i$ for all values of i.

These congruential generators produce integers on the range $(0, m - 1)$ and this integer series is converted to values on the range $(0, 1)$ by dividing the integers by m. That is:

$$\{U_i\} = \{X_i/m\} \qquad \text{for } i = 0, 1, 2, \ldots, n$$

where $\{U_i\}$ is over the range $(0, 1)$ and X_i is over the range $(0, m - 1)$.

Table 10.2 Cyclic behaviour of a trivial congruential pseudo-random number generator

i	X_i	$3X_i$
0	4	12
1	2	6
2	1	3
3	3	9
4	4	12
5	2	6

When referring to "random numbers" in the rest of this chapter, this term will mean that they are uniformly distributed over (0, 1), unless stated otherwise.

10.2.4   General requirements for these generators

It is clear, from the simple example above, that the selection of the values given to the parameters a, c and m is crucial in determining whether the random number generator will be of any practical use. In general, we wish to ensure that the generator has a number of features:

(1)   The numbers produced should be uniformly distributed over the interval (0,1). That is, all values within this range should occur with equal frequency.

(2)   The numbers produced should be independent of one another. That is, any particular value cannot be predicted from the remainder of the sequence. In statistical terms, this means that the sequence of values ($\{X_i\}$ and $\{U_i\}$) should have no serial correlation. This means that all values should be equally likely to occur anywhere in the sequence, as should all pairs of values, triples and n-tuples.

(3)   The cycle length (or period) should be as long as possible. The maximum period for a congruential generator is m, as the values may range from 0 to $m - 1$. Some generators do not have a full period, since some values are missed. The larger the value of m, the longer the maximum period of the generator. Whether the generator will have a full period will depend on the values chosen for the entire set of parameters.

(4)   Since many discrete simulations require a large number of random numbers, the arithmetic needs to be fast so as to ensure efficiency at run-time.

Number theory provides the key to the selection of values for the parameters so as to meet these four requirements. For a useful survey of this theory and its application see Knuth (1981). Fishman (1978) and Ripley (1987) also provide good coverage of the same issues.

10.2.5   Multiplicative congruential generators

These are simpler than the general form, as they have the increment c set to zero. Their recurrence relation is therefore as follows for their underlying integer sequence:

$$X_i + 1 = aX_i \pmod{m} \qquad \text{for } i = 0, 1, 2, \ldots, n$$

The maximum period for a multiplicative generator is $m - 1$, since the integer sequence must exclude the value 0. To ensure a full period within this range, the integer seed (X_0) and the modulus (m) must be relatively prime. That is, their only common divisor must be 1. Perhaps the simplest way to ensure that this condition is met is to use a large prime number for the modulus. One commonly used generator that has good statistical properties and a maximum period of $m - 1$ uses the following values:

$$a = 16,807 \quad \text{and} \quad m = 2^{31} - 1,147,483,647$$

this value of m being the largest integer if 32-bit arithmetic is used. This generator is very simple to program using integer arithmetic in any computer that permits 32-bit-long integers.

Fishman (1978) suggests that the same value of $m = 2^{31} - 1$ can be used with a multiplier of $a = 630,360,016$ and that the generator will behave well. Kleijnen and van Groenendaal (1992) add the values of $397,204,094$ and $950,706,376$ to this list. Hence, with 32-bit integer arithmetic, the following values are held to be the basis of reasonable multiplicative congruential generators:

m	2,147,483,647			
a	16,807	630,360,016	397,204,094	950,706,376

However, it should be noted that unless m is a prime number, which is the case with the value 2,147,483,647, then the generator should always be given an odd number as its seed. For a larger list of possible values for a, with $m = 2^{31} - 1$, see Fishman and Moore (1986).

It is straightforward to program the prime modulus generator described above, being sure to use long integer (32-bit) arithmetic. If only 16-bit arithmetic is available, then some programming languages (e.g., Turbo Pascal and Borland C) allow integer overflow. What this means is that, with integer arithmetic, if the result of a computation returns a number that exceeds the maximum integer value ($2^{15} - 1$, or 32,767, for 16-bit arithmetic) its sign is reversed and 32,768 is subtracted from its value. This, of course, only applies if the number is in the range 32,768–65,535. In this way, the period of the generator can be extended from 32,787 to 65,535. As ever, care must be taken to ensure that suitable values are used for a and for X_0.

If faced with the task of programming a multiplicative congruential random number generator in machine code then the arithmetic is much faster if m is put to some power of 2. This is because the division necessary to compute the modulus operation is replaced by a shift, m places to the left. This is analogous to division by some power of 10 in decimal arithmetic. For example, if the number 123,456 is divided by 1,000 (that is by 10^3), then the division produces 123.456 (i.e., the decimal point has shifted 3 places to the left). This means that 123,456 (mod 10^3) is immediately seen to be 456 (i.e., the right-hand three digits). The same principle applies in binary arithmetic.

Clearly, if m is made some power of 2 then the seed X_0 must be an odd number to guarantee much from the generator. The selection of a value for a, the multiplier, is also important if m is some power of 2. Knuth (1981) gives proofs for the assertion that, if a computer employs w-bit arithmetic, then suitable values are guaranteed if the following conditions hold:

$m = 2w - 1 \quad$ where $w \geq 5$
$a = 3$ or 5 (mod 8)
(i.e., $a = \pm 3 + 8k$ where k is some positive integer)

This implies that X_0 is an odd number, as will be all further values $\{X_i\}$ in the integer sequence. This means that the period will be, at most, $m/4$. Although multiplicative generators using m as some power of 2 may provide good, uniform coverage of their period, there is no guarantee that they will be well behaved from a statistical point of view.

10.2.6 Improving on simple congruential generators

Multiple recursive generators

A number of ways of improving on simple congruential generators have been suggested and two, both of value, are discussed here. The first, known as multiple recursive generators, use linear combinations of previous values as follows:

$$X_{i+1} = a_1 X_i + a_2 X_{i-1} + \cdots + a_t X_{i-t-1} \ (\text{mod } m)$$

Thus, they rely on the storage of a number of previous values generated by the congruential recurrence relationship. As an example:

$$X_{i+1} = (19{,}031X_i + 9{,}298X_{i-1}) \ (\text{mod } 65{,}536)$$

is a generator with a long period, but whose statistical properties are poor—as will be seen later. A better example:

$$X_{i+1} = (10{,}7374{,}182X_i + 104{,}480X_{i-4}) \ \text{mod}(2^{31} - 1)$$

is reported by L'Ecuyer (1994), who claims that it passes virtually all statistical tests applied to pseudo-random number generators and can therefore be wholeheartedly recommended.

The advantage of such combinations is that they produce generators with a long period, but understanding their statistical properties can be very difficult.

Shuffling

A second approach is to use a composite generator and shuffle its output. These can be used with 16-bit generators that have an inherently short period and they work as described in the following example. Consider two multiplicative congruential generators, g_1 and g_2:

(1) Fill a vector **V** with the first k values from g_1, which gives $\mathbf{V} = (V_1, V_2, \ldots, V_k)$.
(2) Use g_2 to generate a value i on $U(1, 2, \ldots, k)$.
(3) Select the ith value of **V**, and use V_i as the required sample.
(4) Generate another value from g_1 and use it to replace V_i.

These generators produce behaviour which is statistically very good and which has a very long period. Their only snag is that it is hard to determine seeds that allow sampling to begin at some defined point in the cycle.

10.2.7   Using inbuilt random number generators

Most programming languages and spreadsheets provide their own inbuilt random number generators but the manuals are often remarkably coy about the details. If in doubt, the advice is to test the generator using one of the methods described in the following sections. There is a further problem with many of these inbuilt generators and this is that each run of a program may only permit the user to use a single seed. As will become clear in the next chapter, this is often not good enough if we wish to minimize the sampling errors that occur due to short(ish) run lengths.

10.3   TESTING RANDOM NUMBER GENERATORS

It is important to realize that the selection of values for a, c and m when designing a suitable congruential generator is done with the aim of meeting the requirements listed in Section 10.2.4. These refer to independent uniform distribution, to long periods and to fast generation. The current section is concerned with tests that may be applied to the output of a generator to see whether it is statistically well behaved.

As mentioned earlier, randomness is a rather difficult property to define for pseudo-random sequences. Knuth (1981) quotes Lehmer (1951) as saying that a random sequence "is a vague notion embodying the idea of a sequence in which each term is unpredictable to the uninitiated and whose digits pass a certain number of tests, traditional with statisticians and depending somewhat on the uses to which the sequence is put." Knuth (1981) tries to make this rather vague statement more precise by specifying the mathematical properties necessary if a sequence is to be considered as random.

The testing of the sequences produced by these generators is mainly concerned with establishing whether they display the statistical properties that would be expected in a sequence produced by a truly random generator. Thus, most of the tests are used to examine a sequence for uniform distribution and for statistical independence. Note, however, that uniformity is guaranteed with a full period generator, which simplifies the task of checking a purpose-designed generator. The literature of random number generation contains many suggested tests and these include variations on most standard non-parametric statistical tests. Generators designed for very specific purposes may need to be tested in very specific ways.

It ought to be true that the generators provided with commercially produced discrete simulation software are known to be good. However, this cannot be guaranteed and, unless published evidence is available, it is as well to remain sceptical about these generators. This means that, when using such software for the first time, it is worth spending some effort in testing the generator or in getting the software vendor to show that the generator is sound.

10.3.1   Scatter plots

Before getting immersed in the conventional statistical tests of random number generators, it can be illuminating to take a different approach by the use of scatter plots. If a series of values $\{U_i\}$ is being examined, then a scatter plot may be displayed on a computer screen with the vertical axis representing U_k and the horizontal axis representing U_{k-n}, where n is the lag or interval between the two values. What is being sought is a random scatter of points around the square (i.e., there should be no obvious patterns). If obvious patterns are apparent then this suggests that the random number generator which produced the sequence may have its problems. The person most associated with these plots is Ripley (1977) who provides an overall approach to such spatial patterns.

As an illustration, consider the two scatter plots of Figures 10.4 and 10.5. That of Figure 10.4 was produced by a generator which clearly has problems. The generator is a linear combination congruential one of the form:

$$X_{i+1} = 19{,}031X_i + 9298X_{i-1} \pmod{65{,}536}$$

It utilizes the overflow available for 16-bit integers within Turbo Pascal. The scatter plot shows the first 1,000 pairs of consecutive values. The regular lattice is apparent after only a few hundred pairs of values are plotted. The generator also has a short period—indeed, the number of pairs needed before the lattice is complete is a good indicator of the period of the generator.

The next plot, shown in Figure 10.5, is from a rather better generator, this time the simple multiplicative generator with the form:

$$X_{i+1} = 16{,}807X_i \pmod{2^{31} - 1}$$

As with the previous figure, the plot of Figure 10.5 shows the first 1,000 pairs of values and, although not perfect, has no obvious lattice structure. Indeed,

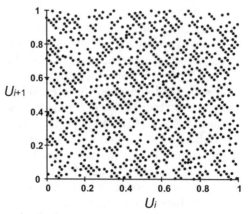

Figure 10.4   Scatter plot: bad generator, $n = 1{,}000$

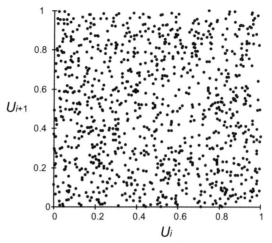

Figure 10.5   Scatter plot: better generator, $n = 1,000$

allowing the generator to run for 30,000 pairs produces a nicely filled square. This generator has a long period as it is based on 32-bit arithmetic.

10.3.2   Auxiliary sequences

The tests that follow can sometimes be applied to the $(0,1)$ series $\{U_i\}$ or must, otherwise, be applied to a sequence of integer values. If the tests are being applied to a purpose-designed generator for which the underlying integer series is accessible, then they may be applied to that sequence $\{X_i\}$. If this sequence is not accessible then the integer tests must be applied to an auxiliary sequence $\{Y_i\}$, which consists of integer values distributed on the interval 0 to $d-1$ obtained by computing $d.\{U_i\}$ and putting $\{Y_i\}$ equal to the integer part of $d.\{U_i\}$.

The following tests assume that those which require integer values are applied to the auxiliary sequence $\{Y_i\}$, but they could be applied to the underlying integer sequence $\{X_i\}$ if that is available.

10.3.3   Frequency tests

These tests aim to check whether the values are uniformly distributed in the sequence. They are not needed if a full period generator is being used. Two basic forms are in use. The first applies a chi-square test to either the auxiliary series $\{Y_i\}$ or to the $(0, 1)$ series $\{U_i\}$.

If the auxiliary series $\{Y_i\}$ is being tested, then for each integer in the period of the generator (which will be 0 to $d-1$) count the number of times that the value occurs in a sequence of n values. For the chi-square test, this gives an expected frequency of n/d for each integer. These may be compared with the observed count of these integers on $d-1$ degrees of freedom.

If the series $\{U_i\}$ is being tested, then the usual approach is to divide the range (0, 1) into s equal subintervals with the intention of counting the number of values found in each subinterval. Thus, if a sequence of n values is being examined, their expected frequency will be n/s in each subinterval if they are uniformly distributed. These may be compared with the observed frequencies on $s - 1$ degrees of freedom. Alternatively, a Kolmogorov–Smirnov test may be applied directly to the series $\{U_i\}$.

10.3.4   Serial test

This, and the other tests that follow, aims to assess whether the values in the sequence are independently distributed. A simple version of this test takes pairs of values from the auxiliary sequence $\{Y_i\}$ and examines the frequency with which they occur by applying a goodness-of-fit test to the observed and expected values.

Assuming a sequence of length $2n$, consider the pairs of values:

$$(Y_0, Y_1), (Y_2, Y_3), (Y_4, Y_5), \ldots, (Y_{2k}, Y_{2k+1}), \ldots$$

There are d^2 such values on the integer interval $(0, d - 1)$, and thus a chi-square test with $d^2 - 1$ degrees of freedom may be used, the expected frequencies of each pair being $2n/d^2$.

The same idea can be extended to triples and to higher k-tuples, though the value of d that is used to generate the auxiliary sequence must be chosen to avoid small observed frequencies.

10.3.5   Gap test

This is based on a search for the gaps between occurrences of ordered values within a specified range and may be applied directly to the series $\{U_i\}$. Consider a subinterval (a, b) within the (0, 1) range and any two real numbers r_i and r_{i+k}. If these two numbers occur within the interval (a, b), but the intermediate values of $r_{i+1}, r_{i+2}, \ldots, r_{i+k-1}$ do not, then there is a gap of length k in that interval.

Given that the series $\{U_i\}$ should be uniformly distributed over (0, 1), then the probability that r_j lies within the interval (a, b) is $(b - a)$. Hence, the expected frequencies of each gap can be computed because the probability of a gap of length k is $(b - a)(1 - b - a)^{k-1}$. A chi-square test with $k - 1$ degrees of freedom may be used to compare the observed and expected frequencies.

10.3.6   Other tests

The tests described above should give a reasonable indication of whether a generator is suitable for general purpose use. If a generator is to be used in ways that might test its randomness to the limit, then there are many other tests that can be applied—although it should be noted that, according to

Kleijnen and van Groenendaal (1992) there can still be no cast-iron guarantee that it is a good generator. Thorough descriptions of these tests are given in Fishman (1978), Knuth (1981), L'Ecuyer (1994) and Ripley (1987). It should be noted that L'Ecuyer finds fault with virtually all of the generators that are in common use; however, some of these failings may be less important in the type of simulations carried out within management science.

10.4 GENERAL METHODS FOR RANDOM SAMPLING FROM CONTINUOUS DISTRIBUTIONS

Most random sampling procedures used in discrete simulation rely on the availability of one or more random numbers, which may then be transformed into a sample from the required distribution. This may be done via a look-up table or via the use of some suitable algorithm. This section describes the main general algorithms that have been developed to cope with continuous probability distributions.

10.4.1 Inversion

This method is more or less equivalent to top-hat sampling and may be applied to some continuous probability distributions. It relies on the formal definition of a probability density function (p.d.f.), which is as follows.

Consider a continuous random variable X that takes values x, as shown in Figure 10.6:

$$\Pr(x < X < x + \delta x) \approx f(x)\,\delta x \qquad 0 \le x \le \infty$$

where $f(x)$ is the p.d.f. of X. The cumulative density function (c.d.f.) of X is as follows.

$$F(x) = \Pr(X \le x) = \int_{-\infty}^{x} f(t)\,dt$$

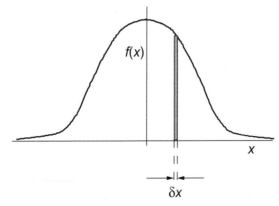

Figure 10.6 Definition of a p.d.f.

As with top-hat sampling, the vertical axis of the c.d.f. is replaced by U, where U is a uniform random variable distributed on the interval $[0, 1)$ (i.e., by a random number generator). Thus any value of U may be transformed into a value of x from the curve $F(x)$. Expressed algebraically.

$$\text{If } U = F(x) = \int_{-\infty}^{x} f(t)\, dt \qquad \text{then } x = G(u) = F^{-1}(u)$$

where $G(u)$ is known as in the inverse cumulative function and is employed to transform a value u into a sample x.

Inversion may be used if two conditions hold. The first is that $f(x)$, the p.d.f., is known. The second is that the p.d.f. is tractable so that the inverse cumulative function, $G(x)$, can be formed by integration.

Negative exponential distribution

One of the most common uses of inversion is to take samples from a negative exponential distribution, sometimes known as the exponential distribution. This has the following p.d.f.

$$F(x) = \int_{0}^{x} \lambda e^{-\lambda t}\, dt$$

$$= 1 - e^{-\lambda x}$$

$$\therefore u = 1 - e^{-\lambda x}$$

$$\therefore (1 - u) = e^{-\lambda x}$$

$$\text{or } \log_e(1 - u) = -\lambda x$$

$$\therefore x = -\frac{1}{\lambda}\log_e(1 - u)$$

Now, if u is uniformly distributed on $[0, 1)$ then so is $(1 - u)$. Hence the required sample is obtained from:

$$x = -\frac{1}{\lambda}\log_e(u)$$

Uniform distribution

The method of inversion also makes sense of the common-sense method of sampling from a uniform distribution such as that shown in Figure 10.7. The common-sense method relies on the realization that to transform U, a

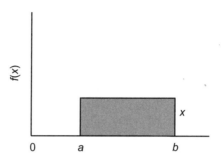

Figure 10.7   A uniform distribution

uniform $(0, 1)$ variable into one distributed over the interval (a, b), then the value of U must be scaled and shifted. The inversion proceeds as follows:

$$f(x) = \frac{1}{(b-a)}$$

$$\therefore F(x) = \int_a^x \frac{1}{(b-a)} dt = \frac{(x-a)}{(b-a)}$$

$$\therefore u = \frac{(x-a)}{(b-a)}$$

$$\therefore x = a + u(b-a)$$

That is, u is scaled by multiplying it by $(b-a)$ and then shifted by a.

Triangular distribution

This was used to demonstrate in Section 4.3.2 how a spreadsheet can be used to manage risk and uncertainty in investment decisions. It is often used when it is possible to estimate a maximum, minimum and mode for a distribution but data is scarce or non-existent. Johnson (1997) suggests that it can be used instead of a beta distribution in risk analysis. Figure 10.8 shows its p.d.f., which is as follows:

$$\text{If } x \le b, \text{ then } f(x) = \frac{2(x-a)}{(c-a)(b-a)} \qquad \text{else } f(x) = \frac{2(c-x)}{(c-a)(c-b)}$$

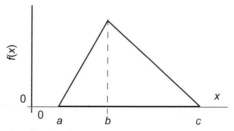

Figure 10.8   A triangular distribution

where a is the minimum, b is the mode and c is the maximum of x. Integrating over the appropriate intervals gives the c.d.f.:

$$\text{If } x \leq b, \text{ then } F(x) = \frac{(x-a)^2}{(c-a)(b-a)} \quad \text{else } F(x) = 1 - \frac{(c-x)^2}{(c-a)(c-b)}$$

Using the usual inversion procedure, this leads to the following:

$$\text{If } x \leq b, \text{ then } x = a + \sqrt{u(c-a)(b-a)} \quad \text{else } x = c - \sqrt{(1-u)(c-a)(c-b)}$$

where u is a uniform random number on $(0, 1)$.

10.4.2   Rejection

This approach is suitable for any continuous random variable with a known p.d.f. and a defined range, even if the c.d.f. cannot be formed by direct integration. Conceptually, the method is like throwing darts at a dart board and only counting those that strike certain values—assuming that the aim is random, which is reasonable in the author's case! It is equivalent to the use of the Monte Carlo method of numerical integration.

The basic method works as follows. Consider a random variable X, as shown in Figure 10.9, with known p.d.f. $f(x)$, such that:

$$0 \leq f(x) \leq M \quad \text{for } a \leq x \leq b$$

and $f(x) = 0$ elsewhere

Suppose that we have two uniformly distributed random variables, r on the range (a, b) and s on the range $(0, M)$. These may be used to define the coordinates of points within the rectangle that encloses the distribution as shown in Figure 10.9. If the coordinates lie within the distribution, then the pair of values is accepted and r is returned as the sample of X. Otherwise the pair is rejected and the process is repeated until the point (r, s) lies under the curve of $f(x)$.

The practical use of this procedure works by scaling the c.d.f. $f(x)$ so its

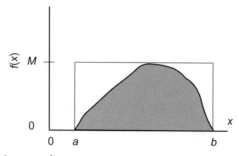

Figure 10.9   Rejection sampling

maximum value is 1 and by generating a sample from a uniform distribution over the interval (a, b). Hence the practical procedure is as follows:

(1)   Choose a constant c, so that $c.f(x) \leq 1$ for $a \leq x \leq b$.
(2)   Redefine x so that $x = a + u(b - a)$ where u is uniformly distributed on $[0, 1)$.
(3)   If $u_2 \leq c.f(a + u_1(b - 1))$, then accept u_2 and use $x = a + u_1(b - a)$ as the sample, otherwise reject u_2 and repeat the procedure.

It is clear, that the closer that the enclosing rectangle fits the distribution, then the more efficient this procedure will be.

The proportion of values rejected is:

$$\frac{(b - a) - c}{(b - a)}$$

10.4.3   Composition

This approach, sometimes called decomposition and sometimes called the method of mixtures, relies on a creative realization that some complicated distributions may be represented by a combination of several simpler ones.

The procedure is illustrated for sampling from a normal distribution in Section 10.6.3. Composition may be a preferred approach for sampling from negative exponential distributions when a very large number of samples are required. Fishman (1978) gives a composition algorithm for the negative exponential distribution.

10.5   RANDOM SAMPLING ALGORITHMS FOR DISCRETE DISTRIBUTIONS

Not all random variables are continuous, some are discrete (i.e., they take only certain integer values). An example would be a Poisson distribution, which represents the number of events per unit time in some random processes. More specifically, if the interval between successive arrivals at a service point follows a negative exponential distribution, then the number of arrivals expected in any unit time (say each hour) should follow a Poisson distribution. General methods for sampling from discrete distributions are similar to those for continuous random variables.

10.5.1   Sampling from histograms

Section 10.1.2 introduced top-hat sampling for histograms and the approach can be formalized to show how samples may be taken from many discrete distributions. A discrete random variable whose p.d.f. may be represented by a histogram can be defined as follows. Consider a discrete random variable X, taking values x_i, such that:

$i = 0, 1, 2, \ldots, n$
and $x_k > x_j$ for all values of x_k and x_j in which $k > j$.

Referring back to Figure 10.3 which shows a histogram and its cumulative form, the task of top-hat sampling can be thought of as a form of search. In the simplest case, the search begins with the first value of X (i.e., with x_1). It continues, as if climbing up the stairs formed by the cumulative histogram, until it reaches the correct level. Expressed in pseudo-code, an algorithm might rely on the following data structures:

p[ ] : a one dimensional array of real values, to be used a vector that contains the values $\{x_i\}$, for $i = 0, 1, 2, \ldots n$
x : an integer, which will be the required sample
u : a real variable, which will hold a uniform $[0, 1)$ random number

Thus, the algorithm might be as follows:

```
u : = Rand();          {Take a random number}
x : = 0;               {initialize x}
While (p[x] < u) do
x : = x + 1;           {climb up p[ ], looking for the correct value}
Return x.              {the required sample from the histogram}
```

This use of repeated trials characterizes many algorithms used for random sampling from discrete distributions. Clearly, if the histogram has a large number of cells then some more efficient search procedure may be used in place of this algorithm. An obvious improvement would be to begin the search half way up the range, rather than at the first value.

10.5.2   Implicit inverse transformation

Section 10.4.1 introduced the idea of inversion sampling from continuous distributions and a similar approach may be used with discrete distributions. The only requirement is that the p.d.f., now expressed as $\Pr(X = x)$, is known:

where X is the random variable, and x is the set of values $(0, 1, 2, \ldots, n)$ taken by X.

By definition:

$$\Pr(X \leq x + 1) = \Pr(X \leq x) + \Pr(X = x + 1)$$

and also

$$\Pr(X = x + 1) = A_{x+1}\Pr(X = x)$$

where A_{x+1}, depends on the distribution as well as on the value of x. Its effect, as with the systematic approach to sampling from histograms, is to provide a way of climbing up the c.d.f. in a systematic manner.

The data structures of a general algorithm for implicit inverse transformation could be as follows:

p : a real, to be used to hold the $\Pr(X = x)$.
b : a real, to hold the value of the $\Pr(X \leq x)$.
$A[\ ]$: a real array to hold the A_{x+1} values.
x : an integer, which will be the required sample.
u : a real variable, which will hold a uniform $[0, 1)$ random number.

Thus, the algorithm might be as follows:

```
x: = 0;           {initialize the counter}
p: = 0;           {initialize the probability}
b: = p;           (initialize the cumulative probability}
u := Rand();      {Take a random number}
While (u < b) do  {climb up the cumulative}
   x: = x + 1;    {increment x}
   p: = p * A[x]; {compute the next value of p}
   b: = b + p;    {compute the cumulative probability}
Return x.         {the required sample from the distribution}
```

Geometric distribution

As an example of the use of this approach, consider the geometric distribution, which can be thought of as the discrete equivalent of the negative exponential distribution. Imagine a container that contains two types of ball, A and B, in known proportions. Suppose that we wish to find a type A ball but that we cannot see inside the container and must take balls from it until we find one that is type A. The distribution of the number of type B balls that we pick before we find a type A ball, follows the geometric distribution. In general it models the number of failures in some trial before there is a success. Suppose that the proportion of type A balls is p, therefore the proportion of type B balls is $1 - p$.

The Geometric p.d.f. is as follows:

$$\Pr(X = x) = p(1 - p)^x$$

where $x = 0, 1, 2, \ldots$; p is the probability of success and x is the number of independent trials before a success is recorded.

Hence, $\Pr(X = x + 1) = p(1 - p)^{x+1}$, which means that $A_{x+1} = (1 - p)$.

Poisson distribution

This approach may also be used to sample from a Poisson distribution for which the p.d.f. is:

$$\Pr(X = x) = \frac{e^{-\lambda}.\lambda^x}{x!} \qquad \text{where } x = 0, 1, 2, \ldots$$

where λ is the mean number of occurrences per unit time and x is the actual number of occurrences per unit time. It is obvious that:

$$\Pr(X = x + 1) = \frac{e^{-\lambda}.\lambda^{x+1}}{(x+1)!} = \frac{e^{-\lambda}.\lambda^x}{x!} \cdot \frac{\lambda}{(x+1)}$$

$$\therefore A_{x+1} = \frac{\lambda}{(x+1)}$$

Thus the implicit inversion algorithm can be simply applied to a Poisson distribution, without even the need to store the values of A_{x+1}, since they can be computed at each step.

10.5.3 Discrete rejection—samples from a Poisson distribution

As with inversion, a discrete version of rejection (see Section 10.4.2) may also be employed in some cases. As an example, consider a Poisson distribution as this provides a second way to sample from this distribution in addition to an implicit inverse transformation. In this case, the method relies on the well known result that, if the number of events per unit time follow a Poisson distribution, then the intervals between those events follow a negative exponential distribution. That is, if a discrete random variable x follows a Poisson distribution:

$$\Pr(X = x) = \frac{e^{-\lambda}.\lambda^x}{x!} \qquad \text{where } x = 0, 1, 2, \ldots$$

then the interval between the events y, follows a negative exponential distribution as:

$$f(y) = \frac{1}{\lambda}.e^{-y/\lambda}$$

The method uses an inversion of $f(y)$ to generate successive exponential deviates $t_0, t_1, t_2, \ldots$ until:

$$\sum_{i=0}^{x} t_i \leq 1 < \sum_{i=0}^{x+1} t_j \qquad \text{where } x = 0, 1, 2, \ldots$$

That is, compute a succession of exponential deviates, keeping a running sum of their values until that sum exceeds the length of the unit interval with which the Poisson distribution is concerned. At which point, the number of deviates (the value x) follows a Poisson distribution with mean λ. If inversion sampling is used for the exponential distribution of y, then the condition can be rewritten as:

$$-\frac{1}{\lambda}\sum_{i=0}^{x}\log_e(u_i) \leq 1 < -\frac{1}{\lambda}\sum_{i=0}^{x+1}\log_e(u_i)$$

that is

$$\sum_{i=0}^{x}\log_e(u_i) \leq \lambda < -\sum_{i=0}^{x+1}\log_e(u_i)$$

which is the same as

$$\prod_{i=0}^{x+1}u_i < e^{-\lambda} \leq \prod_{i=0}^{x}u_i$$

This result allows the following algorithm to be used for sampling from a Poisson distribution. The data structures might be as follows:

M: real, the parameter of the Poisson distribution.
x: integer, the sample from the Poisson distribution.
u: real, random numbers.
b: real, the running product of the uniform variates generated so far.

The algorithm might then be as follows.

$x := -1$;	{initialize the counter}
$b := 1$;	{initialize the running product}
Repeat	{take successive random numbers, compute their
$\quad u := \text{Rand}()$;	running product and increment x until the product is
$\quad b : b * u$;	less than e^{-M}}
$x := x + 1$;	
Until $(b < \exp(M))$;	
Return x.	

There are other, more efficient, algorithms that may be employed for Poisson distributions that have a large mean value, see Fishman (1978)) for details.

10.6   SAMPLING FROM THE NORMAL DISTRIBUTION

The normal distribution merits special attention for two reasons. First, it is a distribution that is needed in many simulations and second, its p.d.f. is rather awkward. It is usual to work with a standard normal distribution of z which has a mean of 0 and a variance of 1, for which the p.d.f. is as follows:

$$f(z) = \frac{1}{\sqrt{2\pi}} e^{-z^2/2}$$

which can be converted to a normal distribution of x, with mean μ and variance of σ^2, by using the conversion formula $x = (z - \mu)/\sigma$.

By way of caution, it should be noted that the normal distribution covers the entire range from plus to minus infinity. Thus, the methods employed may produce extreme values. In fact, in most discrete simulations, the processes that are being represented by normal distributions are truncated at certain values, specifically at the value zero in many cases, since negative activity durations are most unwelcome! Hence the output from any algorithm employed should be checked and rejected, causing a resample, if the value lies outside the required range. Therefore, the methods themselves need to sit inside the protection of a rejection/acceptance shield.

10.6.1   The original Box–Müller method

Although it is impossible to use a full inversion procedure on a normal distribution, Box and Müller (1958) devised an ingenious partial inversion. The method is exact and it produces two standard normal deviates from a pair of random numbers. When implementing the algorithm, care should be taken to use both values in each pair, and not to throw half of them away.

The joint distribution function of two independent standard normal variables x and y is as follows:

$$f(x, y)\delta x . \delta y = \frac{1}{2\pi} . e^{-(x^2 + y^2)/2} . \delta x . \delta y$$

If x and y are regarded as the Cartesian coordinates of some point, then these coordinates may be transformed into their polar forms:

$$x = r\cos\theta \qquad y = r\sin\theta$$

where

$$r^2 = x^2 + y^2 \qquad \theta = \tan^{-1}(y/x)$$

and it can be shown that the joint distribution of these polar variables r and q is as follows:

$$f(r, \theta)\delta r . \delta\theta = \frac{1}{2\pi} . e^{-r^2/2} . \delta r . \delta\theta$$

and that this implies that $r^2/2$ and θ are independently distributed, θ with a uniform distribution over $(0, 2\pi)$ and $r^2/2$ with a negative exponential distribution whose mean is 1.

If U_1 and U_2 are uniform random variables on $[0, 1)$, then they can be substituted into the above formulae to give:

$$U_1 = \exp(-r^2/2) \quad \text{which implies that } r = \sqrt{(-2\log_e U_1}$$

$$U_2 = \theta/2\pi \quad \text{which implies that } \theta = 2\pi U_2$$

These results can be used to generate a pair of independent standard normal variates from a pair of random numbers as follows:

$$z_1 = \sqrt{(-2\log_e U_1}\cos(2\pi U_2)$$

$$z_2 = \sqrt{(-2\log_e U_1}\sin(2\pi U_2)$$

This result is simple to program and produces exact samples. However, the following polar variation of this method is to be preferred since the computation of trigonometric functions can be very slow.

10.6.2 Box–Müller polar variation

This variation on the original Box–Müller was suggested by Marsaglia and Bray (1964) and it incorporates a rejection procedure. Like the original Box–Müller method, this takes two random numbers and produces a pair of independent standard normal variates. In this algorithm, the two random numbers, V_1 and V_2, are distributed across $[-1, +1)$ rather than $[0, 1)$ and the sum of their squares W, is constrained to lie within the interval $(0, 1)$. This is equivalent to considering points within a circle, centred at $(0, 0)$ that has a radius of 1. From this transformation:

$$\sin 2\pi U_2 = \frac{V_1}{\sqrt{(V_1^2 + V_2^2)}} \qquad \cos 2\pi U_2 = \frac{V_2}{\sqrt{(V_1^2 + V_2^2)}}$$

Hence, the two standard normal variates can be computed from:

$$z_1 = V_1 \cdot \sqrt{\frac{-2\log_e W}{W}} \qquad z_2 = V_2 \cdot \sqrt{\frac{-2\log_e W}{W}}$$

where $V_i = -2 \cdot U_i + 1$, if U_i are uniformly distributed across $[0, 1)$ for $i = 1, 2$ and $W = (V_1^2 + V_2^2)$, with $W \leq 1$.

Hence, a suitable algorithm might utilize the following data structures:

$v1, v2$: real, the two random numbers on the interval $[-1, +1)$.
w : the sum of squares.
$z1, z2$: the two standard normal variates.

The basic algorithm may therefore be as follows:

```
Repeat
    v1 := 2 * Rand() −1;                    {Compute v1 and v2, form w}
```

$v2 := 2 * \text{Rand}() - 1;$
$w := v1 * v1 + v2 * v2;$
Until $(w \le 1);$ {Reject w if too large}
    $z1 := v1 * \text{SQRT}(-2 * \text{LOG}(w)/w)$ {Form $z1$ and $z2$}
    $z1 := v2 * \text{SQRT}(-2 * \text{LOG}(w)/w)$
Return $z1$ and $z2$.   {Return with standard normal variates}

Atkinson and Pearce (1976) and Fishman (1978) report that the polar variant is about 30% faster than the original method. Hence, for most purposes, this is the algorithm of choice when normal variates are needed.

10.6.3   Sampling from a normal distribution by composition

Section 10.4.3 introduced the idea of sampling by composition, in which one distribution is broken down into others that are more convenient to handle. Despite the high quality of the polar Box–Müller method, there are occasions when a composition approach is to be preferred. Essentially these are circumstances where a very large number of normal variates are needed. Under these circumstances, even the polar Box–Müller method may be too slow according to Atkinson and Pearce (1976).

The common algorithm, developed by Marsaglia, MacLaren and Bray (1964) composes a normal distribution of the four components shown in Figure 10.10.

(1)   A set of rectangles that account for about 86% of the area under a normal curve between ±3 standard deviations.
(2)   A set of triangles, that sit on top of the rectangles, and account for a further 11% or so of the area under the normal curve between ±3 standard deviations.
(3)   A set of strange shaped residual densities that account for about a further 2% of the area between ±3 standard deviations.
(4)   A small area of under 0.3% that relates to the extreme tails of the distribution.

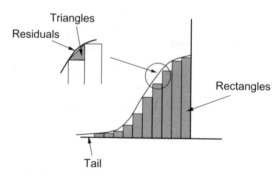

Figure 10.10   Sampling by composition

The method will always need at least two random numbers for each sample. It produces only positive values and so each variate needs to be given a random sign in order to produce a standard normal variate. The algorithm works as follows, assuming that all of the random numbers u_i are from the range $[0, 1)$.

> Generate u_0
> If $(u_0 \leq 0.8638)$ then return $z = 2(u_1 + u_2 + u_3 - 1.5)$ which samples from the rectangles
>> Else if $(u_0 \leq 0.9745)$ then return $z = 1.5(u_1 + u_2 - 1)$ which samples from the triangles
>>> Else if $(u_0 \leq 0.9973002039)$ use a rejection method for the residuals
>>>> Else use a modification of the polar Box–Müller method to sample from the tails.

The reason that this method is fast is that, on about 97% of the occasions, it takes fast samples from the rectangles or the triangles.

10.6.4 A poor way to sample from the normal distribution

By way of a cautionary tale, some people still insist on using an approximate algorithm for generating normal variates. The method in question relies on the Central Limit Theorem, which states that: "the sum of n identically and independently distributed random variates is approximately normally distributed when n is large". Hence, the method in question relies on the generation of n random numbers and the computation of their sum, which should have a mean of 0.5 and a variance of $1/12$.

If $n = 12$, then this sum is approximated a standard normal deviate z, where:

$$z = \sum_{i=1}^{12} U_i - 6$$

However, this is only an approximation and it has the special defect that it is impossible for $|z|$ to exceed 6, which means that it will not provide a good representation of the tails of a normal distribution. In general, this method is to be avoided, since it is neither fast nor accurate.

10.7 DERIVING ONE DISTRIBUTION FROM ANOTHER—LOG-NORMAL VARIATES

Sometimes, one distribution may be formed from another and the easiest example of this type to understand is the log-normal distribution. If a random variable X is distributed normally with mean μ_X and variance σ_X^2, this is usually represented as:

$$X \sim N(\mu_X, \sigma_X^2)$$

If there is another random variable Y, where $Y = e^X$, then Y is log-normally distributed with mean μ_Y and variance σ_Y^2. This is usually represented as:

$$Y \sim \text{LN}(\mu_Y, \sigma_Y^2)$$

Hence to compute a log-normal variate, first compute the appropriate underlying normal variate and then exponentiate the value to get the required sample.

It is important to be sure which mean and variance are being used, as these could be for the log-normal distribution of Y or for the underlying normal distribution of X. It can be shown that the following results allow conversion from one to the other:

$$\mu_Y = \exp\left(\mu_X + \frac{\sigma_X^2}{2}\right)$$

$$\sigma_Y^2 = \mu_Y^2[\exp(\sigma_X^2) - 1]$$

Or, if the distribution is expressed the other way, that:

$$\mu_X = \log_e(\mu_Y) - \frac{1}{2}\log_e\left(\frac{\sigma_Y^2}{\mu_Y^2} + 1\right)$$

$$\sigma_X^2 = \log_e\left(\frac{\sigma_Y^2}{\mu_Y^2} + 1\right)$$

10.8   SAMPLING FROM NON-STATIONARY PROCESSES: THINNING

The sampling methods described so far have all related to stationary distributions (i.e., to distributions whose parameters are constant through time). This is not always the case in practice, most commonly when simulating arrival processes. For example, if the arrivals at a service centre are random then it may be reasonable to simulate them with a Poisson process that allows us to generate the inter-arrival times from a negative exponential distribution (see Section 10.4.1). However, it may be the case that the arrival rate varies through the day, as shown in Figure 10.11. Thus in Figure 10.11, the arrival rate is at its highest between 08.00 and 10.00 and between 15.00 and 17.00. Hence, the inter-arrival times should be lower in these periods.

There are two ways of handling this problem, only one of which is to be recommended. The wrong way of handling this problem is to divide the day into discrete time periods and to establish an arrival rate (or average inter-arrival time) for each of these periods. Hence, if there were 10 such periods in the day, the arrival rate λ, would take values $\lambda_1, \lambda_2, \lambda_3, \ldots, \lambda_{10}$. Thus, in this non-recommended method, a different arrival rate (and thus, a different average inter-arrival time) would be applied, depending on the current clock time in the simulation.

The problem with this approach is that, if a period with a low arrival rate comes just before one with a high arrival rate, the result of the low arrival

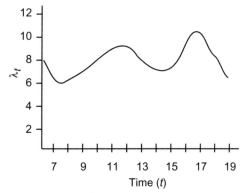

Figure 10.11   Non-stationary arrival rate

rate will be a long inter-arrival time. This long inter-arrival time may mean that the next arrival is due quite some time into the period of a high arrival rate. Hence this period of more intense arrivals may begin in the model too late, causing an underestimate of the average arrival rate and a poor estimate of congestion at busy periods. Instead, an approach known as thinning may be used.

This approach was suggested by Lewis and Shedler (1979) and it works by rejecting samples in periods of low intensity. The method involves generating the arrivals by a stationary Poisson process that uses the maximum arrival rate, which is shown as $\lambda_{\max}$ on Figure 10.11. This will, of course, generate too many arrivals during most of the day, since it has used the maximum value. In turn, if a negative exponential distribution is being used to generate the time of the next arrival, then the use of $1/\lambda_{\max}$ will lead to inter-arrival times that are too short during most periods.

If a graph like that of Figure 10.11 can be produced for the non-stationary process then, if the simulation clock has reached time t and the simulation needs to generate the interval to the next arrival, thinning works as follows:

(1) Use a stationary distribution with $\lambda_{\max}$ to generate the time of the next arrival.
(2) Generate a uniform $[0, 1)$ random number U and use this to reject the sample if $U > \lambda_t/\lambda_{\max}$, accepting the sample otherwise. Repeat this step until a value is accepted.

That is, a second random number is used to reject a proportion of the samples at those times when the arrival rate is lower than the maximum. This approach provides good estimates of congestion in non-stationary Poisson processes.

EXERCISES

(1) If you have a simulation system available (a language or a VIMS), investigate what control it permits over random number generation.

Plot lagged pairs as shown in Figures 10.4 and 10.5 to assess whether the generator is a good one.

(2)   If you have a simulation system available (a language or a VIMS), apply the serial and gap tests to the random number generator.

(3)   Using a spreadsheet with which you are familiar, generate 1,000 random numbers and plot lagged pairs as shown in Figures 10.4 and 10.5. If the generator looks a poor one, investigate why this is so.

(4)   Using a spreadsheet with which you are familiar, apply the serial and gap tests to the random number generator.

(5)   Using a programming language or a spreadsheet with which you are familiar, program one of the random number generators recommended in this chapter. Plot lagged pairs as shown in Figures 10.4 and 10.5.

(6)   Using a programming language or spreadsheet with which you are familiar, write a program to generate negative exponential variates. Collect the results from 1,000 variates and use statistical inference to decide whether the sample appears to come from the negative exponential distribution.

(7)   Using a programming language or spreadsheet with which you are familiar, write a program to generate standard normal variates using the polar Box–Müller method. Be sure to use both values generated. Collect the results from 1,000 variates and use statistical inference to decide whether the sample appears to come from the normal distribution.

(8)   Modify your algorithm developed for the standard normal distribution (Exercise 7) so as to generate values with a mean of 10 and variance of 4.

(9)   Modify the algorithm developed for the non-standard normal distribution (Exercise 8) so as to avoid negative values.

(10) Modify your algorithm for the negative exponential distribution (Exercise 3) so as to enable non-stationary distributions to be simulated.

REFERENCES

Atkinson A.C. and Pearce M.C. (1976) The computer generation of beta, gamma and normal random variates. *J. R. Stat. Soc. A.*, **139**, 431 ff.

Box G.E.P. and Müller M.E. (1958) A note on the generation of normal deviates. *Annals of Mathematical Statistics*, **28**, 610–1.

Carter E. (2003) Random Number Generation. Taygeta Scientific Inc. http://www.taygeta.com/random.xml

Fishman G.S. (1978) *Principles of Discrete Event Digital Simulation*. Wiley-Interscience, New York.

Fishman G.S. and Moore L.S. III (1986) An exhaustive analysis of multiplicative congruential random number generators with modulus 231–1. *SIAM Journal of Statistical Computation*, **7**, 24–45.

Hellekalek P. (2003) Theory and practice of random number generation. http://random.mat.sbg.ac.at/

Johnson D.G. (1997) The triangular distribution as a proxy for the beta distribution in risk analysis. *Journal of the Royal Statistical Society – Series D (The Statistician)*, **46**(3), 387–98.

Kleijnen J.P.C. and van Groenendaal W. (1992) *Simulation: A Statistical Perspective*. John Wiley & Sons, Chichester, UK.

Knuth D.E. (1981) *The Art of Computer Programming (2nd edn), Vol. 2: Seminumerical Algorithms*. Addison-Wesley, Reading, MA.

L'Ecuyer P. (1994) Uniform random number generation. In: O. Balci (ed.), *Annals of Operations Research, Vol. 23: Simulation and Modeling*. J.C. Balzer, Basel, Switzerland.

Lehmer D.E. (1951) Mathematical methods in large-scale computing units. *Annals of the Computing Laboratory, Harvard University*, **26**, 141–6.

Lewis P.A.W. and Shedler G.S. (1979) Simulation of non-homogeneous Poisson process by thinning. *Naval Research Logistics Quarterly*, **26**, 403–13.

Marsaglia G. and Bray T.D. (1964) A convenient method for generating Normal variables. *SIAM Review*, **6**(3), 260–4.

Marsaglia G., MacLaren M.D. and Bray T.D. (1964) A fast procedure for generating Normal deviates on a digital computer. *Journal of the ACM*, **7**, 4–10.

RAND Corporation (1955) *A Million Random Digits with 100,000 Normal Deviates*. The Free Press, Glencoe, IL.

Ripley B.D. (1977) Modelling spatial patterns. *Journal of the Royal Statistical Society B.*, **39**(2), 172–212.

Ripley B.D. (1987) *Stochastic Simulation*. John Wiley & Sons, New York.

Tocher K.D. (1963) *The Art of Simulation*. English Universities Press, London.

Planning and Analysing Discrete Simulation Output

11.1 FUNDAMENTAL IDEAS

11.1.1 Simulation as directed experimentation

The usual purpose of a computer simulation is to bring about some improvement in the system being simulated. Hence the output of the simulation should be interpreted with some care, the risk being that wrong decisions will be taken. Assuming that the simulation model is considered valid and that all computer programs used have been verified, further difficulties remain in most discrete event simulations because they commonly include stochastic elements. As shown in Figure 11.1, a simulation experiment involves subjecting the model to inputs (or factors) at various levels and interpreting their effects on the output (or responses).

As a simple example, consider again the problem of the harassed booking clerk introduced in Chapter 5. Possible measures of performance might be the average waiting times of personal enquirers and phone calls, or the numbers waiting to be served. Thus, the queue lengths and the waiting times would be the response variables for which estimates need to be found. The inputs whose effects are being investigated are in two groups:

(1) Those parameters which define the configuration of the system. For example, the number of booking clerks or the priority rules for different types of customers.
(2) The random samples from the various probability distributions, such as those for inter-arrival times. Some of these samples may be exogenous (i.e., they stem from outside the controlled system). For example, the

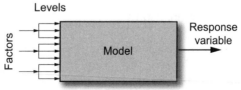

Figure 11.1 Formal simulation experimentation

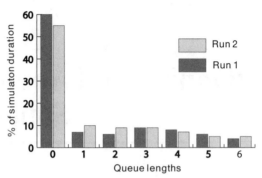

Figure 11.2   An example of sampling variation

arrivals come from the world outside. Others may be endogenous (i.e., they are a result of the activity within the system).

Suppose that the management of the theatre wishes to investigate the effect of a variety of system configurations: such as one or two clerks, or no priority to personal enquirers. The inputs include stochastic elements (i.e., random samples, and simulating the same configuration with different sets of random numbers will produce results that differ, at least slightly). This effect, due to sampling variation, is clearly seen in Figure 11.2. This shows the length of the queue of personal enquirers during two simulations employing different sets of random numbers. Thus, the analyst simulating even such a simple system needs to be sure that different estimates of the average queue length are due to the system configuration and are not just the result of sampling variation.

Generalizing from this simple example, it is important to distinguish clearly between the effects of sampling variation and those effects that result from the system configurations, or policies, being examined. Making this distinction and maintaining this separation is one of the key issues in planning a discrete simulation and interpreting its output. This is because the response variables are random variables, whose estimation requires careful statistical analysis. This chapter introduces the basic ideas of this analysis and suggests how the major problems should be faced in practical terms.

For a thorough treatment of the main issues in output analysis, see Fishman (1973, 1978) or Kleijnen (1974, 1975, 1987). As with discrete simulation software (Chapter 9), the annual Winter Simulation Conference includes tutorials on output analysis (e.g., Alexopoulos and Kim (2002), Barton (2002) and Nakayama (2002)).

11.1.2   Estimation and comparison

Because the response variables are random variables, simulations are often used to determine the parameters (mean, variance, etc.) of their distributions. For example, an airport might be simulated to gain estimates of its capacity under a particular operating condition. Another possible use for a simulation is to compare different policies or configurations, for example, to compare different ways of operating the airport. This too involves the estimation of response variables, but it also requires their comparison and, sometimes, this may be easier than gaining a precise estimate of a single random variable.

Comparison can, of course, be reduced to the problem of estimating a statistic that is some function of the difference between two variables. In such cases, estimating the difference may be easier than giving a precise estimate of either of the single variables. This is because sampling variation may easily lead to bias in estimates of the variables. If some way can be found to ensure that this bias equally affects both variables involved in the comparison, then working with the difference of the two variables will remove the bias. As will be discussed in Section 11.4, a number of so-called variance reduction techniques have been developed to support the production of better estimates of random variables.

11.1.3 Three important principles

In analysing the output from discrete simulations, three principles need to be borne in mind:

(1) Most such simulations include a number of sampling processes and these samples are combined to give one or more response variables. Hence it is sensible to regard these simulations as complex sampling experiments. It can sometimes be very difficult to understand the effects of these combinations, and were the effects of these combinations straightforward, then it is unlikely that a simulation approach would be needed at all.

(2) Because these simulations run through simulated time, many output variables take the form of timeseries and the observations may, therefore, include significant serial correlation. This means that the observations are not statistically independent. Therefore, care must be taken in any analysis because the presence of this serial correlation means that many classical statistical analyses are inappropriate. There are ways of coping with this problem and these will be discussed later in this chapter.

(3) Although there are many similarities between simulation output analysis and classical experimental design, there is one important difference. Simulation output is the result of running a created model through time and the inner workings of that model can be explored and manipulated. By contrast, much classical experimental design assumes that it is a game against nature. When analysing simulation output it is sensible to take advantage of any knowledge that is available about the inner workings of the model. Many variance reduction techniques (see Section 11.4) make use of this knowledge.

It is very common for a simulation approach to be used to find which policy, amongst several, is the best for operating a system. For example, how many tellers do we need in a bank branch, should there be a single queue or a queue for each teller? The challenge when analysing simulation output is to distinguish between variation that comes from the policy and that which comes from the random sampling processes within the simulation model.

11.1.4 Some preliminary advice

Do not get carried away by complicated statistical methods. Sometimes they are needed, but often a little common sense will go a long way. Many simulation software packages include optimization routines designed to support the process of simulation optimization. These are useful, but are no substitute for thinking about what is likely to be the result of a simulation. In particular, do not despise the use of simple arithmetic to narrow down the alternative options to be considered in full experiments.

For example, consider a queuing system with n servers in which each server takes a time to serve a customer distributed normally, with a mean of 10 and variance of 4, truncated at 2 and 18 minutes. Customers arrive at intervals, which are negative exponentially distributed with a mean of 3 minutes. Suppose that we wish to know how many servers are required. It is very sensible to do some straightforward calculations with mean values before even thinking about a simulation. The ratio of service time to inter-arrival times is $10/3 = 3.333$. Thus, at least 4 servers will be needed. Whether we need 4, 5 or 6 will depend on the service targets that we are trying to meet. But there is no point including any option of less than 4 servers in any experiments, unless we are happy to see infinite queues develop. It is quicker to do the calculations than to let a simulation optimizer discover this.

11.2   DEALING WITH TRANSIENT EFFECTS

11.2.1   Terminating and non-terminating systems

Some systems, and therefore some simulations, can be regarded as self-terminating. What this means is that some natural event terminates the operation of the system. As an example, the flight of a missile is expected to terminate when it hits its target, or it hits some other object or it passes harmlessly into oblivion. Another example would be a one-off task such as an evacuation, which begins with a serious incident and ends with (we hope) a successful evacuation.

By contrast, some systems are not self-terminating in this way, because there is no such natural event that terminates the system's operation. An example might be an air traffic control system in which any day, week or month is just a snapshot in a continuous stream of activity. Most factory and logistics simulations are non-terminating. This does not mean that they are eternal, it merely implies that the simulation provides a moveable window on their activity.

Finally, some systems sit between the two extremes and may be treated one way or other. For example, consider a factory in which work begins at 08.00

and ends, each day, at 17.00. In one sense this is a self-terminating system, since there is a natural event (reaching 17.00) that closes down the operation of the system. However, in another sense, the system is clearly a continuing one, since work will continue at 08.00 the next day. On this next day the model will probably use as its starting work-in-progress that which was left at the end of the previous day. In these cases, the analyst may need to make an arbitrary decision about how the system is to be regarded.

- Although there are exceptions to this rule, in general, our interest is as follows. In self-terminating systems it is normal to be interested in transient behaviour, for this transience will be what brings the system to its climax. The data which capture this behaviour may be highly correlated and data analysis must take this into account. Many self-terminating systems never achieve a steady state of any kind.
- In non-terminating systems it is common for interest to centre on the long-run or steady-state behaviour of the system and the main concern is with average values and their confidence limits. It is also important to ensure that the transient effects, due to initial bias, are lost before embarking on a steady-state analysis.

In most cases, therefore, the analysis of non-terminating systems focuses on the steady state. This concept is not as obvious as it may seem and any useful definition embodies two linked ideas. The first is that, when a simulation is in a steady state, this is a state of dynamic equilibrium in which the effects of the starting conditions of the simulation have been lost. The second, more formal view, is that a simulation is in a steady state "if the probability of being in one of its states is governed by a fixed probability function" (Kleijnen, 1974, p. 69). This does not mean that the system does not change state, but rather that the probability of it being in any of its states can be determined. If, for example, a simulation of the harassed booking clerk problem were to be in a steady state, then the length of the queue of personal enquirers waiting for service would vary somewhat and this variation would be predictable, in statistical terms.

When planning simulation experiments and analysing their output, it is crucial that the analyst considers whether the analysis is to focus on the steady state or on the transient effects. For example, if a manufacturing job shop is being simulated, then measurements of the mean waiting time for the jobs are best taken when the simulation has reached a steady state. If, on the other hand, the simulation is of a doctor's consulting room in which the clinic opens with 20 or more patients already waiting, then these starting conditions may be crucial when deciding on, say, an appointments system—which might be the reason for the simulation. That is, in this second case, a major focus of the simulation may be the effect of the initial conditions of the model.

As will become clear later, the response variables are random variables, whose values are therefore determined by probability distributions. Hence, to estimate those distributions requires multiple values for the response variables. This means that the sample size is a crucial aspect of the analysis of discrete simulation output. If the simulation reaches a steady state, then observations made at intervals (e.g., of queue lengths) can be treated as statistically independent. If no such steady state is reached, then a more creative approach is needed.

11.2.2   Achieving steady state

The easiest way of bringing a simulated system into a steady state is to control its starting conditions. For example, suppose that the simulation model is of a commercial airport and that its main purpose is to see the effect of increasing its runways from one to two. A commercial airport is never wholly idle, except on the very first day that it is open. Hence, if a simulation were to begin with no activity in progress, then that starting state would not be typical in any way. If the simulation were, however, started in that null state and then were left to run for some time then, if the simulation model is valid, it should eventually move into steady states that reflect the actual operating conditions of the airport. This, of course, assumes that the real airport operates in some form of steady state. The problem is that, if the main focus is on this steady-state operation, then any observations taken whilst the simulation model moves from its initial null state into a steady state are not relevant for analytical purposes.

In general, when attempting to analyse the steady-state behaviour of a non-terminating system, it is important to ensure that initial bias is lost before collecting data for analysis. Even an analysis of a single run needs to be rid of the early transience if steady-state estimates are required. Also, if policies are being compared, then the same treatment of transience is essential for all policies. Two approaches have been suggested for achieving this end: typical starting conditions and run-in periods (sometimes known as warm-up periods). If, on the other hand, transience is the main interest (as is often the case in self-terminating systems), then these approaches should not be used.

The idea of typical starting conditions is deceptively attractive, but not to be recommended. The basic notion is that the simulation should begin in some state that is believed to be typical of the system when it is operating in "reality". Hence, in a simulation of a factory, someone might assume certain initial values for work-in-progress and for machine occupancy at the start of the simulation. There are a number of clear problems with such a proposal:

- We may not know the typical conditions because the system may not actually exist.
- We may not know the typical conditions because we are investigating how the system might operate under novel circumstances.
- We may be comparing policies and we may unwittingly bias our comparison by giving an unfair advantage to one policy rather than the other through the choice of initial conditions.

As a further example of this problem, consider the hypothetical airport simulation mentioned earlier. It would be reasonable to suppose that an airport with three runways would end up, at steady state, coping with more traffic than with just two runways. Hence, it would seem reasonable to start the simulation with the two policy options loaded somewhat differently. If the aim of the simulation is to find whether the third runway is worthwhile, then a simulation started in this way looks dangerously like a self-fulfilling prophecy.

Conway (1963) expressed the problem elegantly as follows:

(1)   I wished to compare two systems, A and B.
(2)   I anticipated that system A would yield a greater mean value of attribute M than would system B.
(3)   I conducted an experiment in which the initial value of attribute M for system A was greater than for system B.
(4)   The experimental results demonstrate that the mean value of attribute M for system A is significantly greater than for system B.

Put in these terms, using "typical" starting conditions seems unwise.

11.2.3 Using a run-in period

Using a run-in period takes a little more care, but is much better, as it addresses the problems mentioned above. The idea is that a simulation run should begin with some unrealistic, and effectively null, system condition. The simulation should then be run until it is believed to have achieved some steady-state condition. Data collection for analysis purposes should begin at that point. Most modern software allows the user to specify the time at which data collection is to start—the end of the run-in period.

The practical question to be asked is, "How long should the run-in period be?" If it is too long, then time will be wasted (although computer time is an increasingly cheap resource). If it is too short, then transient effects may be included by mistake and the results may, unintentionally, be biased. Robinson (2002) suggests the use of an approach based on statistical process control and also provides a useful set of references covering the main approaches. A commonly used approach that is not too data intensive was suggested by Welch (1981, 1983) and is described below. However, there is no straightforward technique that will always determine a suitable run-in period.

A simple way to proceed is to select some suitable variable (or variables) and to treat it (or them) as a response variable(s) about which data may be collected as timeseries from the start of the simulation. This variable(s) can be displayed on a graph as the simulation proceeds. In most cases, such a graph will indicate when the initial transience is over and, from this, the time for the start of data collection can be determined. Welch's approach does this, but with a smoothed series. For example, if the variable is of queue lengths in the simulation, then if these are still generally increasing, the initial transience may not have been lost—or it implies that there are insufficient service

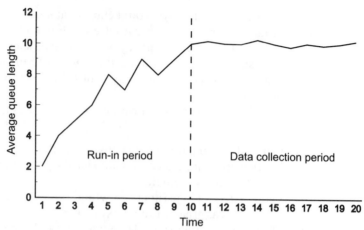

Figure 11.3   Using a run-in period

resources in the system to manage the demand from customers. The basic idea is shown in Figure 11.3.

11.2.4   Welch's method for determining the run-in period

Welch (1981, 1983) suggests a simple way to decide how long the run-in period should be by smoothing the simulation output and plotting the resulting series. Its basic approach is to make a few (say 5 or 10) pilot runs of the simulation. Each run should be a replicate, but with different random numbers for each run. It involves the calculation of a smoothed series by moving averages and then uses the display of the smoothed series to enable a decision about the length of the run-in period.

Some nomenclature

Suppose that we are interested in a response variable Y, which produces values $y_1, y_2, y_3, \ldots, y_m$. Suppose, too, that we make n independent replications of the run. Thus, we end up with a two-dimensional matrix of value y_{ij}, where $j = 1, \ldots, n, i = 1, \ldots, m$.

The method

(1)   Make n independent replications ($n \geqslant 5$), each of length m, giving values y_{ij}.

(2)   Compute the mean for each observation: $\overline{Y}_i = \sum_{j=1}^{n} y_{ij}/n$ for $i = 1, \ldots, m$. (Note that: $E(\overline{Y}_i) = E(Y_i)$, but that $VAR(\overline{Y}_i) = VAR(Y_i)/n$, i.e., the variance is reduced.)

(3) Compute the moving average of length w:

$$\overline{Y}_i(w) = \begin{cases} \dfrac{\displaystyle\sum_{s=-w}^{w} \overline{Y}_{i+s}}{2w+1} & \text{for } i = w+1, w+2, \ldots, m-w \\[2em] \dfrac{\displaystyle\sum_{s=-(i-1)}^{i-1} \overline{Y}_{i+s}}{2i+1} & \text{for } i = 1, 2, \ldots, w \end{cases}$$

(4) Plot the moving average for $i = 1, 2, \ldots, m - w$ and choose l (the run-in period) beyond which the moving average series seems to have converged.

11.3   DEALING WITH LACK OF INDEPENDENCE

During a discrete event simulation a system's behaviour unfolds through time, in a model that approximates these changes as a sequence of discrete states. Because the progress of the model is a sequence of state changes, then it is highly likely that observations of response variables (such as queue lengths), which are taken as the simulation proceeds, will not be independent. That is, the value at some instant will be a function of its previous value or of previous values. In statistical terms, the timeseries of the observations will display significant serial correlation. This will be true whether or not the initial bias has been removed from the set of results. How then should the data that comprises the simulation results be analysed? Is it acceptable to make what some cynics describe as "the declaration of independence"?

11.3.1   Simple replication

Perhaps the simplest strategy is to make many independent runs of the simulation, taking just a single reading from each run. In this way multiple replications of the same operating conditions are made. This is achieved by ensuring that different random numbers are used for each replication of the simulation under the same policy. For example, if a random variable X is of interest in the simulation, then running the simulation n times under the same conditions, but with different random numbers, should result in n independent observations of X. If these observations of X are x, then a suitable estimate of the mean value of X might be $(\Sigma x)/n$.

This, of course, implies that the random number streams can be fully controlled, so that different random number streams are used for each replication of the simulation. In practice, this means that different seeds are applied to each replication of the simulation since, as discussed in Chapter 10, the random number generators in common use are cyclic (see Figure 11.4) and the random number seed selects the starting point of the generator in its cycle. This in turn implies that the random number generator needs to have a

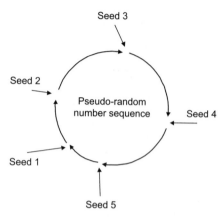

Figure 11.4   A pseudo-random number generation cycle

very long period, otherwise the replications may employ correlated subsequences. If these subsequences turn out (by accident) to overlap significantly, then even "independent" replication will not produce truly independent observations. If a suitable random number generator is used, which should lead to independent observations of the response variable(s), the variance reduction techniques described in Section 11.4 may be used. If a run-in period is being employed, then this should obviously be used for each and every replication.

11.3.2   Using batch means

Rather than run a simulation many times, each time wasting results during a run-in period, an alternative approach is to make one long run of the simulation and then to divide the results into a sequence of batches. The idea is to ensure that observations within one batch are independent of those within any other batch. In a simple queuing simulation, the run might extend to, say, 100,000 customers and these might be broken down into, say, 10 batches, each of 10,000 customers. The hope is that, although customer n is clearly likely to be affected by what happened to customer $(n-1)$, customer n is unlikely to be much affected by what happened to customer $(n-10,000)$. Kleijnen (1987) and Kleijnen and van Groenendaal (1992) suggest tests that might be applied to such batches to see if they are independent, but a few rules of thumb also present themselves for practical application.

The first problem is to decide how long each batch should be. Suppose that a long run is divided into n batches, each of which consists of k observations of some random variable X. Thus, batch 1 takes the values $x_1, x_2, \ldots, x_k$, batch 2 takes the values $x_{k+1}, x_{k+2}, \ldots, x_{2k}$ and so on. Each batch provides a sample from which a single estimate of the parameters of X may be made. Hence, from batch j, the estimate of the mean of X might be:

$$\bar{x} = \frac{1}{k} \sum_{i=1}^{k} x_i$$

The overall estimate of the mean of X would be the grand mean of the n samples, that is:

$$\overline{X} = \frac{1}{nk} \sum_{j=1}^{n} \sum_{i=1}^{k} x_i = \frac{1}{n} \sum_{j=1}^{n} \bar{x}_j$$

and the overall variance would be the sum of the batch variances, if the batches are independent. This is likely to hold if k is made large enough, which also has the advantage that the central limit theorem will apply to the observations in each batch. Similarly, if n is large enough, the central limit theorem will apply across the batches, which means that classical methods of statistical inference can be applied.

Hence, the practical advice is to make k very large (batches of several thousand)—since if there is correlation between the batches, then the method collapses. As with deciding on run-in periods, it may be sensible to plot the batch means that result from the batching, just to make sure that there is no pattern in their sequence. The number of batches n needs to be large enough to apply the central limit theorem with some confidence, Schmeiser (1982) suggests that, in most practical cases, between 10 and 30 batches will suffice.

11.3.3 Overlapping batch means (OBM)

It is desirable that the number of batches n be between 10 and 30 and that k, the batch size, be large. This is not always possible with wholly separate batches. Hence, Meketon and Schmeiser (1984) introduced the idea of overlapping batch means in which the first batch consists of $x_1, x_2, \ldots, x_k$ and the second batch consists of $x_2, x_3, \ldots, x_{k+1}$ and so on. This gives an OBM estimator for μ as follows:

$$\overline{X}_o = \frac{1}{n-k+1} \sum_{i=1}^{n-k+1} x_i(k)$$

for which

$$X_i(k) = \frac{1}{k} \sum_{j=1}^{i+k-1} X_j$$

are the batch means for $i = 1, 2, \ldots, n - k + 1$, and the sample variance is

$$\frac{1}{n-k} \sum_{i=1}^{n-k+1} (X_i(k) - \overline{X}_o)^2$$

It can be shown that the overlapping batches are relatively independent. The approach produces more batches than non-overlapping batches from the same data series which means that variance of the estimator will be lower than for non-overlapping batch means. Hence overlapping batches are to be preferred in most cases.

11.3.4   Regenerative methods

Some stochastic systems and, therefore, some simulations, return to special states from time to time in which the events prior to their occurrence are independent of those after their occurrence. Hence, the data before and after a regeneration point can be analysed separately. For some queuing systems, an obvious example is the state in which all servers are free and all waiting lines are empty. When a new customer arrives whilst the system is in this state, an independent cycle of activity is beginning—if the arrivals are governed by a Poisson process. In one sense, this approach resembles the batching method, except that the length of the batches varies and their start and finish is determined by the activity in the model and not by the analyst.

The point at which one cycle ends and the next one starts is usually known as the regeneration point. The lengths of the cycles are known as epochs, or as regeneration cycles. As with batching, the intention is that each epoch should be treated as a set of observations that is independent of the previous epoch. In this way, the central limit theorem, and all of the classical statistics that go with it, may be applied to the simulation output. Kleijnen and van Groenendaal (1992) argue that the use of regenerative methods has a further advantage in that it removes the need for the analyst to determine a run-in period (see Section 11.2.3). This is because the period from the start of the simulation to the first regeneration point is simply one epoch in the series to be analysed.

One practical problem is that true regeneration points may occur very rarely. For example, if the servers in a queuing system are over-worked (i.e., the traffic intensity is high), then such a state will occur only rarely. Hence there will be few independent epochs for analysis. One suggestion is that "nearly renewal" states may be used. An example might be the state when there is just a single customer waiting. This is clearly less likely to generate truly independent epochs, but it may be good enough for many practical purposes. Fishman (1978) provides a thorough coverage of regenerative methods. It should be noted that this approach, like many aspects of the analysis of simulation output, relies on the privileged position of the analyst. The model is not a black box that is not understood; rather, it is the product of human endeavour which the analyst should understand. Regenerative methods are one example of the ways in which this knowledge may be used to support appropriate analysis.

11.4   VARIANCE REDUCTION

There are many techniques in use that claim to help reduce the variance of the output variables. They are needed because the response variables of discrete simulations often display somewhat large variance and this makes the

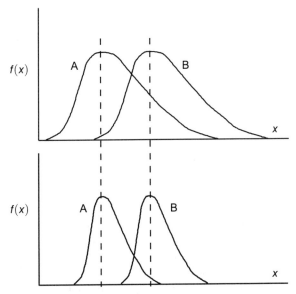

Figure 11.5   The effect of variation on inference

problem of estimation and comparison rather difficult at times. As can be seen from Figure 11.5, the size of the output variance makes a great difference to the confidence that can be placed in any comparison of two or more policies. The top part of Figure 11.5 shows the distribution of the response variables from two policies A and B. Because both response variables have a large variance, then there is a high probability of wrongly concluding that policy A has a higher mean value of X than policy B. The bottom part of Figure 11.5 shows something much more satisfactory. This is because the variances of the response variables are much lower, meaning that a comparison is much more likely to lead to the correct conclusion.

11.4.1   The basic problem—sampling variation

To understand the basic problem, consider a simulation from which someone wishes to estimate the mean value of some random variable X. The common-sense way to do this would be to run n independent replications of the simulation, each time collecting a new value of x. Hence, a suitable estimator for the mean value of X might be the arithmetic mean of the values of x, which could be bounded by some confidence limits. These limits provide upper and lower bounds on a confidence interval in which there is some known probability that the true mean of X lies within the interval. Expressing this in algebraic terms produces the following:

$$\mu = \overline{X} \pm a_n \frac{s}{\sqrt{n}}$$

where μ is the true mean of X and s is the sample standard deviation.

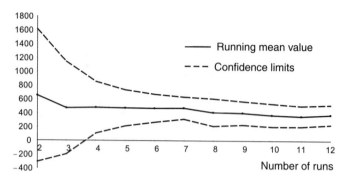

Figure 11.6   Converging confidence limits

This gives confidence limits on the estimate of the mean value of X. The value taken by the parameter a_n is distribution dependent as well as dependent on the degree of confidence that we are seeking. As an example of this, consider Figure 11.6. The dashed lines shown are 95% confidence limits from a simple discrete simulation and the solid line is the sample mean. Note that the confidence limits converge as the number of runs (i.e., the sample size) increases. However, the problem is that this convergence is only rapid in the first few samples, thereafter it is slow. This is because the convergence is a function of the square root of the sample size. Thus, the convergence in moving from two samples to four is rapid, but to make an equivalent reduction again will require sixteen samples and so on.

Thus, a sure-fire way to end up with reasonable estimates that have narrow confidence limits is to run a huge number of replications. But this is time consuming and there are better ways to proceed than this blunderbuss approach. Variance reduction techniques are employed to help this convergence along a little. Kleijnen (1974) lists the following variance reduction techniques:

- Stratified sampling.
- Selective sampling.
- Control variates.
- Importance sampling.
- Antithetic variates.
- Common random numbers.

Of these, only common random numbers, control variates and antithetic sampling are widely used in the types of discrete simulation carried out within management science.

11.4.2   Set and sequence effects

It can be quite illuminating to think about the sources of the variation that is seen in simulation output, which stems from the use of random sampling algorithms to develop finite samples in which:

- The moments of the sample distribution may not be what they should be (the shape and position may be wrong).
- The sequence in which samples are combined might also make its effect known, even though the individual random numbers are found to be "properly" random.

This is because random numbers are used for two purposes in the standard random sampling algorithms. They are used to select a set of values and also to ensure that this set is presented in a pattern-free (i.e., random, sequence). These two aspects can be captured in two effects (which have been studied by analysis of variance techniques; Saliby, 1980):

- *The set effect.* These are errors due to the set of values produced by the sampling process. With a finite sample size, we may be unlucky and may end up with a poor, unrepresentative coverage of the distribution. If we use random numbers to select the set of values then these errors are inevitable unless we employ huge sample sizes.
- *The sequence effect.* This is a bit more subtle and results from the sequence in which the random numbers (and the resulting samples) are produced and combined.

With care, the set effect can be partially controlled, but the sequence effect is more problematic. To illustrate this, consider two sampling processes that are combined within a simulation. Suppose that these are known as X and Y and that both produce integer values; where X is $\{0, 1, 2, \ldots, 9\}$ and Y is $\{0, -1, -2, \ldots, -9\}$. Imagine that we wish to estimate $Z = X.Y$ and that there is some way to ensure that the set effect is eliminated, so that all 10 values for X and Y are included in each 10 samples of each variable. Consider two runs of the simulation and suppose that they produce the results shown in Table 11.1.

Table 11.1 The sequence effect in combining samples

Sample	Run 1			Run 2		
	X	Y	$Z = XY$	X	Y	$Z = XY$
1	2	−9	−18	6	−5	−30
2	1	−6	−6	3	0	0
3	3	−5	−15	0	−4	0
4	0	−3	0	9	−8	−72
5	5	−4	−20	7	−7	−49
6	6	−2	−12	4	−6	−24
7	7	−8	−56	2	−1	−2
8	4	0	0	8	−3	−24
9	9	−7	−63	5	−2	−10
10	8	−1	−8	1	−9	−9
Mean	*4.50*	*−4.50*	*−19.80*	*4.50*	*−4.50*	*−22.00*
SD	*0.96*	*0.96*	*6.97*	*0.96*	*0.96*	*7.44*

In the first case, the estimate of Z is -19.8, and in the second case, the estimate for Z is -22.0. The difference in these estimates for $Z = X \cdot Y$ is purely a result of the short sequences in which the values produced are combined. This effect will occur in all discrete simulations that incorporate random sampling, since all such simulations will have finite sample sizes. It is important to realize that these errors, whether due to the set or sequence effect, are undesirable. In planning a simulation and analysing its output, the stress is on good estimates and on error-free comparison. Neither is possible if there is much sampling error. It so happens that much of the set effect is reasonably straightforward to control; however, the sequence effect is less straightforward. The following variance reduction techniques are attempts to reduce the sampling error.

11.4.3   Common random number streams and synchronization

This approach, sometimes known as streaming, is used when the aim is to compare the effect of different policies on a response variable. In the simplest case, consider a simulation which is used to compare two policies, X and Y, which produce random variates x and y in their output. We wish to estimate $Z = X - Y$.

If the two policies are compared via a set of runs that are statistically independent, then:

$$VAR(Z) = VAR(X) + VAR(Y)$$

However, if we ensure that the sampling is not independent, then:

$$VAR(\hat{Z}) = VAR(X) + VAR(Y) - 2COV(X, Y)$$
$$\text{If } COV(X, Y) \text{ +ve}, VAR(\hat{Z}) < VAR(Z)$$

Thus, if we can induce positive correlation between the runs, then we end up with an estimator with a reduced variance. In essence, this approach gives good control of the set of values (it ensures, as far as is possible that all policies suffer the same bad sampling and then removes this bias by working with the difference). It gives some control over the sequence effect.

To gain the fullest effect from common random numbers, we need random number streams that have a large, complete period and in which a large (preferably unlimited) number of entry points is possible. If a simulation contains k sampling processes and there are n runs for each policy, then we need $k.n$ different random number seeds. For example, consider the harassed booking clerk example in which there are three clerks. In this case, eight seeds are needed, this being one each for the two arrival processes, one for each clerk's personal service and one for each clerk's phone conversation.

If eight such streams were available then this would ensure, as far as it is possible, that the sampling processes were fully synchronized in each run. The idea of synchronization is to ensure that the same random number is used for the same purpose in each policy comparison. In fact, perfect synchronization is rarely, if ever, possible in simulations in which the effect of the different policies is to change the sequence in which events may occur. In many cases, this change of event sequence will lead to the individual random numbers being used for different purposes. Thus, if the idea of the simulation is to try different queue disciplines, the effect of this will be to change the sequence in which customers are served. This in turn will prevent full synchronization.

There is no guarantee that common random numbers will give complete control over the set effect because, in many random sampling algorithms, there is no one-to-one correspondence between random numbers and the samples. This is particularly the case in methods that rely on rejection approaches—which are surprisingly common. Nevertheless, it is hard to conceive of circumstances in which the use of common random numbers would lead to an increase in sampling variation. Thus, they can be generally recommended for those cases in which different policies and configurations are compared.

Although the use of common random numbers seems straightforward, this is not always the case in practice. This is because not all commercial simulation software packages allow the analyst full control over random number generation. Some packages only allow a maximum number of streams per run, some even permitting only a single stream per run of a simulation. Also, even in those cases in which the analyst may employ as many "streams" as needed, it is important to realize that these are rarely proper streams. Instead, the analyst may specify as many seeds as required, with the hope that each will lead to an independent substream (see Figure 11.4).

11.4.4   Control variates (regression sampling)

This is a way of using inside knowledge so as to control the sampling variation. It relies on our knowing at least something of how the simulation should behave, were the sampling to be properly controlled. It may be used to gain a better estimate of a single random variable, whereas common random number streams are used for comparison between policies and configurations.

Consider a single server queue with a known service time distribution. If the observed service time in the simulation is higher than the known mean, then the observed queue lengths should be higher than would otherwise be the case, assuming that other aspects of the model are performing normally. This information can be used to control the undesirable sampling variation by allowing for a "bad" set of samples as shown in Figure 11.7. In this example, the fact that the observed service time is too high is used to drag the queue length distribution back into its "proper" position.

Using a single server queuing system as an example, suppose that Q is the random variable that represents queue length and that it takes values q. Defining the following variables:

μ_Q = true (population) queue length

$\bar{q}$ = observed (sample) queue lengths in the simulation

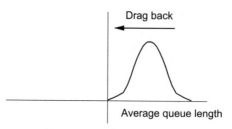

Figure 11.7   Using control variates to "rescue" bad sampling

If the aim of the simulation is to estimate the mean queue length, an obvious way of estimating the mean queue length would be to use:

$$\mu_Q = E(\bar{q})$$

But, instead, the estimator could incorporate the knowledge that we have about the relationship between queue lengths and service times:

$$\hat{q} = \bar{q} - \delta(\bar{s} - \mu_s)$$

where μ_s is the true (population) mean service time, $\bar{s}$ is the observed mean service time in the simulation and δ is the control variate.

Hence, the original estimator of the mean queue length is to be "dragged back" by some multiple of the difference between the actual and the expected service times. This multiplier δ is known as the control variate. The new estimator is unbiased, since:

$$E(\hat{q}) = E(\bar{q}) - \delta . E(\bar{s} - \mu_s)$$
$$= \mu_Q - \delta . (\mu_s - \mu_s)$$
$$= \mu_Q$$

Using the usual variance algebra:

$$VAR(\hat{q}) = VAR(\bar{q} - \delta . \bar{s})$$
$$= VAR(\bar{q}) + \delta^2 . VAR(\bar{s}) - 2\delta . COV(\bar{q}, \bar{s})$$

Rearranging this gives:

$$VAR(\hat{q}) - VAR(\bar{q}) = \delta^2 . VAR(\bar{s}) - 2\delta . COV(\bar{q}, \bar{s})$$

If the variance is to be reduced, then the following condition must hold true:

$$VAR(\hat{q}) - VAR(\bar{q}) < 0$$
$$\Rightarrow \quad \delta . VAR(\bar{s}) < 2 . COV(\bar{q}, \bar{s})$$
$$\Rightarrow \qquad \delta < \frac{2 . COV(\bar{q}, \bar{s})}{VAR(\bar{s})}$$

This means that some value of the control variate δ must be selected so as to guarantee this. The usual suggestion is that such a value may be found via a simplified analytical model or from preliminary simulations. This example has developed a control variate for the mean of a distribution, but a similar idea could be used for the other moments of the distribution and for more than a single distribution in a simulation. Any variance reduction induced by control variates is a result of gaining some control of the set effect by dragging the values in the set closer towards their "true" values.

11.4.5   Antithetic variates

This is often recommended, but there is very limited evidence that it works very well. It is mentioned here for completeness. As with control variates, the approach is used when the aim is to gain a better estimate of a response variable for a single policy, unlike common random numbers, which are used for policy comparison. Suppose that a simulation produces a response variable X and that two runs of the simulation produce estimates X_1 and X_2. An obvious unbiased overall estimator would be to use $Z = (X_1 + X_2)/2$, for which the variance is:

$$VAR\left[\frac{(X_1 + X_2)}{2}\right] = \frac{1}{4}VAR(X_1) + \frac{1}{4}VAR(X_2) + \frac{1}{2}COV(X_1, X_2)$$

However, if some way can be found to make the covariance term ($COV(X_1, X_2)$), whilst leaving the variance terms more or less unchanged, then the variance of Z can be reduced.

The obvious way to do this is to introduce negative correlation between runs 1 and 2. If this finds its way through to the output, then the resulting variance of Z should be reduced. In essence, the idea behind antithetic sampling is to correct for poor sampling. Thus, if a sample turns out to be "too low", then its antithetic should turn out to be "too high" (see Figure 11.8). Taking the arithmetic mean of the two should drag the result back to some "true" value. (The words "too low", "too high" and "true" are in quotes, because when a system is simulated the true values are usually unknown—this is why the operation of the system is being simulated.)

In practice, this method is implemented in a number of ways of which the most popular, suggested by Tocher (1963), is to take each simulation run and repeat it with a complementary, or antithetic, run. The first run might use m random number streams that produce values $\{u_{m,1}, u_{m,2}, \ldots, u_{m,i}\}$ for all m. The second, or antithetic run, might use $\{1 - u_{m,1}, 1 - u_{m,2}, \ldots, 1 - u_{m,i}\}$. This will ensure negative correlation, at least in the input streams. This can be shown to be very effective in simple queuing simulations, but the practical problems with this approach stem from the fact that samples from different distributions are combined and the effect of this can be very hard to discern.

Page (1965) proposed a different antithetic procedure for a simple queuing problem in which he interchanged the random stream for service with the

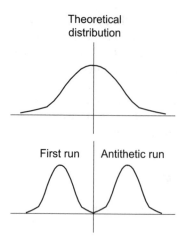

Figure 11.8 Using antithetic sampling to "rescue" bad sampling

one used for arrivals to gain an antithetic run. Saliby (1980) analysed the variance that resulted from simulations of a simple queuing system using both approaches, concluding that Page's interchange of streams led to a greater reduction in output variance.

However, it is as well to be cautious in the use of antithetic sampling since there are circumstances in which the method might actually lead to an increase in output variance rather than to a reduction. The basic problem is the difficulty of ensuring that the deliberately induced negative correlation between the input variables finds its way through to the response variables. This is because most discrete simulations are complicated sampling experiments in which samples are dynamically combined. This results in complex transformations that make it hard to be sure what effect changes on the inputs will have on the outputs—that is why, in most cases, the simulation is being conducted. In essence, there is a loss of synchronization. Whereas common random numbers can always be recommended, the same is not true of antithetic sampling.

11.5   DESCRIPTIVE SAMPLING

11.5.1   Basic idea

Descriptive sampling was proposed by Saliby (1980) and is similar to a selective sampling, suggested by Brenner (1961). It offers almost complete control of the set effect and partial control of the sequence effect. Kleijnen (1974) argues that selective sampling will always lead to biased samples. Saliby demonstrated that this is not true of descriptive sampling. Whereas the usual variance reduction techniques are attempts to staunch the flow of blood from damaged samples, descriptive sampling attempts to prevent these accidents from ever happening. It does so by separating the two functions of sampling into separate operations as follows:

(1) Select values from the distribution so that full and proper coverage of its values is given and this will guarantee that the moments of the sample distribution are correct. Random numbers are not used for this purpose.
(2) Place these values in a sequence and select from them at random, without replacement, using random numbers for this purpose.

Saliby and Pacheco (2002) provide an empirical comparison of the effectives of descriptive sampling with conventional random sampling using two examples.

11.5.2 Procedure

Consider a random variable X, with a known p.d.f. $f(x)$. Saliby's original approach relies on the use of inversion sampling (see Section 10.4.1) to generate samples x, from the distribution of X. The first stage is to determine the size (n) of sample that will be needed in the simulation. This is, of course, problematic, and it is better to err on the side of caution by selecting a sample size that may be slightly too large. This known sample size n is then used to divide the $(0, 1)$ range into n subintervals as follows:

$$U_i = n/2 + (i-1)/n \qquad i = 1, \ldots, n$$

where $\{U_i\}$ are the midpoints of the subintervals.

The second stage is to take a full set of samples from the cumulative distribution, using the U_i values as shown in Figure 11.9. Thus:

$$\{x_i\} = F^{-1}(u_i) \qquad i = 1, \ldots, n$$

Finally, random sampling without replacement is used to generate the random sequence in which the values are used in the simulation.

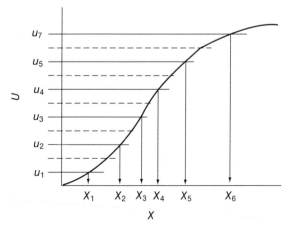

Figure 11.9 Descriptive sampling on the c.d.f.

Table 11.2   Descriptive sampling versus random sampling

Sample number	Random sampling		Descriptive sampling	
	U_i	$x_i = 10 * \ln(U_i)$	U_i	$x_i = 10 * \ln(U_i)$
1	0.53	6.35	0.05	29.96
2	0.81	2.11	0.15	18.97
3	0.29	12.38	0.25	13.86
4	0.13	20.40	0.35	10.50
5	0.39	9.42	0.45	7.99
6	0.35	10.49	0.55	5.98
7	0.01	45.05	0.65	4.31
8	0.30	16.09	0.75	2.88
9	0.71	3.42	0.85	1.63
10	0.34	10.79	0.95	0.51
Mean		*13.75*		*9.66*
SD_{n-1}		*12.60*		*9.17*

As an example, consider a negative exponential distribution with a mean of 10. If inversion sampling is used, then samples of X result from $x_i = -10 * \log_e(u_i)$. Table 11.2 shows two sets of samples, the first from the usual method of random sampling, the second is from a set of 10 descriptive samples. It is clear that the descriptive sample gives a better estimate of the mean and standard deviation, despite its small size.

There are two practical problems when using descriptive sampling. The first is the need to specify the sample size in advance—which may be problematic in some simulations. One practical approach to this is to take the samples in stages. For example, the (0, 1) interval might be divided into 1,000 subintervals. Descriptive samples could then be taken by using the midpoints of the subintervals. If more samples are needed, a different point could be chosen in each subinterval, leading to another 1000 samples and so on. There would, of course, be some waste, but the resulting output variance should be much lower than if random sampling had been employed. The second practical issue is that many distributions cannot be sampled by inversion, and this still remains an issue to be tackled, although Saliby (1990) makes some suggestions.

11.6   EXPERIMENTATION

11.6.1   Basic ideas

Many simulations are carried out so as to compare system configurations or policies for operating the system. The basic idea of this was shown in Figure 11.1. The inputs that are controllable and which are thought to affect the system response are known as factors. These can be quantitative variables (e.g., the number of clerks serving in the theatre booking office). They might also be qualitative (e.g., the priority rule that determines whether personal enquirers are served before phone calls). The aim of the simulation may be to determine how many clerks are needed and what priority rule produces the best result.

Although it is normal to focus on the controllable factors in the simulation, one advantage of a simulation is that some uncontrollable effects can also be simulated. For example, the arrival rate of customers is not directly controlled by the theatre manager. Yet she may wish to find the clerk/priority combination that copes best with a range of arrival rates.

In the simplest possible experiments there are just two things to compare. If this is a single factor that can take two values, then these values are referred to as levels. Hence the simplest case is either one of two factors, both at one level, or one factor at two levels. In either case, the experiment is designed to assess which of the two produces the most favourable response from the model. Various approaches may be used to make this comparison, and care must be taken (as discussed) earlier if classical statistical methods are to be used.

The field of experimental design is one which has occupied statisticians for many years, since the pioneering work of Fisher (1951). There are many texts on this subject (see, e.g., Box and Draper, 1987; Cochran and Cox, 1957). The mathematical statistics involved can seem very daunting, but the basic principles are simple enough. The aim is to ensure that any experiment is conducted in such a way that the comparisons made are fair and that sampling variation is properly accounted for when drawing conclusions from the results of the experiments. Careful design of an experiment takes time, but can save a lot of heartache and should actually save time in the long run. This book can only scratch the surface of the possibilities but for more detail see Kleijnen (1975), who discusses many of the ideas that are valuable in the context of discrete simulation.

It is important, as mentioned at the start of the chapter, to realize that there is an important difference between the experiments conducted by simulation analysts and those carried out by many other people. Much of the theory that underlies experimental design assumes that the experiment is some kind of black box and that the analyst has little or no inkling of what goes on within. Hence, the aim of the experimentation is to untangle the effects of the various factors that may be causing the distinctive behaviour of the system. In simulation experimentation, by contrast, the analyst has the great advantage of knowing what lies within the model. The model is not a black box; rather, it is a creation of the human mind and any inside knowledge may be used to good effect.

11.6.2 Factorial experiments

When an experiment must be designed to consider the combined effects of rather more than two levels or two factors, the common recourse is to a factorial experimental design. Such experiments are usually analysed by the analysis of variance, often shortened to ANOVA. Factorial experiments aim to compare the effects of each level of each factor with each level of each other factor being considered. In this way, the possible effects of the interacting factors and levels may be considered.

Suppose that a simulation experiment involves three factors, each of which may operate at any of three levels. This means that there are $3^3 = 27$ factor–level combinations to consider in the experiment. Because of the stochastic variation inherent in discrete event simulations, each factor–level combination must be replicated several times. Even if each factor–level combination were only to be replicated three times, this would lead to 81 runs of the model. In general, an experiment with n factors each operating at m levels and with k replications will need $n.m.k$ runs if the experiment is to be properly analysed. Hence, such experimentation can clearly be a very time-consuming process. There is, of course, no particular reason why each factor should operate at the same number of levels.

In an experiment in which three factors were being considered, each at two levels, then this would be a 2^3 factorial experiment. If there are n factors at m levels, then this is described as an nm factorial experiment. With three factors X, Y and Z, such an experiment would aim to uncover the following:

- *The main effects.* These are due solely to the factors X, Y and Z as they are individually changed without altering the other factors. Thus, for example, these might include the effect of changing the number of clerks, whilst keeping everything else the same.
- *The interaction effects.* These are due to simultaneous change in one or more of the X, Y and Z factors. If two factors are changed simultaneously, this is known as a second-order effect. It is a third-order effect if all three factors are altered at the same time.

The analysis of variance attempts to examine the results of an experiment so as to unscramble these various effects. This unscrambling is not attempted by a form of magic, but by an attempt to split the total variation of the response variables into independent components. The intention is that each of the components should represent one of the main effects or one of the interaction effects. How these components are identified will depend on the assumptions that underlie the analysis of variance. As with most classical statistical analyses, the idea is to see if the effects that are detected in the components is significantly different from zero. That is, does the analysis support the view that the observed variation is due to the effect of the factors and their levels, or is it just due to chance variation?

Although it is often necessary to resort to the full panoply of the analysis of variance, this is not always the case. Indeed, the best starting point is to find some suitable way to plot and to tabulate the results. It may be that, from these plots and tables, it is very obvious what is going on. Failing this, a proper analysis of variance may well be necessary.

EXERCISES

(1) Use a spreadsheet to investigate the effect of random number streaming, by comparing a sequence of streamed values with unstreamed values.

(2) Investigate the effect of random number streaming on the results from the harassed booking clerk program of Chapter 7.

(3) Use descriptive sampling to take a sample of size 10 from a triangular distribution.

(4) Use a spreadsheet to compare descriptive sampling with random sampling from a triangular distribution.

(5) Using a spreadsheet, generate a long sequence (say 20,000) of serially correlated values. Investigate the batch sizes that would be needed to implement batching in an attempt to gain independent samples.

(6) Find a simulation case study from the literature and critically review the simulation output analysis as it is presented in the case study.

REFERENCES

Alexopoulos C. and Kim S.-H. (2002) Output data analysis for simulations. In: J.M. Charnes, E. Yücesan and C.-H. Chen (eds), *Proceedings of the 2002 Winter Simulation Conference, December 2002, San Diego, CA.*

Barton R.R. (2002) Designing simulation experiments. In: J.M. Charnes, E. Yücesan and C.-H. Chen (eds), *Proceedings of the 2002 Winter Simulation Conference, December 2002, San Diego, CA.*

Box G.E.P. and Draper N.R. (1987) *Empirical Model-building and Response Surfaces.* John Wiley & Sons, New York.

Brenner M.E. (1961) Selective sampling—a technique for reducing sample size in simulations of decision making situations. *Journal of Industrial Engineering,* **14**, 291–6.

Cochran W.G. and Cox G.M. (1957) *Experimental Designs* (2nd edition). John Wiley & Sons, New York.

Conway R.W. (1963) Some tactical problems in digital simulation. *Management Science,* **10**, 47–61.

Fisher R.A. (1951) *The Design of Experiments.* Oliver and Boyd, Edinburgh.

Fishman G.S. (1973) *Concepts and Methods in Discrete Event Digital Simulation.* Wiley-Interscience, New York.

Fishman G.S. (1978) *Principles of Discrete Event Digital Simulation.* Wiley-Interscience, New York.

Kleijnen J.P.C. (1974 and 1975) *Statistical Techniques in Simulation* (2 volumes). Marcel Dekker, New York.

Kleijnen J.P.C. (1987) *Statistical Tools for Simulation Practitioners.* Marcel Dekker, New York.

Kleijnen J.P.C. and van Groenendaal W. (1992) *Simulation: A Statistical Perspective.* John Wiley & Sons, Chichester, UK.

Meketon M.S. and Schmeiser B.W. (1984) Overlapping batch means: Something for nothing? *Proceedings of the 1984 Winter Simulation Conference, IEEE, Piscataway, New Jersey, November 1984, Dallas, TX.*

Nakayama M.K. (2002) Simulation output analysis. In: J.M. Charnes, E. Yücesan and C.-H. Chen (eds), *Proceedings of the 2002 Winter Simulation Conference, December 2002*, San Diego, CA.

Page E.S. (1965) On Monte Carlo methods in congestion problems: II. Simulation of queuing problems. *Operations Research*, **13**, 300–5.

Robinson S. (2002) A statistical process control approach for estimating the warm-up period. In: J.M. Charnes, E. Yücesan and C.-H. Chen (eds), *Proceedings of the 2002 Winter Simulation Conference, December 2002*, San Diego, CA.

Saliby E. (1980) A re-appraisal of some simulation fundamentals. PhD thesis, Lancaster University.

Saliby E. (1990) Understanding the variability of simulation results: An empirical study. *Journal of Operational Research Society*, **41**(4), 319–27.

Saliby E. and Pacheco F. (2002) An empirical evaluation of sampling methods in risk analysis simulation: Quasi-Monte Carlo, descriptive sampling, and Latin hypercube sampling. In: J.M. Charnes, E. Yücesan and C.-H. Chen (eds), *Proceedings of the 2002 Winter Simulation Conference, December 2002*, San Diego, CA.

Schmeiser B.W. (1982) Batch size effects in the analysis of simulation output. *Operations Research*, **30**, 556–68.

Tocher K.D. (1963) *The Art of Simulation*. English Universities Press, London.

Welch P.D. (1981) On the problem of the initial transient in steady state simulations. Technical Report, IBM Watson Research Center, Yorktown Heights, NY.

Welch P.D. (1983) The statistical analysis of simulation results. In: S. Lavenberg (ed.), *The Computer Performance Modelling Handbook* (pp. 268–328). Academic Press, New York.

12

Model Testing and Validation

12.1 THE IMPORTANCE OF VALIDATION

In some sense or other, management scientists strive to be scientific in their work, although what this can mean will vary somewhat between individuals and may depend on the work they are doing. One important aspect of this scientific ideal is the notion that models should be thoroughly tested or validated before use. The idea is that the management scientist should ensure that the model is wholly adequate and appropriate for the task for which it is intended. Simple though this notion of validation may sound, in practice it can be very difficult to validate a simulation model properly. As it happens, the same is true of other types of model used by management scientists and a review of these more general issues can be found in Pidd (2003).

This chapter considers the problems of validating the types of simulation model commonly used in management science. It shows why this is sometimes difficult and suggests approaches to validation that are practically useful and which are also based on a sound theoretical framework. It focuses on the issues that arise when simulations are performed as part of management science projects, rather than on those that arise in very large-scale simulation projects such as those found in the defence sector. Given the importance of simulation modelling in defence and, also, given the scale of some defence simulations, the question of model credibility and validity looms large in this domain. Thus the USA's Defense Modeling and Simulation Office has put considerable effort into this topic and its website (`https://www.dmso.mil/public/transition/vva`) maintains a set of relevant references and offers useful advice. For thorough discussions of the issues that arise in the large-scale defence simulations, see Balci (1994), Miser and Quade (1988) or Sargent (1982).

12.1.1 Validation is impossible, but desirable

A naive approach to validation would be something like the following:

A model is a representation of the real world, or of at least part of it. Therefore, the validation of the model is really quite straightforward—in principle. All we have to do is check that the model behaves as the real world does under the same conditions. If it does, then the model is valid. If it doesn't, then it isn't.

Though this view is appealing in its simplicity, there are reasons why it is described as naive.

Underlying the naive approach is what might be termed another "declaration of independence": an implicit view that the problems on which management scientists work are independent of the observer or of other people. They are somewhere "out there". But is this true, is the management scientist clearly separate from the context of the problem? Writing about modelling in management science, Pidd (2003) argues that problems are social and psychological constructs that need to be negotiated between the management scientist and the client or user. That is, the simplification that is part of any systems model, and which gives the model its power, means that the model is not independent of the modeller or modelling team. Instead, it reflects the views of an individual or group about what should be included within the model.

This does not mean that such inclusion is random or casual: great efforts may have been made to uncover the significant factors in the system to be simulated. However, it does lead us to a sombre conclusion: validation, if taken to mean a comprehensive demonstration that a model is fully correct, is impossible. What, then, is possible, and is this better than nothing? It would perhaps be best to answer the second question first. Validation is best regarded as an ideal towards which we must strive if we are to be at all faithful to the idea that management science aims to support action in the real world. It actually matters whether our models are wrong, as this may cause people to embark on action that has very negative consequences. Hence, management scientists have a responsibility to aim at some form of validation, but should begin by recognizing that this may be limited. Among many scientists it is recognized that theories and knowledge can never be comprehensively demonstrated to be true, and yet these same theories turn out to be very useful. They also have an impact on the world outside the scientific community, especially if they resonate with wider social concerns and needs.

12.1.2 Some practical issues

Why is validation of a simulation model so important? There are two fundamental reasons. First, from a practical standpoint, the simulation model is usually being developed with a view to taking some action in a human activity system. Sometimes the model is of a system that already exists but some new insight into its operation is required. For example, manufacturing facilities are increasingly automated and may run at high speed but with little in the way of in-process stocks. It is not unusual for such systems to perform somewhat below the efficiency specified at the design stage. Simulations are often used to understand why this should be so.

On other occasions, the target system exists but the aim of the simulation is to demonstrate that some new mode of operation would be preferable. To take the automated plant example again, having understood why the plant is not performing well, the next stage is to find some way of operating it so as to bring its performances up to the specification. That is, the model can be used for experimentation. This is somewhat more difficult from a validation point of view, because the suggestion may be that the plant is operated in wholly novel ways. There is thus no existing "real" system with which to compare the results of the simulation experiments.

A third case occurs when the model is of a system which does not yet exist but where possible new designs are being considered. To continue with the automated plant example, the designer usually has several possible plant configurations to consider and must select the one which best meets whatever performance and cost criteria have been agreed. An obvious way to do this is to try to simulate the options and then to compare the results of the various simulations. As with the second case above, the validation problem occurs because there is no "real" system with which to compare the model.

As well as these practical considerations, there is an important theoretical point to be weighed. The simulation model is, in some sense, a set of beliefs and assumptions about how a system should behave or is intended to behave. The model incorporates rules that are believed to govern the behaviour of the elements and objects of the system. If learning and progress are to occur, then it is important that these beliefs and assumptions be tested in some way or other. Organizations whose beliefs and assumptions are closest to "reality" are likely to be in a good position to achieve their goals.

12.1.3   The "real" world, the model and observation

Though this is not intended to be a philosophy text, it is important to consider what is meant when we think of comparing a model with what is so often called the "real" world. Only by understanding this concept of the "real" world can the difficulty of validation be appreciated.

The easiest concept of all is the model: after all, this is the creation of the modeller or analyst and is intended to be a representation of some system or other. The model may be entirely external and concrete, say as a scale model of a building. On the other hand, it may exist solely within the mind of the modeller as a set of ill-defined concepts and beliefs and may thus be termed a mental model. Between these two extremes of implicit mental models and explicit concrete models are various other possibilities, including the models usually associated with computer simulation in management science. The main characteristic of such models is that they are the creations of an individual or a group of people. To be cruel, there is therefore, no excuse for the modeller not understanding the model which he/she has created.

What then of the "real" world? To avoid too many problems, this discussion assumes that some form of reality exists external to an observer. It assumes too that it is possible for two or more independent observers to experience that external reality, even though their descriptions of that same reality may differ. That is, for present purposes it will be assumed that the external reality and the observations of it can exist quite separately. This is an important point, for what is often meant by the "real" world is some set of observations made by one or more people. If the notion of validation implies a comparison between a model and the "real" world, this usually implies a comparison between two sets of observations. One set comes from the model, which should be intimately known by its creator, and the other set comes to the observer from the "real" world. The notion of validity rests very heavily on these observations.

12.1.4   The hypothetico-deductive approach

Popper (1959) argues that scientific methodology is best seen as theory-driven rather than being driven by independent observation. Hence, scientific observation is always biased (not necessarily in a sinister way) by pre-existing theory and is not wholly disinterested. Thus, the role of scientific experimentation is the provision of observations that are relevant to particular hypotheses and theories. After all, the experiments are devised to test the theories in some way or other. Popper's main argument is that scientific work depends on the generation of hypotheses from which deductions can be made. These deductions can be tested by properly designed experiments that aim to show whether or not the deductions, and therefore the hypotheses, are correct. More precisely, the experiments may produce observations which support the hypotheses or which refute it.

In another work, Popper (1965) takes this idea slightly further by arguing that conjectures, hypotheses and theories can never by proved in an absolute sense but can only be refuted. That is, all knowledge is in some sense conjectural. A common way of explaining this is to think of the following conjecture:

All swans are white.

Testing this conjecture is simple enough and involves straightforward observation of all swans—if that were possible. In practice, the experimenter would have to settle for a finite sample of swans and see whether their colour supported the hypothesis. But this creates a problem. Even if all the swans in the sample were white, this does not rule out the possibility that somewhere else there might be a black, blue, green, red or yellow swan. Visitors to New Zealand quickly discover that black swans are very common. Thus, the experiment could never demonstrate that the conjecture is wholly true. The most decisive experimental result of all is one which refutes the conjecture and which leads on to other conjectures.

In Popper's view, therefore, a scientific theory is a conjecture about the "real" world which may be tested by some form of experimentation. The experimentation may support the theory or may, decisively, refute the theory by demonstrating that it is false. What are popularly referred to as scientific "laws" are no more than theories which have not been refuted—usually within very specific assumptions (e.g., Newton's laws of motion). That is, they are found to be valid for certain specific purposes.

12.1.5 The importance of process and other aspects

Balci (1994) points out that computer simulation studies are cyclic, in that models are refined gradually so that simple models become more complex as time progresses. This fits well with the principle of parsimony espoused in Chapter 5. In a proper sense, therefore, assessment and validation are activities which should continue throughout a simulation project. The same should be true of any quantitative modelling in management science that follows the principle of parsimony. Therefore, it would be wrong to focus all the assessment and validation effort at the end of a modelling project. Instead it should be a fully-fledged part of all stages of the modelling work, part indeed of a critical approach. Balci (1994) suggests tests and assessments that can be made at each point of the simulation modelling cycle. He suggests that many of these could be built into simulation support environments.

Also writing about computer simulation, Robinson (1996) points out that, "Three terms are often used in the context of simulation models and simulation study assessment: validity, credibility and acceptability." He quotes Schruben (1980) as arguing that, "credibility is reflected in the willingness of persons to base decisions on the information obtained from the model." This is clearly as much a feature of the trust that the model user or client places in the analyst or group building the model as it is in the credibility of the model itself. Acceptability is usually a reference to the entire study, which includes the model and is also clearly a reflection of the relationship between the modeller(s) and the user or client.

12.2 VALIDATION AND COMPARISON

With what can a simulation model be compared for validation? Ideally, it would be compared directly with the system that it will simulate—but, as shown above, this is not always straightforward. This is because the comparison is between two sets of observations, one of the model and one of the "real" system. Thus, at best, the modeller can be satisfied that the observations of the model display identical characteristics to the observations from the "real" system. More likely, the two sets are not identical but are similar enough for the purpose in hand. However, it is always possible that some other observations could be made of both systems (model and "real") in which there is massive disagreement between the two. Thus, in Popperian terms, a valid model is one that is unrefuted within some specific assumptions.

This means that simulation models cannot be shown to be true or valid in any absolute sense. There always remains the possibility of making observations of the model or the "real" system which are in conflict. What can be said is that a model is valid for some particular purpose (i.e., under certain specific assumptions). Validation, then, is to be seen against the intended use of the model and not in an absolute sense.

12.2.1   Experimental frames

Chapter 3 briefly introduced the idea of experimental frames as suggested by Zeigler (1976). This idea is defined by Zeigler (1984) in terms of set theory, but the basic idea is quite simple. This is that, when considering the question of the validity of a model, this can only be done against the backdrop of this experimental frame, which defines the use to which the model will be put. The same term is used by the developers of the simulation language SIMAN (see Chapter 9), although the meaning is rather different in that context.

Zeigler (1976) is careful to distinguish between the following, which are shown in Figure 12.1.

- *The real system.* Zeigler defines this as the source of observable data. Even if we do not understand the real system, we can still observe its behaviour. The observable data consist of a set of input/output relations, which may not be simple.
- *An experimental frame.* This is defined as the limited set of circumstances under which the real system is to be observed or experimented with.
- *The base model.* This is defined as some hypothetical model which would account for all of the input/output behaviour of the real system. This may not exist in any tangible form and must be imagined if there is no real system in existence—such as when a new system is being developed from scratch.
- *A lumped model.* This is defined as an explicit and simplified version of the base model and is the one which will be used in management science.
- *A computer program.* In which the lumped model is implemented and which is intended to generate the input/output relations of the lumped model.

Thus, the idea is that, when faced with the need to develop a model of some complex system, we begin with a base model, which we have in mind as we try to build the lumped (or conceptual) model, which may then be implemented in a computer program. The intention is that the models should be used in relation to the purposes defined by the experimental frame.

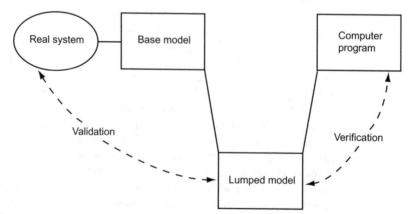

Figure 12.1   Zeigler on modelling

Zeigler (1984) develops a notation system, based on set theory, which allows the convenient expression of some useful ideas. In this chapter we will just use one of these ideas, that of an input/output relation. This embodies the idea of a reference system (Zeigler's real system) as a form of black box that can be observed and from which we can relate inputs to outputs. This is known as the input/output relation of the real system. Zeigler points out that we wish to know the true input/output relation of this system but that in fact we can only observe it at some point of time t (of which there may be many). Ideally, the input/output relation of the model should be the same as that of the computer program and the same as that of the real system.

12.2.2   Program verification and model validation

In Zeigler's terms, verification is a process by which we try to assure ourselves that the lumped model is properly realized in the computer program. In one sense this is straightforward, since the lumped model is, by definition, fully specified and the computer program exists in a tangible form. Validation is a process whereby we assess the degree to which the lumped model input/output relations map onto those of the real system. This implies the existence of the experimental frame. At its simplest, therefore, Zeigler sees validation and verification as black box in approach—see Section 12.3.

This distinction between program verification and model validation is very important in the development of large-scale simulation models that are implemented via proper computer programming and which may be used repeatedly over a long time period. In these terms, verification focuses on the computer program(s) that are supposed to embody the lumped or conceptual model. This implies that the lumped model needs to be unambiguously stated if verification is to be properly done. Hence, for these large-scale exercises, model documentation that is separate from program documentation is absolutely crucial. Verification itself proceeds by a series of formal tests on the simulation program and its components to see if it properly embodies the lumped model.

The first such tests focus on the program code itself and are based on "walk-throughs" in which the program code is examined line by line, preferably by third parties. The use of programming languages that are expressive (see Chapter 9) is a great help in this regard. The second set of tests take program modules and subject them to defined inputs to see if the output is as expected. The third group take the entire simulation program and also check its input/output relations.

As frequently pointed out in this book, many management science simulations make use of Visual Interactive Modelling Systems (VIMS) and there is no separate program code as such. In addition, the conceptual model may not exist separately from its VIMS realization. This is because the model and its realization may have been developed in a stepwise manner through time. In such cases, the distinction between verification and validation is artificial and can be abandoned.

12.3 BLACK BOX VALIDATION

As was introduced in Section 3.4.3, it is useful to consider two approaches to the validation of simulation models. As with all such simple typologies, there is bound to be some overlap between the two, but there are also important differences between black box validation and white box validation.

12.3.1 Black box validation: a model's predictive power

As the name suggests, the basic assumption here is that both the model and the "real" system are black boxes. That is, that the inner workings of both are unknown but that it is possible to observe their results. Thus, the intention is to analyse the function of both so as to decide whether their functioning is sufficiently similar. Notice that this basic assumption of black box validation is quite false, for the modeller actually has little or no excuse for not understanding the detailed working of the model. Despite this, there is still something to be gained from this approach.

The practical strategy of black box validation is simple enough. The behaviour of the "real" system is observed under specified conditions and the model is then run under conditions which are as close as possible to these. If the model is valid in a black box sense, then the observations of the model should be indistinguishable from those of the "real" system.

12.3.2 How valid?

If the two sets of observations are to be compared, then some comparison methodology must exist so as to inform that comparison. Most commonly, the comparison is performed using the methods of statistical inference—details of which can be found in most texts on statistics (see, e.g., Wonnacott and Wonnacott, 1982). The notion here is that the observations may be used to test some specific hypothesis, the credibility of the test being expressed as a probability value. For example, the modeller may wish to know whether there is a statistically significant chance of a difference between the mean values of some observations of the model and of others from the "real" system. This chance is usually expressed as an acceptable probability of error, the idea being that there is a less than $x\%$ chance that the hypothesis is wrongly accepted or rejected.

It should be noted here that the same caveats about classical statistics mentioned in Section 11.1.3 also apply here. That is, if the observations of the model or of the "real" system form a series in which each value is in some way dependent on one or more previous observations (i.e., there is autocorrelation in the series), then the methods of classical hypothesis testing must be used with great care. Most classical hypothesis tests assume that the observations are independent (uncorrelated) and care must be taken to ensure that this is the case. Chapter 11 gives more details.

12.3.3   Validation errors

Statisticians usually distinguish between two types of possible error in hypothesis testing. These are known as Type I and Type II errors and can be applied to black box model validation as follows:

- *Type I errors*. In classical hypothesis testing, these occur when a correct hypothesis is wrongly rejected. In modelling, a Type I error occurs when a valid model is wrongly rejected. Why should this happen? It occurs because of the nature of statistical inference in which there is a finite probability that an error may occur. That is, the tests are designed to achieve a certain percentage reliability. Most users of such tests unthinkingly plump for significance values of 95% or 99%. That is, they allow a 5% or 1% chance that an error may occur. In general, the smaller the acceptable chance of error then the larger must be the samples to test the hypothesis.
- *Type II errors*. These occur when a hypothesis which is actually false is accepted as true by the user of a hypothesis test. Thus, in simulation modelling, such an error occurs when an invalid model is taken to be valid. As with Type I errors, errors of Type II are inevitable from time to time—how often depends on the confidence levels set for the test.

As well as these two error types, it is as well to accept that a much more severe type of error is possible both in hypothesis testing and in model validation. This is usually known as a Type Zero error. Type Zero errors occur when the modeller/tester simply asks the wrong questions altogether. The result is a model which does totally the wrong thing, possibly in a highly sophisticated and rapid manner. This is probably the most important mistake to avoid in any validation of a simulation model. Expressing it in other terms, it happens when the model is found to be utterly and wholly valid on statistical grounds but turns out to be useless in practice because it addresses the wrong issues. Less severely, a model may include unnecessary detail which leads, due to a shortage of time, to a loss of important detail elsewhere in the model.

12.3.4   Testing model components

A black box approach can be applied to the parts of a model as well as to the whole creation. If the model represents a system that does not yet exist, then such partial validation is one of the few options open to the would-be validation. In most such simulations, various subsystems of the proposed "real" system do already exist and their performance can be compared with their simulated counterparts. The problem is that there is no guarantee that the whole model is valid just because most of the parts have been tested.

12.4   WHITE BOX VALIDATION

12.4.1   Detailed internal structure

In some ways "white box" is an unfortunate name, for the assumption is that the model and "real" system are transparent rather than white. That is, the assumption is that the internal structures of both are well understood. Clearly, this should be the case for the simulation model, so long as the modeller is in tune with his/her own creation. For the "real" system, this can never be wholly true but can be true enough for useful comparison to occur. White box validation most usefully takes place while the model is being constructed rather than after the event, and is usually applied to the model components in turn. As far as possible, it is also applied to the interaction of the model components.

Whereas the stress in black box validation is on the predictive power of the model as captured in hypothesis tests, the emphasis in white box validation is on the detailed internal workings of the model. In particular, such validation will need to focus on the following aspects at least.

12.4.2   Input distributions

In a discrete event simulation much of the model behaviour depends on the statistical distributions which are chosen to model the objects of the system. The distributions are used to model uncertain or indeterminate behaviour—such as the varying intervals between successive arrivals at a queuing system. They are appropriate when the process that produces this behaviour cannot be understood in any deterministic sense. Most commonly they are used to represent the varying time taken to complete some activity within the simulation.

Selecting the appropriate distribution is sometimes rather difficult and two guidelines may be followed. The first is rather obvious, and that is to select a distribution which behaves in the same way as the object being modelled. Usually, this behaviour of the "real" object is understood from a statistical analysis of a sample of observations. Thus, the analyst may calculate the mean, variance and higher moments of the distribution. The idea is to specify some distribution for the model with the same values for the mean, variance and other moments. The usual way to do this is to compare a theoretical distribution with the sample data using a goodness-of-fit test, as described in most statistics textbooks. Ideally, the distribution will be a perfect fit to the data sample. This sounds simple enough, but in practice it is almost unknown for any distribution to be a perfect fit over the sampled data. This is not because of incompetent sampling, but is expected from the theory of sampling. The result is that there may be several candidate distributions for the part of the model under scrutiny. None will fit perfectly and several may have their own distinct advantages. Which should be chosen?

To avoid this difficulty, the modeller should follow the second guideline. This is to bear in mind the assumptions which underlie the behaviour of the object in the "real" system and the assumptions of the distribution. Ideally these should be well suited to one another in at least the following ways:

(1) *Discrete or continuous variables.* Some distributions (e.g., the negative exponential and normal distributions) are continuous (i.e., the variable may take any of the infinite set of values in the specified range). Others (e.g., the binomial and Poisson distributions) are discrete (i.e., the variable may only take integer values within the specified range). It should therefore be obvious that the selected distribution should be continuous or discrete, depending on the variable being modelled.

(2) *Infinite or finite range.* Some distributions (e.g., the normal distribution) actually assume that the variable is distributed from negative infinity to positive infinity. Others (e.g., the negative exponential) assume that the value may range from zero to positive infinity. A third group, such as the uniform distribution, may be specified over a finite range. The modeller must ensure that the distribution selected has a range appropriate to the values taken by the variable.

(3) *The process producing the values.* All analytical distributions have underlying assumptions which specify how the distributed values arise. For example, the Poisson, negative exponential and Gamma distributions assume there is an underlying Poisson process. Put simply, if a source of entirely random occurrences is imagined, then it is a Poisson process if:
- The number of occurrences in any non-overlapping time intervals is entirely independent.
- The distribution of the number of occurrences in any interval depends only on the length of that interval.
- In any very small time interval there is a negligible chance of more than one occurrence.

For a more mathematical statement of these assumptions see any mathematical statistics text, such as Meyer (1970). Other distributions have their own assumptions, which need to be understood. Thus, it is important for simulation modellers to have a good grounding in statistics in order to appreciate the limitations of any of the distributions which they might select for a particular model.

12.4.3 Static logic

Most simulations include some static logic, which governs the behaviour of the objects of the system. In a discrete simulation these are rules of the type:

```
If <conditions> then <actions>
```

For example, a rule might specify that a machine cannot be started unless its tools are set, the operative is available, a job is waiting for completion and the material supply exists. These rules are intended to mimic those that govern the objects of the "real" system. In a continuous simulation they are more likely to be rules which govern the behaviour of the system in extreme conditions, such as when a variable reaches a critical value. Rules of this latter type are obviously also present in discrete simulations. If this static logic is wrong then the model cannot correctly mimic the behaviour of the "real" system and thus it is of some importance to subject them to detailed scrutiny. It is better that this is done before the model is fully programmed, although sometimes such logic errors only become obvious when a programmed model is in use.

The key to checking for such errors is to use the knowledge of all the people involved in the study and not just that of the modeller. Most commonly, the client of the study and the users of the results will know more about the system than the modeller. It is therefore crucial to tap into this knowledge in some way or other. The problem is the technical jargon that surrounds most computing studies. There are two approaches to this problem and ideally they will be used together. It is crucial to have some form of conceptual model to express the static logic in non-technical ways. Hence, before the computer model is built the modeller could use natural language descriptions of the logic or could rely on simple flow diagrams such as activity cycle diagrams (see Chapter 5). The idea is to allow the clients and users to participate in the validation and to use their knowledge. If possible, the users could participate in the construction of such diagrams or verbal descriptions during a joint session.

12.4.4   Dynamic logic

If a simulation were simply concerned with the static logic of the objects of the system then it would be quite unnecessary. Why simulate what is already fully understood? A simulation is used to mimic the dynamic behaviour of a system and not just of its individual components. Thus it is important to be able to validate the dynamic performance of the model as it runs—or, at the very least, during a run.

Perhaps the best way of doing this is to make sure that animated displays are an integral part of the simulation program. Thus, important variables and the system state can be monitored as the program runs and this can make it relatively easy to spot errors in the dynamic logic of the model. As with the static logic, it is sensible to make use of the knowledge of the clients and possible users of the simulated system by making the dynamic display as easy to understand as possible. Before the availability of cheap graphical systems and interactive operating systems, this was a tedious task which involved sifting through piles of printout. Fortunately, this is rarely necessary nowadays.

The key then, is the dynamic display of crucial features of the system state as the program runs on the computer. If the system state is represented by carefully chosen icons, tables and graphs it is easily possible to monitor the progress of the system as the model runs. It is also possible to interact directly with the running program; then it may be possible to force the simulation into extreme conditions as a further test of its validity. If the simulation model is built in a VIMS as discussed in Chapter 8, then this is no problem. The same is true if a graphical systems dynamics package such as Stella, Powersim or Vensim (see Chapter 14) is used, since these two are VIMS. Even better, a well-designed VIMS allows rapid modification to a model, which is very useful in model development and testing. It is usually more difficult to use graphics in a conventional simulation language, since detailed programming may be necessary. Nevertheless, the extra effort can be well worthwhile.

12.5   TYPE ZERO ERRORS

Section 12.3.3 introduced the concept of Type Zero, Type I and Type II errors, the latter pair being well known to statisticians. Type Zero errors arise from an inadequate attempt at problem structuring and are as liable to occur in simulation modelling as in any other management science activity. Throughout this book runs an assumption that simulation models evolve over time and are extremely unlikely to be correct on a first attempt. Hence, earlier chapters lay great stress on modelling and programming practices which lead to modular programs which are relatively easy to modify. Accepting that the first attempts to build a particular model are likely to end in, at best, partial success is the starting point for avoiding serious Type Zero errors.

12.5.1   Over-elaboration

One common mistake in simulation modelling is to make the model too elaborate in an attempt to capture as much realism as possible. This occurs because a simulation approach offers a relatively low level of abstraction, compared say, to mathematical models. Thus, it is possible to develop very detailed simulation models which mimic very closely the fine interaction of the objects of the "real" system. This is not always a good thing.

For example, consider a simulation of an arrivals terminal of an international airport. As passengers disembark from the aircraft, they must pass through customs, immigration and (sometimes) an agricultural checkpoint. Meanwhile, their baggage should be unloaded from the aircraft hold and routed to the correct carousel for the passengers to collect. When designing a new arrival area, one consideration is that passengers should not be subject to unnecessary delay. As in a factory, the key to this is the sizing and speed of operation of the sequence of processes through which the passengers pass. An important feature of this is the size of baggage carousels—thus, baggage-handling systems have been the subject of several simulation studies. It is very tempting, partly because this is encouraged by some of the commercial simulation software, to try to track each individual item of baggage and each passenger through the system. In most cases, this is quite unnecessary as all that matters is whether congestion occurs at certain points within the system and not whether particular (simulated) bags or customers are involved. This avoids having to build an elaborate and slow-running simulation model which addresses the wrong issues.

12.5.2 Over-simplification

On the other hand, it is all too easy to over-simplify and the result may be a model with insufficient detail to handle the full complexity of the simulated system. In the case of a handling system for specialized cargo, it may be crucially important to know how long it takes to process particular types of object. In such cases, it may be necessary to track the individual lives of each item as objects of the simulation model.

12.5.3 Steering a sensible course

There are two keys to avoiding over-simplification and over-elaboration. The first is to ascertain, as soon as possible, the intended use of the model. If detailed results are needed then a detailed model may be required—at a cost. The second is to adopt an explicit and evolutionary approach to model and program development. If the model starts simply, it can probably be elaborated gradually as the need arises. It is better to get a skeleton, but simple, model working than to have an over-elaborate disaster that no one understands.

REFERENCES

Balci O. (1994) Validation, verification and testing techniques throughout the life cycle of a simulation study. In: O. Balci (ed.), *Annals of Operations Research, Vol. 23: Simulation and Modeling*. J. C. Balzer, Basel, Switzerland.

Meyer P.L. (1970) *Introductory Probability and Statistical Applications* (2nd edition). Addison-Wesley, Reading, MA.

Miser H.J. and Quade E.S. (1988) Validation. In: H.J. Miser and E.S. Quade (eds), *Handbook of Systems Analysis: Craft Issues and Procedural Choices*. John Wiley & Sons, Chichester, UK.

Pidd M. (2003) *Tools for Thinking: Modelling in Management Science* (2nd edition). John Wiley & Sons, Chichester, UK.

Popper K.R. (1959) *The Logic of Scientific Discoveries*. Hutchinson, London.

Popper K.R. (1965) *Conjectures and Refutations*. Routledge, London.

Robinson S.W. (1996) Service quality management in the process of delivering a simulation study. *Proceedings of the 14th Triennial Conference of the International Federation of OR Societies, July 8–12, Vancouver, BC*.

Sargent R.G. (1982) Verification and validation of simulation models. In: F.E. Cellier (ed.), *Progress in Modelling and Simulation*. Academic Press, London.

Schruben L.W. (1980) Establishing the credibility of simulations. *Simulation*, **34**(3), 101–5.

Wonnacott J.R. and Wonnacott R.H. (1982) *STATISTICS: Discovering Its Power*. John Wiley & Sons, New York.

Zeigler B.P. (1976) *Theory of Modelling and Simulation*. John Wiley & Sons, New York.

Zeigler B.P. (1984) *Multi-faceted Modelling and Discrete Event Simulation*. Academic Press, New York.

Part III

System Dynamics

Structure, Behaviour, Events and Feedback Systems

13.1 EVENTS, BEHAVIOURS AND STRUCTURES

13.1.1 System simulation

In management science, a simulation model is usually built to support an investigation of the dynamic behaviour of a human system. In abstract terms, a system is a set of related elements within some defined boundary. Designed systems that involve human beings exist for some purpose (e.g., to provide health care or to produce goods). Most writers agree that system definition is, in part at least, arbitrary and depends on the stance of the person making the definition. Others go further and question whether systems really exist or are just convenient fictions; an issue discussed in Checkland and Holwell (2004). The interaction of the system's elements with one another and with the system's environment leads to the characteristic behaviour of the system. Since this behaviour is distinct from that of the systems components and emerges from the system as a whole, this is sometimes known as emergent behaviour.

Discrete event simulations, covered in Part II, focus on the detailed rules that govern the interactions of the system entities through time. Discrete event simulation software provides ways to model those rules and interactions and to check that they occur as intended within the model. Hence, most discrete event simulations are microscopic in their focus and involve considerable detail. They may include appropriate probability distributions if the system behaviour is stochastic.

It is, though, possible and often useful to model system behaviour at the rather more macroscopic level. This is the usual focus of the system dynamics approach, which occupies Part III. System dynamics is less concerned with detail than discrete event simulation and focuses, instead, on the ways in which system structures affect system behaviour. Since a systems perspective underpins system dynamics, this has led some system dynamicists to claim the name "systems thinking" for their approach. One example is the popular book *The Fifth Discipline* (Senge, 1992), which shows how the ideas of system dynamics can be used to support organizational learning. As Jackson (2003, chapter 5) points out, such a high ground claim to "systems thinking" is unwise, since there are other communities that engage in systems thinking who do not use a system dynamics approach.

13.1.2　The importance of system structure

Understanding how system structures lead to system behaviour and to system events is fundamental to contemporary system dynamics. But what does this distinction mean? An example may help: someone may notice that the sales of a product have increased. This leads them, and others, to try to understand why that happened—that is, to construct a causal argument that links the observed increase in sales with some other event(s). It is, though, a mistake to think only in terms of individual events and a sequence of events through time since the fluctuating pattern of sales is what is meant by system behaviour). Thus, events have a short, possibly immediate, timescale whereas system behaviour represents the observed fluctuations over a longer time period.

The question then is, what causes this behaviour? A fundamental assumption in system dynamics is that behaviour is a result of structures—both inside the system and in its environment. However, these are not structures as might often be understood—such as the number of staff employed or the layout of a factory. Instead, they are the underlying, general structures that can be observed across many types of system. At their most basic, these are the feedback loops and delays that are present in most organizational systems.

If it is true that the behaviour of a business process is a function of its characteristic system structures then this suggests that any redesign of such a process needs to concentrate on re-thinking those structures. Even when the most able people are employed in a poorly designed business process, they are unlikely to be high performers. The presence of delays in transmitting information and in moving goods and services around may mean that the root cause of observed events is some distance away in space and time. That is, analysis of symptoms may not lead to the true causes unless there is deep understanding of the operation of systems structures. The structure of business processes causes (much of) their behaviour.

In order to model feedback systems it is important to concentrate on their structure rather than their content. The structure defines how the variables interact but the content is the meaning of those variables for the organization. Two systems may have similar structures but quite different content. For example, a supermarket and the control room of a fire station may both be analysed in terms of their queuing structure. Both systems have customers who are served, but the meaning (and importance) of the customers differ. In the fire station the customers are calls awaiting response, whereas in the supermarket the customers are the shoppers. Coyle (1977) points out that the management scientist has to maintain two views of a system at the same time. To model it, the system must be seen in terms of its structure, but to consider making changes it is crucial to keep in mind the meaning of the variables. Only then will it be clear which changes are feasible.

13.2   FEEDBACK SYSTEMS

13.2.1   Hierarchical feedback systems: an example

Consider a company that produces spares and replacement parts for the motor trade. Suppose that it does not produce original equipment and is dependent on wholesalers and retailers to reach its customers. Suppose, therefore, that it has two groups of final consumers of its products:

(1)   Garages who fit the parts to their customers' vehicles.
(2)   DIY motorists who fit the parts themselves.

The company has no direct contact with either of these groups of consumers.

To make its products, the company buys in raw materials and processes them. Thus, it creates two distinct sets of stocks within its own boundary: raw materials and finished goods. These stocks must be financed and will be subject to some control. The finished goods are sold to motor factors who themselves hold stocks as wholesalers. The motor factors buy in large lots from the manufacturer and sell in smaller batches to the retailers or the garage trade. The DIY motorists buy in units from the retailers. This produces the overall hierarchical system shown in Figure 13.1.

A DIY motorist enters a retail outlet to buy parts, and as individual sales occur the retailer's stocks are reduced. In time, possibly as a result of a call from a salesman, the retailer places an order with the motor factor. As several such orders are met, the motor factor's stocks are also run down. At some stage the motor manufacturer receives an order from the factor, which in turn will deplete the finished stocks of the manufacturer. Eventually, the effect is felt on the raw material stocks and so an order is placed on the raw material supplier. Most likely, the parts manufacturer operates a production plan that calls for production of particular parts in batches at regular time intervals. Hence, though variations in demand may appear smooth at the

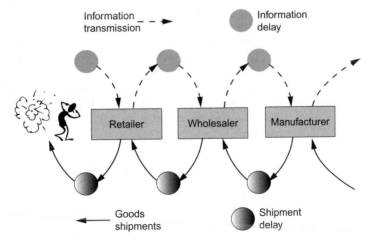

Figure 13.1   A motor parts distribution system

retailers, the result could be a very lumpy production schedule at the manufacturer.

Several things are apparent in moving up this chain of supply from the DIY motorist to the manufacturer. First, the batch sizes of stock replenishments increase—meaning that mistakes are more costly higher up the chain. Second, the purchasing decisions move further and further away from the consumers' behaviour. Hence, both the cost and the risk of wrong action increase higher up the chain. A third feature is the presence of delays in the system. For example, the manufacturer does not respond to individual orders from factors by attempting to maintain a constant finished stock level. Rather, batches are made and added to the stocks at intervals. Similarly, the retailer may place weekly or monthly orders with the wholesaler.

The presence of these delays, feedback and batching can produce interesting, not to say, strange behaviour that is hard to manage. Suppose, for example, that DIY motorists suddenly reduce their demand for parts for some reason or other. What happens?

(1) The depletion of the retailers' stocks slows down. This occurs immediately.
(2) Rather later, the factors' stocks are also higher than normal. If parts ordered from the manufacturer a month earlier begin to arrive in stock, then this makes things even worse. Eventually, the factors reduce their orders to the manufacturer. If things get too bad, they may stop ordering for some time.
(3) Meanwhile, in the absence of market intelligence, the manufacturer may be blissfully unaware of all this. While the downturn in DIY demand is happening, the regular production plan of the manufacturer continues. Then suddenly, to the unaware manufacturer at least, demand dries up. This causes severe problems. Raw material stocks are too high and more supplies are already on order. Finished stocks are also mounting and there is no prospect of moving the stock. Thus, the manufacturer has either to reduce production, which will create severe labour problems, or devise some means of shifting the stocks. One way might be to offer a special price promotion.
(4) Remember that these problems hit the manufacturer some time after the original downturn in DIY demand. If their luck is bad, and sometimes it is, the price promotion may coincide with a resumption in DIY demand. The price promotions may inflate this demand still further. This causes frantic calls for deliveries at all levels in the hierarchy. Thus, there is a risk that the manufacturer may end up over-producing to meet this artificial demand.

What happens next? That depends, but there is a clear risk of catastrophic overshoot in production. Of course, this scenario is not entirely realistic. However, similar effects do occur in systems of this type. Small decisions at a low level can have much amplified effects further up the system. Such multilevel systems need to be modelled with the aim of exploring their stability and response.

13.2.2   Causal loop diagrams

In a dynamic feedback system, the various factors combine to produce the observed system behaviour. To model these systems, therefore, we need to understand the various factors and their interactions. In particular, we need to model the system structure. This could be done in a textual form such as "... delays to in-stock replenishment lead to lower stocks, which in turn may affect demand ..." However, once the interactions become complicated, it becomes very difficult to follow through the number of possible links. Hence, most people find that a diagramming approach is helpful. On a diagram, it is fairly easy, with care, to show multiple interactions that can be understood by other people. Causal loop diagrams, first suggested by Maruyama (1963) are a simple way of mapping out the interacting elements of feedback systems. The idea is to show which factors cause other factors to change in a dynamic system. Causal loop diagrams are used to map the system structure so as to try to understand how the system may behave.

As a simple example unconnected with management science, consider a thermostatically controlled domestic central heating system, for which a causal loop diagram is shown in Figure 13.2. Gas is burned to provide heat; heat input to the room causes the room temperature to rise; as the temperature rises, this trips a thermostat, which cuts off the gas supply. If the temperature drops below some pre-set temperature, the thermostat causes the gas supply to be restored. Notice the following conventions:

(1)   The direction of the arrowhead indicates causality. For example, an increase in room temperature causes (via the thermostat) the gas supply to be cut off.

(2)   The sign at the arrowhead indicates the effect of the causality. When an increase in one factor causes an increase in another, other factors remaining unchanged, then a plus sign is used. If an increase in one leads to a decrease in another, other factors being unchanged, then a minus sign is called for. Sometimes both effects are possible and a question mark should be used. In the central heating example, increased

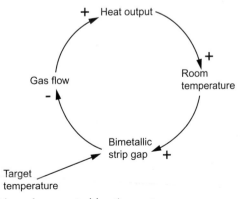

Figure 13.2   Causal loop for a central heating system

heat output should lead to an increase in room temperature—hence a plus sign is shown.

The diagram can be used to consider the nature of any loops. In Figure 13.2 there is only a single loop, which consists of three positive arrows and one negative arrow. Counting the number of negative signs helps us determine the causality of the loop. An odd number of negative links indicates a loop in which there is negative feedback—which is the case in Figure 13.2. Negative feedback of some kind is essential if a self-contained system is to remain in control.

A good introduction to the use of causal loops and their value in qualitative analysis is given in Wolstenholme (1990) but a further example may be helpful at this point. Section 2.3.1 worked through a simple deterministic simulation which used a time-slicing approach and which could be implemented on a spreadsheet. It described the recruitment problems of Big Al, a somewhat unsuccessful gangster. Section 2.3.2 developed a set of equations to consider what Big Al might do and it can also be instructive to examine the causal loops that determine what is going on. These are drawn in Figure 13.3 (note that unless the sign of a link is given, it should be assumed positive). It shows that several negative feedback loops control the behaviour of the system. In particular, two deserve mention. The first controls the recruitment rate by measuring the gap between the current mob size and Big Al's target— the smaller the gap, the lower the recruitment rate. The second control comes from the arrest rate (the rate at which Big Al loses mobsters) and is directly related to the current mob size. To achieve his goal, Big Al will have to find ways of beating these two controls—either by making mob membership more attractive as the mob size increases or by keeping his men out of jail.

Of course, the systems investigated by management scientists are much more complex than these two examples. The control function in particular is much more complicated and, most likely, is fairly diffuse. At one extreme, control may be exercised via simple programmed rules or procedures that are rigorously followed. For example, jobs of certain types may always be allocated to specified machines in a job shop. At the other extreme is the adaptive behaviour by which any organization ensures its continued existence. This is characterized by conscious responses to changes in the organization's environment, which present both threats and opportunities. For instance, companies manufacturing cameras in the late 1990s needed to be ready for the digital revolution. Some were not.

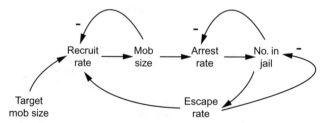

Figure 13.3 Causal loop diagram for Big Al's recruitment problem

13.3   MODELLING FEEDBACK SYSTEMS

Jay Forrester is the originator of system dynamics, initially giving it the name Industrial Dynamics (Forrester, 1961). The system dynamics approach focuses on system structure, emphasizing that observed behaviour and events can be understood by concentrating on three aspects of system structure: delays, levels (or stocks) and flow rates. The basic idea is that an organizational system consists of flows of information, cash and material items that flow at varying rates. The flows are accumulated in levels (e.g., stocks of goods and cash balances) and may be subject to delays (e.g., it takes time to get the goods from A to B). In an organizational system, the behaviour of the system is subject to management control by the implementation of control policies. Expressed in these terms, the system dynamics approach can seem a little inhuman, but this need not be so.

13.3.1   Delays

Information and materials (or whatever make up the "stuff" of the system) are rarely transmitted and received instantaneously. To give a simple example, orders may be sent by customers to their supplier by ordinary mail, thus introducing a delay of at least one day. Similarly, a company may have good reason to increase its production by 30% but may face a lead time of four weeks to do so because of the need to train more staff. Delays occur for all sorts of legitimate reasons and often these may be reduced at a cost. Companies with geographically dispersed distribution depots once had to transmit information about stock levels using the postal system. This was replaced by fax and then by electronic data transfer. Reducing delays always seems a good idea, but unless the system structures are redesigned accordingly, the reduction may not make things any better. Instead, the backlog may be shifted somewhere else and doing so might even cause a reduction in overall system performance.

Delays, of whatever type, can have profound effects within feedback systems. As a trivial example, most people have had the distressing experience of trying to control the temperature of a shower with a manual mixing valve. Typically, such a valve mixes water from separate hot and cold sources. The mixed water then passes to the showerhead and thence drops onto the person in the shower. Unfortunately, it takes time for the water to travel from the mixing valve to the showerhead. Hence the familiar pattern of events unfold:

(1)   Bather enters shower area and turns on the water, but the water is too cold because the shower was last used some time ago.
(2)   Bather turns the mixer valve so as to increase the water temperature.
(3)   No immediate effect, therefore the bather turns the mixer valve further towards hot.
(4)   Scalding water now hits the bather who frantically turns the mixer valve to the cold side.

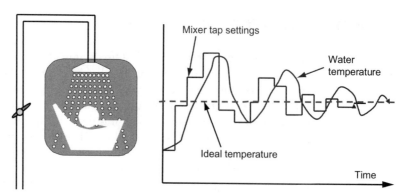

Figure 13.4   Temperature variations under a shower

(5)   Water still too hot, so the bather turns the mixer valve still further towards the cold side.

(6)   Bather now hit by cold water! Therefore, the bather turns the mixer valve towards hot, but with no immediate effect.

And so the process continues. With stable water flows and intelligent action by the bather, the temperature oscillations should decrease in amplitude until the right temperature is achieved. All this is because of a delay in a simple system. Figure 13.4 shows the temperature oscillations and their eventual damping.

To avoid such oscillation, the answer is to reduce the delay. Thus, the temperature should be sensed as close to the mixing valve as possible. Hence, if a thermostat is to be used, it should be placed in the circuit immediately after the valve.

Returning to organizational system, the motor parts manufacturer of Section 13.2.1 has real difficulties in trying to control production runs and stock levels. As it stands, the system includes far too many delays; also decisions about the production rates are too far removed from the behaviour of the consumers. One objective of the manufacturer, if more control is required, may be to reduce the effect of these delays. That is, the manufacturer must be more in touch with the state of the market. This does not mean that the management must respond to every fluctuation in the market. However, they ought to be in a position to decide whether or not to react. Thus the consideration of delays is an important part of the analysis of feedback systems. Section 14.3 discusses how different types of delay are handled in system dynamics.

13.3.2   Levels and stocks

Organizational systems contain accumulations of one kind or another. In system dynamics these are usually called levels or stocks. Often, levels are clearly recognizable such as stocks of raw materials or of finished goods. Some are less obvious, partly because our day-to-day language does not label them as stocks—such as cash balances, which are produced by inflows and outflows of funds. A slightly less obvious example might be a labour force with numbers of employees at different grades and experience. As in the case of Big Al's mob (Section 2.3.1) recruitment causes the number (level) of workers to increase and resignations cause it to decrease. Levels can be less tangible than this, too. Another similar example, also involving people, might be a medical waiting list for treatment or diagnosis. Even less tangible, perhaps, the order book maintained by a make-to-order manufacturing company is also a level or stock; representing a backlog of work.

Levels continue to exist (in principle, at least) even if all activity ceases (Forrester, 1961). Hence, if a make-to-order business ceased trading, its order book would remain—though would never be fulfilled unless someone else took on the business. The financial assets of an individual are, likewise, assessed at death in order to determine what taxes are due and what people will inherit. In system dynamics, the current conditions of the levels within a system correspond to the system state. That is, the levels/stocks are state variables. Generally, these levels are subject to some control by the management of the organization. By examining the levels within the system the system state can be understood and appropriate corrective action may be taken.

Hence, a crucial part of any system dynamics modelling of feedback systems is the identification of the relevant levels of the system. Though causal loop diagrams do not distinguish between levels and other aspects of system structure, they are necessary for developing a simulation model. The stock flow diagrams used by the software discussed in Chapter 14 rely on the clear identification of levels if they are to work.

13.3.3 Rates and flows

Activity continues in any dynamic system and this is represented by dynamic flows between the levels. Levels have inflows and outflows and will rise and fall according to whether the inflow exceeds the outflow or vice versa. Thus, cash balances are affected by the rates at which money flows into and out of the organization. The labour force is affected by the rate at which people are hired and leave. A hospital waiting list is determined by the rate at which people are added to the list and leave it—for whatever reason. To use the system dynamics modelling software discussed in Chapter 14 it is essential to distinguish between the levels (or stocks) and the flow rates that connect them. This is reflected in the stock flow diagrams used by this software.

Since, in real life, time flows continuously, flow rates mirror this continuous variation and this is captured in the way that flows are modelled within system dynamics. In essence they are treated as continuous variables whose value may be determined at any instant. Flow rates can be usefully measured as average rates over a period. If the period is made small enough, then the rate changes will appear to occur smoothly and will capture something of the continuous variation. This allows the variations to be modelled using differential equations or, in the case of system dynamics, as difference equations.

13.3.4 Policies

It should now be clear that the system dynamics method views feedback systems as interconnected sequences of levels and flows. Matter and information flow from one level to another. Thus, levels are affected by flow rates, which in turn may be affected by information about the levels. As an example, a manufacturer's finished stocks are determined by at least two flow rates:

(1) Despatch rate to customers.
(2) Production rate of finished goods.

This relationship represents, in effect, the "physics" of the system since it is governed by standard notions of conservation of matter.

Reversing the argument, the production and despatch rates are themselves affected by the level of finished stocks. Sometimes this link is also governed by laws of conservation (e.g., goods cannot be despatched if they have not been made). Thus, the despatch rate depends, in some sense, on the level of finished stocks. At other times, the relationship is governed by management policies, and this is a crucial part of system dynamics modelling. For example, if finished stocks are too high, the management may decide to cut production. In system dynamics terms, policies are explicit statements about how levels affect rates and rates affect levels. In feedback systems, policies are expressed as decision rules stating what action is to be taken so as to achieve a given state. A policy might, for example, state the flow rate thought necessary to achieve a certain level. Thus, though this was a mistake, Big Al (Section 2.3.1), wishing to achieve a mob of a certain size, had a recruitment policy based on the current size of his mob and how close it was to its ideal size.

When modelling policies, it is also important to consider the effects of delays (Section 13.3.1). Policies are not based directly on the levels but on information about these levels. This information may be distorted and delayed. The distortion may occur because of mistakes, of malice, or simply because of the way that information is analysed and aggregated. Anyone who has played the game "Chinese whispers", in which a phrase is transmitted from person to person by whispering in the ear of an immediate neighbour, will realize how information can be distorted unwittingly. The effect is worsened by the presence of delays, which may mean that the information is not only distorted but is also out of date and out of phase with any necessary control action.

13.4 THE ORIGINS OF SYSTEM DYNAMICS

It ought to be clear that simulating hierarchical feedback systems calls for methods that are rather different to the discrete event approaches covered in

Part II. In a hierarchical feedback system, the major concern is often with stability (i.e., how does it respond to changes in its inputs?). For example, what will happen if demand increases briefly and then settles down again? Or what effect would the doubling of certain stocks have on production rates in the short term? To answer these and similar questions calls for a simulation method which can cope with delays, with flows of information as well as "material" and which lends itself to the study of transient phenomena.

Forrester and his colleagues at MIT were the originators and continue as the major developers of the system dynamics approach. Originally the approach was known as industrial dynamics, this being the title of the first book on the subject (Forrester, 1961). Despite its long history some management scientists are sceptical of its value and Jackson (2003) provides a useful, brief critique. Possibly there are two reasons for this. First, *Industrial Dynamics* was an ambitious book, perhaps too ambitious. This is particularly seen in Forrester's claim that it presented a revolutionary approach to management. With hindsight, this does seem rather an exaggeration. Even at the time of publication, its mechanistic approach must have seemed a limiting factor to practising managers.

Another possible reason for this scepticism may be that system dynamics is definitely not a highly refined and accurate tool. The aim is to explore the dynamics of feedback systems in terms of their stability and responses to external shocks. In many cases, the presenting instability may be so gross that exact analyses are not required. System dynamics presents a way of approximately modelling and simulating such systems. For the purist, the approximation may seem too great. However, the purist may never have been faced with the need to develop sensibly argued proposals for change in a short time period.

13.4.1 Control theory

The analysis of feedback systems via differential equations has long been a major concern of engineers. Indeed, the design of servomechanisms is a long-standing feature of many engineering curricula. However, once such systems become realistically complex, then their direct analysis by solving the differential equations is often impossible. Instead of direct solution it is common to use other approaches. An early approach was to use analogue computers to simulate the behaviour of the system being studied. Analogue computers are based on a network of selected electrical components whose behaviour can be tuned and can be modelled as differential equations. The components are selected and tuned so that their equations have the same structure as those of the system to be simulated.

Analogue computers allow continuous variables to be represented by continuous properties such as voltage and current. The electrical circuits are subjected to specified inputs and their behaviour is observed and analysed. The components are then rearranged so that the analogue computer has the same mathematical structure as the system being simulated. Hence the term analogue computer is used, since it indicates that the circuit is an analogue of some other system. Since analogue computers can truly operate in continuous time, they actually offer a more accurate way of simulating feedback systems than system dynamics. However, a major difficulty with analogue computers is that they require expertise in the design of electrical circuits and detailed understanding of the underlying mathematics—otherwise, the selection and assembly of the correct components is impossible.

It is possible, though, to use a digital computer to simulate an analogue computer that in turn simulates the system of interest. To do so, the analyst must formulate the system as a set of differential equations that can be represented in an analogue simulation package. This in turn uses standard integration routines to simulate the dynamic behaviour of the system of differential equations. A once popular example was SLAM (ICL, 1972). Rather than use such digital simulators of analogue computers, it is much simpler to use system dynamics when simulating organizational processes.

System dynamics adopts a rather simpler approach in which the differential equations are replaced by first-order difference equations. As will be seen in Section 14.2.4, the usual integration approach of system dynamics should be used with some care, otherwise the results of a simulation could be misleading. Nevertheless, its simplicity can be a great asset in communicating with managers. Forrester gives credit to Tustin (1953) for considering in detail the analogy between servomechanisms and economic systems. Forrester's contribution was to provide a simple and systematic way of simulating such systems, an approach that is still of value 40 years later.

EXERCISES

(1)   Draw a causal diagram of the following system. A biscuit company sells its biscuits to retailers, most of whom demand a price discount which increases with the amount purchased. High discounts mean high sales, but lower unit returns for the biscuit company. On the other hand, low discounts lead to low sales and, sometimes, to no sales. Low sales result, therefore, in low market share, which makes retailers reluctant to stock the biscuit company's products. This leads the retailers to demand yet higher discounts if they are to stock the biscuits. High sales lead to lower unit costs in production and distribution.

(2)   Draw a causal loop diagram of the following system. Bailrigg Computer Services (BCS) provides an on-site maintenance service to customers who pay an annual fee that guarantees the repair of their computer systems within 24 hours on any weekday, apart from Bank Holidays. To this end, 50 service engineers are employed and all are equally skilled. Being a quiet part of the country, BCS have little or no labour turnover but this may be about to change. Nippon MegaCorp Computers (NMCC) are about to open their UK service centre in Bailrigg and will almost certainly try to entice some of the BCS engineers to work for them. Hence, Bill Ritchie, who runs BCS, thinks that he must plan for labour turnover by introducing a training school. His idea is as follows:

Each month he will recruit a number of trainee engineers who will enter a 6-month training scheme. At the end of the 6-month programme they must take a test and those who pass will join the staff of engineers. Those who fail may be found other jobs by BCS, but they will not join the staff of engineers. The problem facing Bill is, what recruitment policy should he adopt? He is inclined to record the number of engineers who leave each month and to use these figures to compute an exponentially smoothed forecast of the expected losses of engineers. In each month he will recruit enough trainees to replace this expected loss to NMCC, adjusted for the proportion of trainees who are expected to fail at the end of the training programme.

(3) Develop a causal loop diagram of the following system. The Sweat Shop is based in one of the Asia Pacific Tiger economies and employs craft workers who manufacture hand-produced articles that sell in the EU. Employment legislation is lax and this means that workers can be hired and fired at will. Working conditions are also rather poor and so the work is tedious and time consuming. No proper work study has ever been conducted but some basic data can be imputed from the meagre records that the owner keeps.
- He reckons that each worker can produce ten items per day.
- The invoices suggest that each day he receives orders that are normally distributed with a mean of 200 items and a standard deviation of 20. However, he suspects that this demand may soon increase, possibly doubling and becoming much more variable.
- Workers are readily available, but need some training (during which time they are unpaid). The training takes 5 days to complete. If he finds that he has too many workers then he sacks them. Being kinder than some owners he gives them 3 days notice, during which time they continue to work normally.
- He prefers to keep about 5 days' demand for finished goods in stock and he has an unlimited supply of raw materials. His son is studying in the UK and, during his last vacation, installed a demand forecasting system based on simple exponential smoothing with an alpha value (smoothing constant) of 0.2. Anything more sophisticated will not be used.

REFERENCES

ICL (1972) *A Simulation Language for Analogue Modelling*. ICL, UK.

Checkland P.B. and Holwell S.A. (2004) "Classic" OR and "soft" OR—an asymmetric complementarity. In: M. Pidd (2004), *Systems Modelling: Theory and Practice*. John Wiley & Sons, Chichester, UK.

Coyle R.G. (1977) *Management System Dynamics*. Wiley-Interscience, London.

Forrester J.S. (1961) *Industrial Dynamics*. MIT Press, Cambridge, MA.

Jackson M.C. (2003) *Systems Thinking: Creative Holism for Managers.* John Wiley & Sons, Chichester, UK.

Maruyama M. (1963) The second cybernetics: Deviation amplifying mutual causal processes. *American Scientist,* **51**(2), 164–79.

Senge P. (1992) *The Fifth Discipline: The Art and Practice of the Learning Organization.* Century Publications, New York.

Tustin A. (1953) *The Mechanism of Economic Systems.* Harvard University Press, Cambridge, MA.

Wolstenholme E.F. (1990) *System enquiry: A System Dynamics Approach.* John Wiley & Sons, Chichester, UK.

14

System Dynamics Modelling and Simulation

14.1 INTRODUCTION

The basic methods that underlie system dynamics simulations have changed little since their introduction by Forrester (1961). However, the way in which they are presented to the modeller and user are very different. Originally, the modeller had to write a set of difference equations that were read by a computer program (DYNAMO). The DYNAMO system then executed a time-sliced simulation using these equations. This was tedious, error-prone and required more computing expertise than most managers (and analysts) possessed. It is possible to develop system dynamics models using spreadsheets and this was done with Big Al's problem in Section 2.3.1, which was a very simple simulation. However, as is well known, spreadsheet models of any kind are very hard to debug and even harder to modify properly. In addition, spreadsheet system dynamics models are very difficult for a non-specialist to follow, which makes them unsuitable if an analyst and client are jointly developing a model. Hence it makes much sense to use properly designed system dynamics software.

Nowadays, most system dynamics simulations are developed using Visual Interactive Modelling Systems (VIMS), specially designed for this purpose. The best-known examples are iThink and its educational cousin Stella (High Performance Systems, 2003), Powersim (Powersim Corporation, 2003) and Vensim (Ventana Systems, 2003). The early versions of Stella/iThink were available only for Apple Macintosh computers, which restricted their use somewhat. All three packages are available for Microsoft Windows based PCs.

The three packages have some significant differences, but at their core are very similar and are based on the same system dynamics approach using difference equations. All three require the modeller to develop a stock and flow diagram and use similar, though not identical, symbols for that purpose. This chapter will use Powersim as its exemplar, but it should be obvious how to develop the same models within Stella/iThink and Vensim.

There are many study materials available for learning system dynamics and a good place to start is the self-teaching material (System Dynamics Road Maps, 2003) available on the Internet. At the time of writing, these were available free of charge.

14.1.1 Stock and flow diagrams

Although verbal descriptions of dynamic systems can be helpful, many people find that diagrams are a useful aid to thinking about how these systems operate. Section 5.3 showed how the simple ideas of activity cycle diagrams can be used to tease out how discrete simulation entities interact. They may also be used as part of a process of automatic program generation, in which the diagram is read by an intelligent computer program that writes a computer program simulating the system represented in the diagram. These same ideas have also been used in system dynamics, based on stock and flow diagrams. The previous chapter introduced the idea of causal loop diagrams, but stock and flow diagrams require more thought and can be used as the basis for visual interactive modelling and simulation.

Figure 14.1 shows the main symbols used in Powersim stock flow diagrams. Forrester (1961) introduced the basic idea of these diagrams for industrial dynamics, though with a slightly more complicated set of symbols. In particular, the industrial dynamics diagrams required the modeller to distinguish between many different types of flow, whereas it is normal, nowadays, to distinguish only between material flow and information flow. The horizontal pipes (double arrows) of Figure 14.1 are the material flows. It is normal in these diagrams for material flows to run either horizontally or vertically and at no other angle. As mentioned in Section 13.3.4, these material flows are part of the "physics" of the system and are subject to conservation laws. The only places at which material flows can be created or destroyed are shown as clouds—the sources and sinks, which are at either end of Figure 14.1. Once a flow leaves a source and until it enters a sink, it is subject to conservation laws.

The other, single arrows on Figure 14.1 are the information flows, which are not subject to conservation laws. They indicate that one factor has an influence on another factor, though it is impossible to be sure what that action is by simply looking at the diagram. In Figure 14.1, *Level* exerts some undefined influence on the rate at which *InFlow* increases its current value. As stated in Section 13.3.4, information is used as the basis for control in a system dynamics model and this information may be distorted or delayed. The information flow that links the Auxiliary circle has two small lines across it about halfway along. In Powersim, this indicates that the flow is

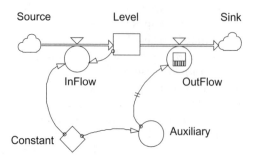

Figure 14.1 Powersim stock flow diagram symbols

subject to some form of delay and several such delay types are built into Powersim and the other system dynamics packages.

Levels are shown in all system dynamics stock flow diagrams as rectangles that may be replenished and depleted by flows. In Figure 14.1, *Level* is replenished by the flow rate *InFlow* and is depleted by the flow rate *OutFlow*. Since both *InFlow* and *OutFlow* are subject to conservation laws, this means that the value taken by *Level* will depend on their relative values. The material flows themselves carry a symbol that also bears their name—this looks like a valve or tap (or faucet, in the USA). This carries the idea that information (the single arrows) is used to control the flow rates by, in effect, opening or closing a valve. The valve for *OutFlow* has a further symbol inside it and this, in the case of Powersim, is because the flow from Auxiliary to it is subject to a delay of some kind. Other system dynamics VIMS use a different diagrammatic notation for this.

The remaining two symbols of Figure 14.1 represent constants and auxiliaries. Constants carry values that are set at the start of a simulation run, though it may be possible to vary them interactively during the simulation— but only by user intervention. Auxiliaries are convenient devices for representing equations in which different information flows are combined. They can make the underlying equations easier to read.

14.1.2 A stock and flow diagram for Big Al's problem

Figure 14.2 shows a stock flow diagram of Big Al's recruitment problem as introduced in Section 2.3.1. Big Al is a mobster who has definite ideas about his ideal mob size and, every week he recruits a number of mobsters in an attempt to achieve it. He also loses mobsters each week, thanks to the vigilance of Happy Harry, the chief cop, who manages to put a number of mobsters in jail each week. Sadly, though, the jail is not escape proof and so, each week, a number of incarcerated mobsters manage to rejoin Big Al. The main material flow is horizontal and shows that new mobsters emerge from a source (shown by a cloud—possibly an appropriate symbol for mobsters) and join the mob at a rate determined by the *Recruit_rate* valve. Big Al's losses to Happy Harry's men are shown by the *Arrest_rate* valve, which also acts as the

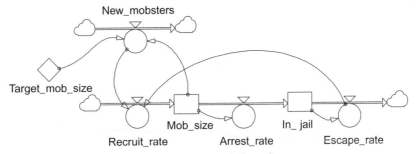

Figure 14.2 Big Al's problem: Powersim stock flow diagram

inflow to the *In_jail* level or stock. The current mob size is represented by the *Mob_size* stock.

What of the escapees from jail? Are they not also a material flow? Yes they are, but Figure 14.2 illustrates a common feature of any model, whether for system dynamics or some other approach. Sometimes it is more convenient to operate at a more abstract level and so escaped mobsters are shown as disappearing into another cloud, this time a sink. The number of escapees is captured in the information flow that runs from the *Escape_rate* back to the *Recruit_rate*. Since the men that Big Al recruits already have form, they need no training whether wholly new to Big Al or returnees. Hence Big Al has no need to distinguish between them. Those recruits that are wholly new mobsters are managed through the *New_mobsters* flow—which, strangely, neither starts at nor ends at a level. In system dynamics terms, this is a catalytic flow that is there for convenience. It allows an information flow to run from the current mob size, since Big Al uses his current number of mobsters to decide how many to recruit. An information flow links this to the actual weekly recruitment rate into Big Al's mob.

Finally, Big Al has definite views about his ideal mob size, which is represented by the *Target_mob_size* constant at the left of the diagram. An information link runs from this to the *Recruit_rate* flow, which also receives an information link from the *Mob_size* level. There are no delayed links on the diagram, which is probably unrealistic, since it assumes that mobsters immediately rejoin Big Al on escaping from jail, whereas they might decide to lie low for a while.

Though Big Al's problem is very simple, its structure, leaving aside the question of delays, is very similar to any manpower planning problem. Staff must be recruited each period and some staff leave for a range of different reasons. If Big Al insisted that his new recruits went through an initial apprenticeship before being accepted into the mob proper, this will be modelled by adding a new level between *Recruit_rate* and *Mob_size*. In turn, the result of this might be that some never make the grade and leave the mob, the remainder become fully fledged mobsters and are fair game for Happy Harry's cops. This type of structure, apart from its criminal tinge, is typical of some manpower planning problems.

14.2   BEYOND THE DIAGRAMS—SYSTEM DYNAMICS SIMULATION

A system dynamics model is a set of difference equations whose variables change their value through time. The approach was developed by Forrester, based on an analogy between physical control systems and the control systems employed in organizations. He provided an approach that is based on the one that most control engineers would use when trying to design or understand dynamic physical systems. The problem that faces such engineers is that, although they are often able to write differential equations that model how a dynamic system might behave, in many cases these sets of equations cannot be integrated directly. Instead, the engineer resorts to a numerical approach, usually with the help of appropriate computer software. Forrester provided a simplified version of this numerical integration in system dynamics.

14.2.1   Time handling in system dynamics

In the terms introduced in Section 2.2.1, system dynamics usually employs a time-slicing approach. That is, as shown in Figure 14.3, within the simulation the values of the variables are computed at distinct points of time separated by an unvarying time increment, dt. The effect is to create linear piece-wise approximations to the smooth curves between each time point, as shown in Figure 14.3.

As in all time-slicing approaches, the modeller must fix the value of dt in advance. If dt is too large, then the simulation will be too coarse and may miss important variation and transient effects. In addition, it should be noted that choosing too large a value for dt may cause the simulation to be very misleading in its dynamic behaviour—this problem is discussed later in Section 14.2.4. If dt is made too small, then this will lead to a model that runs too slowly (which may not matter greatly) but it may also require over-accurate estimates of the parameters of the model. This may, in turn, lead to excessive data collection and, therefore, excessive cost. The usual advice is to choose a value for dt small enough so that it is reasonable to assume that all flow rates in the model can be regarded as constant over dt during the running of the simulation. If in doubt, make dt small.

A system dynamics simulation computes what is happening in the system at regular points in time, each one separated by dt as shown in Figure 14.4. Imagine that time has just reached a known point t at which a sample (actually a computation) is due. Because a fixed time slice (dt) is being used, we know when the previous computation was done (time $t - dt$) and when the next one is due (time $t + dt$).

A system dynamics model has two main types of equation: level or stock equations, and rate or flow equations. As with all such simulation systems, simulated time is moved from point to point and computations are made at

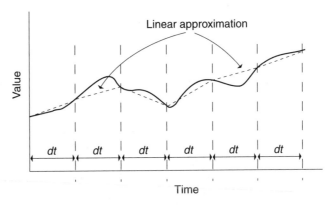

Figure 14.3   Time slicing in system dynamics: linear approximations

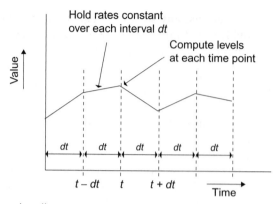

Figure 14.4 Time handling in system dynamics

each point before moving to the next one. The basic method of handling time and of the resulting computations is as follows:

(1) At time t compute the new values for the levels or stocks, using the level or stock equations. Use the current values of the rates or flows, computed at time $t - dt$, for this purpose.
(2) Now compute the values which the rates or flows will hold over the next time interval dt. These will depend on information about the current values of the levels.
(3) Move time forward by one increment (dt) and repeat the process.

Thus, levels are computed for the current point of time and then the rates are computed over the next known interval. Rates are assumed to be fixed over that interval once they are computed and are only revised after the next computation of the levels.

14.2.2 Equation types

A system dynamics model includes two main types of equation: level equations and rate equations. A level equation has a simple format, which can usually be interpreted directly from the system dynamics diagram, as follows:

$$Level\ (Now) = Level\ (Previous) + dt * (InFlows - OutFlows)$$

Thus, at the current time point, the value of the level or stock is simply its value at the previous time point, plus the net inflow or outflow over the interval (dt) that has passed since the last time point. The diagram shows how many such inflows and outflows exist for any level and, therefore, the equation usually follows automatically. Hence VIMS such as Powersim can generate the level equations from the diagram.

Rate equations cannot be inferred from the system diagram, for this shows only which information flows affect the rate computation, not how this influence is exercised. Thus, in Figure 14.1, the *InFlow* rate is seen to depend on two factors: *Level* and *Constant*. How it is affected cannot be determined from the diagram alone, as this is an expression of the way in which the information is used to control the system. This inability to infer the rate equations from the flow diagrams is a serious weakness, for the same links can represent quite different policies, leading to very different behaviours. If system dynamics is to be used for the dynamic simulation of a system, the nature of the rate equations is crucial.

14.2.3   Powersim equations for Big Al's problem

Since the level or stock equations essentially enforce conservation laws, they can be directly inferred from the stock and flow diagram. Hence, systems dynamics VIMS can automatically generate these equations. The different VIMS each employ a slightly different format for their equations. The Powersim level equations for Big Al's problem are shown in Figure 14.5, based on the stock and flow diagram of Figure 14.2. The first two equations, generated automatically by Powersim, are both preceded by a rectangle. This indicates that they are level or stock equations and represent the conserved material flows into and out of the two stocks. For both stock equations, the boxed INIT symbol shows the value given to the variable at the start of a simulation. A zero value is assumed by default, but this can be edited by double clicking on the equation. This opens an edit window that allows the initial value to be altered.

The next four equations relate to flows and these cannot be determined by the Powersim system and must be defined by the modeller. This is done by double clicking on the flow icon in the stock flow diagram, which opens an edit window as shown in Figure 14.6. In this case, the *Recruit_rate* is being defined and, since the Powersim system can determine this from the diagram, the flow or rate equation must use the *Escape_rate* and *New_mobsters*, which

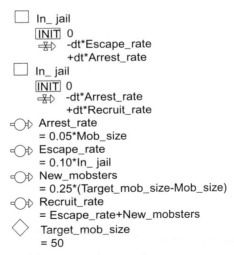

Figure 14.5   Big Al's problem: Powersim equations

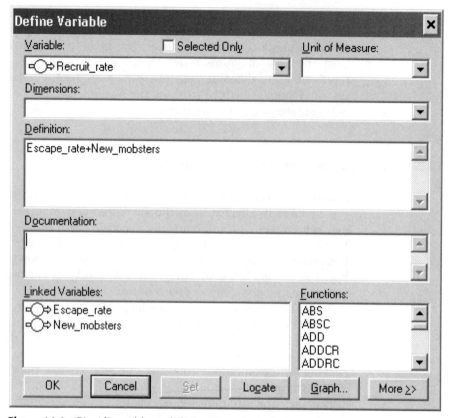

Figure 14.6   Big Al's problem: defining *Recruit_rate* in Powersim

are listed in the Linked Variables window. Though these two variables must appear on the right-hand side of the equation, the form of their relationship must be specified by the modeller and will depend entirely on the system being modelled. The final equation of Figure 14.5 is for the constant *Target _ mob_ size*, which is marked by a diamond shape. The value is given to the constant by double clicking on its icon, which opens another edit window.

The simulation is now ready to run, which is done by using the Simulate menu of Powersim. This allows the user to set the simulation run length, the size of the time step (*dt*) and also the integration method used.

14.2.4   Integration and the value of *dt*

Although it may not be obvious at first sight, what is going on within a system dynamics simulation involves numerical integration. The usual method of achieving this in system dynamics is known as the Euler–Cauchy approach, which was built into DYNAMO, the first system dynamics software. System dynamics VIMS, such as Stella/iThink, Powersim and Vensim allow the user to specify an integration method, although they provide Euler–Cauchy as the

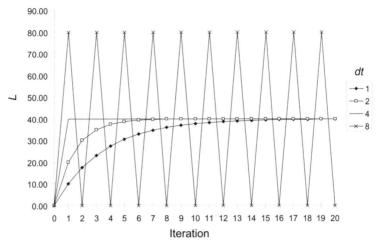

Figure 14.7   Effect of different values of *dt* in Euler–Cauchy integration

default. To illustrate the effect of integration methods, consider the following level–rate pair of equations:

$$Level = dt * InRate - dt * OutRate$$

$$InRate = OutRate/A \qquad \text{where } A \text{ is a constant}$$

This pair of equations could be rewritten as the following differential equation:

$$\frac{dL}{dt} = I - \frac{L}{A}$$

where *L* and *I* represent *Level* and *InRate*. *OutRate* is now implicit. The Euler–Cauchy integration formula for this differential equation is:

$$L(n+1) = L(n) + dt[I(n)L(n)/A]$$

The Euler–Cauchy numerical integration method is iterative, using an interval *dt* in this case. $L(i)$ is the value of *L* at integration step *i*.

Figure 14.7 shows the effect of different values of *dt* when using this Euler–Cauchy approach. It uses an initial value of 0 for *L* and *I*, with *I* rising immediately to a value of 4 and remaining there. Giving *dt* a value of 1 causes *L* to rise gradually and asymptotically towards the value of 4. Increasing *dt* to 2 and then to 4 causes the increase to be much sharper. But when *dt* is given a value of 8, the integration fails and oscillation sets in. In general, the Euler–Cauchy method is sensitive to the size of the integration step *dt*, and also tends to propagate small errors which may be amplified as simulated time proceeds. For *dt*, small is beautiful.

14.3   SIMULATING DELAYS IN SYSTEM DYNAMICS

An important feature of many dynamic systems is the presence of delays that make control of the system rather harder than might seem the case at first sight. The previous chapter described how hard it can be to gain proper control of the temperature in a shower which has a simple mixer valve. As observed earlier, delays are a feature of dynamic systems and affect both material and information flows. The most common are exponential and pipeline delays.

14.3.1   Pipeline delays

These are an analogy with a pipeline of known length into which material is fed and from which it flows once the material has passed through the pipe. In effect, these are delays of known duration, these being due to the length of the "pipe" and the speed at which the material flows. Examples might include delays due to postal systems or the delivery of goods. In effect, an input rate and output rate are separated by a level or stock, and the output rate is the input rate delayed by some interval. The delay time may be fixed (e.g., it may always take a day to confirm and order). Sometimes though it is variable (e.g., the time to complete some work may be wholly a function of the number of machines or people available). Powersim and the other system dynamics VIMS provide built-in functions to model these delays.

14.3.2   Exponential delays

These occur when part of a system takes some time to respond to changes in its input. The response is in effect damped, rather as a car's shock absorbers dampen the effect of the oscillations caused by its springs. This damping is usually very desirable, as it stops the system from over-reacting—but the damping does need to be properly considered. Powersim provides built-in functions to provide exponential delays, but it is instructive to consider how these operate by using the basic building blocks of system dynamics—levels/stocks and flow rates.

It is normal to refer to the *order* of a delay. In effect this relates to the number of times that the input is smoothed before it reaches the output. That is, a third-order delay is a cascade of three first-order delays. Figure 14.8 shows a stock and flow diagram for first and third-order material delays. Using Powersim notation, the equations for the first-order delay are as follows:

init $Level = 0$
flow $Level = -dt * OutRate + dt * InRate$
aux $OutRate = Level/Average\_Delay$
const $InRate = 10$
const $Average\_Delay = 5$

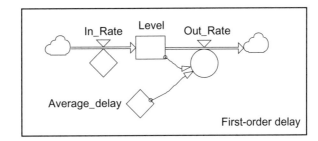

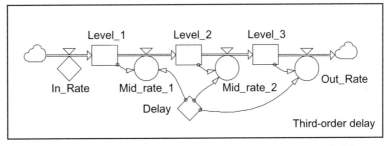

Figure 14.8   Powersim: fundamental structure of exponential material delays

The corresponding equations for the third-order delay are as follows:

init $Level\_1 = 0$
flow $Level\_1 = -dt * Mid\_rate\_1 + dt + dt * InRate$
init $Level\_2 = 0$
flow $Level\_2 = -dt * Mid\_rate\_2 + dt * Mid\_rate\_1$
init $Level\_3 = 0$
flow $Level\_3 = -dt * Outrate + dt * Mid\_rate\_2$
aux $Mid\_rate\_1 = Level\_1/(Delay/3)$
aux $Mid\_rate\_2 = Level\_2/(Delay/3)$
aux $OutRate = Level\_3/(Delay/3)$
const $InRate = 10$
const $Delay = 5$

Though these equations are simple, it is tedious to keep including them in system dynamics models since they are often found. Hence, Powersim, and other system dynamics software provides built-in functions for exponential delays. In Powersim this is the DELAYMTR() function that can be used to model any order of exponential delay for material flows. One of the parameters is the order of the delay.

Figure 14.9 shows the response of *Out_rate* in the two cases to a step change in *In_rate* from 0 to 10, with a total delay of 5 in both cases. As expected, the response of *Out_rate* is damped and it takes time for it to reach the new value of *In_rate*. In the case of the third-order delay, there is a pause before there is any response from *Out_rate*. Thus, a third-order delay can be used to model a damped pipeline delay.

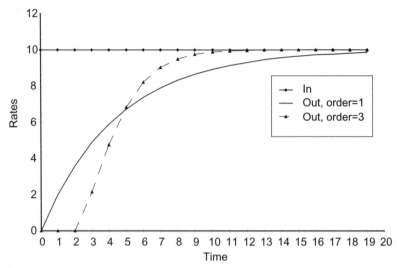

Figure 14.9   Exponential delays: step response

14.3.3   Information delays

As mentioned earlier, information is also delayed. Sometimes these delays are due to information transmission and sometimes because of the ways in which they are processed—stocks may only be checked once each week. The main difference between material and information delays is that material flows are subject to conservation laws. This means that material may be delayed, but it cannot be lost during that delay. If the delay to which material is subject is decreased, then the rate at which it is produced will increase and vice versa.

By contrast, an information delay is a little more complicated, though the difference really only matters if the delay time increases or decreases. An information delay will always produce an output rate somewhere between its minimum and maximum input rates. If the delay time is also a variable, the amount produced will vary between those limits but there is no guarantee that no information will be lost. In effect, this allows the model to allow for the fact that information can simply be outdated and best forgotten. Powersim and the other system dynamics VIMS all provide built-in functions to model information delays.

14.4   SYSTEM DYNAMICS MODELLING

There is much that can be said about developing system dynamics models and much helpful advice can be found on the MIT system dynamics website (`http://web.mit.edu/sdg/www/`). Pidd (2003, chapter 7) suggests that two different strategies may be employed when developing system dynamics models: outside in and inside out.

14.4.1   Modelling from the outside in

This approach relies on an assumption that there are a number of characteristic system structures that will lead to certain types of behaviour. As mentioned above, the modeller begins with some idea of the type of behaviour that would be expected from the system and its components. For example, it might display exponential growth under certain conditions. These types of behaviour can be related to standard structures that are easily modelled in system dynamics terms. The modeller selects the appropriate structures by thinking through the observed behaviours. The model becomes an assembly of these standard structures. It must be noted that standard structures and process will rarely be used in an unmodified form, but they do provide a useful basis from which to begin the modelling. Richmond and Petersen (1994) use this outside-in approach when presenting a set of generic structures that may be employed when modelling in Stella II and iThink. Note though, that even when such structures have been selected, they must still be parameterized—values must be given to the variables in the underlying equations.

The first, and simplest, structure is one that occurs when a level and a flow are connected in such a way that there is exponential growth or exponential decay in the level. This form of growth may be evident in financial systems based on compound interest and in some ecological systems in which there are no limits on available food nor predators to prey on the population. This type of decay happens when a proportion of a level is removed during each time interval. An example of this might be a company reducing its workforce by releasing a proportion in each time period. In the jargon of system dynamics, the proportion applied to the growth or the decay is known as the compounding fraction (shown as CF in Figure 14.10). The compounding fraction itself need not be a constant but could be the result of other factors elsewhere in the model. Figure 14.10 shows Powersim diagrams and the resulting output for these simple compound growth and decay systems.

A second type of generic structure occurs in those systems that aim to keep some value at a target level by feedback control. This is sometimes known as a stock-adjustment process, of which there are many examples. These include make-to-stock manufacturing, which aims to keep finished stock levels at a certain value. Other examples might be the number of people employed in a business after allowing for recruitment and labour turnover, or the number of patients on a hospital ward. The basic process is just an extension of the compounding/decay structure, except that a target is introduced as a way of modifying the inflows and outflows from the level. In the left-hand side of Figure14.11, the target level is set at 30 with an initial value of 10 for the level, thus the actual level increases quickly at first and then it asymptotically approaches the target level. If the initial level had been higher than the target, the level would quickly have dropped towards the target and then would have approached it asymptotically.

The second structure shown on Figure 14.11 is a production process, this term relating to any process in which the output is controlled by reference to another level. Examples might be a manufacturing company in which each

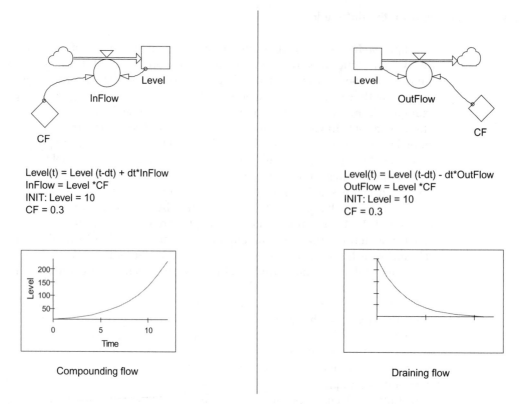

Level(t) = Level (t-dt) + dt*InFlow
InFlow = Level *CF
INIT: Level = 10
CF = 0.3

Level(t) = Level (t-dt) - dt*OutFlow
OutFlow = Level *CF
INIT: Level = 10
CF = 0.3

Compounding flow

Draining flow

Figure 14.10 Powersim structures for exponential growth and decay

machine can produce a specified number of units or a hospital in which each doctor might be expected to conduct a specified number of outpatient clinics per week. In either case, the capacity of the resource is modelled by the extra level, labelled as Resource in Figure 14.11. The unit productivity of the resource is modelled by CF. Clearly, the value taken by Resource could itself be variable and might be the result of other processes elsewhere in the system. It is also clear that the Flow could be bi-directional, resulting in a combined stock adjustment and production process.

14.4.2 Modelling from the inside out

This is the approach that was used to develop the model of Big Al's recruitment problem and is very similar to the way in which a discrete event simulation model might be constructed. Essentially, the first stage is to gain an understanding of the actual structure of the system being simulated. The second stage is to use the elements of a system dynamics model (levels, rates, delays and material and information flows) to represent that structure. Once built, the model can be compared with the system being simulated, if it exists. Thus the validation rules developed in Chapter 12 can be applied.

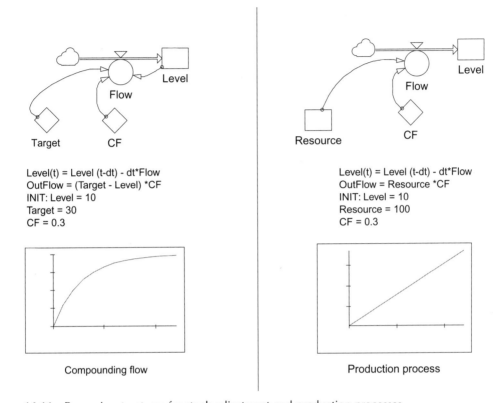

Figure 14.11 Powersim structures for stock adjustment and production processes

EXERCISES

(1) Draw a stock and flow diagram for Exercise 2 from Chapter 13.

(2) Develop a system dynamics model of Exercise 2 from Chapter 13, using the following additional information. If, in any month, the number of engineers on the staff is 50 or higher, then he will recruit no trainees that month. He thinks that he might use a = 0.2 for his forecast, and he reckons that, each month, the number of engineers who leave BCS for NMCC will be normally distributed with a mean = 5 and standard deviation = 2. He also expects that 0.8 of each monthly cohort will be successful in their training and will join the BCS staff of engineers.

(3) Develop a stock and flow diagram and then a system dynamics model to simulate Exercise 3 from Chapter 13.

REFERENCES

Forrester J.W. (1961) *Industrial Dynamics*. MIT Press, Cambridge, MA.

High Performance Systems (2003) http://www.hpc-inc.com

Pidd M. (2003) *Tools for Thinking: Modelling in Management Science* (2nd edition). John Wiley & Sons, Chichester, UK.

Powersim Corporation (2003) `http://www.powersim.com`

Richmond B. and Petersen S. (1994) *Stella II. An Introduction to Systems Thinking*. High Performance Systems Inc., Hanover, NH.

System Dynamics Road Maps (2003) `http://sysdyn.clexchange.org/road-maps/rm-toc.html`

Ventana Systems (2002) `http://www.vensim.com`

15

System Dynamics in Practice

Note: The companies involved in these studies are given pseudonyms to protect their competitive positions. As well as changing their names, it has been necessary to disguise their products to make their identification even more difficult. Both belong to multi-national organizations with turnovers in excess of $500 million per annum. All the divisions involved in these studies are located in the UK. Though the work took place over 25 years ago, the approach is still valid and shows what can be done with system dynamics.

15.1 ASSOCIATED SPARES LTD

Associated Spares Ltd (ASL) makes and sells parts for the domestic appliances and motor trade. They supply original equipment and spares.

15.1.1 The problem as originally posed

In 1977, the general manager of the UK distribution division of ASL put it something like this:

> "The economy seems to fluctuate by about 5% over a 5-year cycle. What I don't understand is why the demand at the central warehouse fluctuates much more than this. Mind you, we have so many products at different stages of their life cycles that I can't prove that this really happens. But I'm fairly certain that it does and it creates enormous problems for my business. Is there any way in which you can help?"

As is so often the case, the initial brief was rather vague and some effort had to be put into problem structuring. After visiting a number of retail outlets and extensive discussions it looked as though a system dynamics approach could be of some use. In particular, it could be used to identify the effect of the various decision rules used in the distribution division of ASL. It could also show the effect of changes in the market.

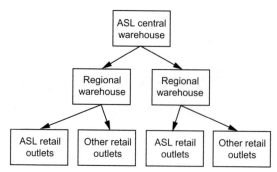

Figure 15.1   The ASL distribution system

15.1.2   The multi-echelon system

Investigation revealed that a multi-echelon distribution system existed. Figure 15.1 shows how it operated. The parts were made in a number of plants throughout the UK and were held in a central warehouse. The UK had been divided into discrete geographical areas, each of which had its own regional warehouse. These received supplies from the central warehouse. Beneath the regional warehouses in the hierarchy were a large number of retail outlets, some of which were owned by ASL. Normally, the retail outlets ordered supplies from the nearest regional warehouse. In exceptional circumstances, urgent orders were despatched direct to the retail outlets from the central warehouse. ASL provided stock control advice for the retail outlets.

Thus, there were large aggregate flows of material and information in a system which included many feedback loops. Management put a great deal of effort into controlling the operation and hence there were a great many decision rules. A further complication was the existence of delays due to forecasting, despatch lead times, batching of orders, etc. Previous knowledge of similar systems suggested that fluctuations of the type suggested by the general manager were indeed possible. Hence system dynamics models were constructed with the aim of studying these dynamic responses.

Four models were eventually built. Three of these were separate models for the retail branches, the regional warehouses and the central warehouse. The fourth model was a combination of the earlier three.

15.1.3   The retail branch model

Construction of this model began with a very simple view of the system as shown in Figure 15.2. Later this was enhanced to include the real-life complications (i.e., the analyst was consciously following the "principle of parsimony"). Starting with this simple model, it was possible to introduce the client to the ideas of system dynamics and thus to gain his confidence. Via the influence diagrams, the analyst and client were able to discuss the obvious shortcomings of the simple model and successive improvements were made.

All that the simple model of Figure 15.2 shows was that stock was created

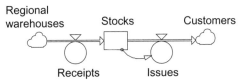

Figure 15.2   ASL simple retail branch model

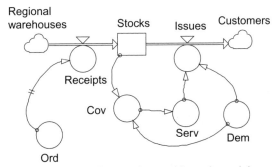

Figure 15.3   ASL first revision to the simple retail branch model

by the difference between receipts and issues in each branch. Obviously, these processes of receipts and issues needed to be modelled. Figure 15.3 shows the first stage in this modelling. Receipts result from the orders placed with the regional warehouse followed by a substantial delay. Issues (sales) stem from customers' demands.

However, there was also the problem of the mix of products in stock to be considered. Figure 15.4 shows the relationship which was found to exist between stock cover and service levels. Stock cover was defined as the total weeks of stock divided by average weekly demand. Thus, a stock equivalent to 6 weeks' demand meant that 83% of customers could be satisfied from stock. The link between issue rate and stock levels was established and built into the system dynamics model as table functions.

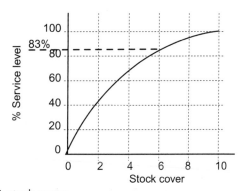

Figure 15.4   ASL stock cover

There was then the order rate to investigate, and it was apparent that the following were important factors affecting order rates:

- Forecast demand (historical demand, current demand and the forecasting system).
- Expected lead time usage.
- Usage between stock reviews.
- Buffer stock held to compensate for demand fluctuations.
- Actual stock levels.
- Outstanding orders.
- Lead times.
- Supplementary orders.

The retail branches were controlled through entirely manual systems which involved a fixed review period. Sales forecasting was via simple exponential smoothing. The smoothing process had the effect of damping out sharp fluctuations (which is good). But it also introduced a delay between changes in demand and their reflection in sales forecasts (which is bad).

The manual stock control system used the sales forecast, modified to allow for delivery lead times, safety stocks and the stock review period. This led to a target stock level which was computed manually at intervals determined by the review periods. Expensive and fast-moving items were reviewed more often than the rest.

Thus for some products, this introduced a delay of several weeks before changes in sales led to revised target stock levels. The difference between free and target stocks led to an order placed on the regional warehouse. The supplies, however, were only received after a lead time delay of several weeks. In the retail branch model this lead time delay was held constant, using the average delay experienced. Figure 15.5 shows the final model of the retail branches.

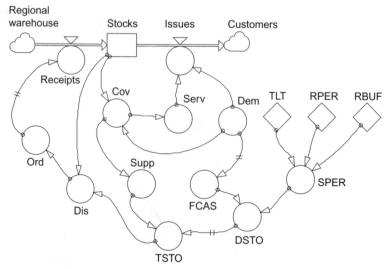

Figure 15.5   ASL final retail branch model

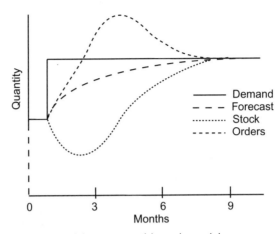

Figure 15.6 Step response of the ASL retail branch model

Figure 15.6 shows the effect of subjecting this retail branch model to a step increase of 5% on a previously steady demand rate. The immediate effect is a considerable decrease in stock levels caused by the sluggish response of the stock control system. The forecast of demand rises steadily until it reaches the new steady state after about 6 months. The orders placed on the regional warehouse display highly erratic behaviour. The order rate initially lags behind the sales rate and then overshoots after about 3 months. Eventually it falls to a new steady-state level. Notice that for a period of about 4 months, the 5% increase in sales leads to an amplified response in the order rate to the regional warehouse.

(1) Why should this happen? A number of reasons are apparent.
(2) The various delays lead to an immediate fall in stock levels. This in turn leads to higher orders being placed on the regional warehouse.
(3) In particular, the stock control system attempted to maintain a constant stock cover of *n* weeks' stock. Thus the increased demand means that stocks are built up, not just to replace the extra sales but also to maintain the stock.

Thus, a simple model of a retail branch brought considerable insight into the effect of demand fluctuations. The delays and the stock cover ratio led to amplification and the system took about 6 months to settle down. And this after only a 5% change in sales rates.

15.1.4 The regional warehouse model

At the regional warehouses, the systems were rather different from those in the regional branches. The stock control was achieved via a computer system which aimed to keep stocks between maximum and minimum levels. Thus the levels were continually monitored and replenishments were ordered as soon as the minimum level was reached. Back orders were also possible

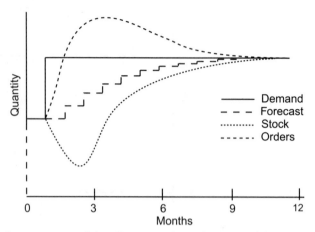

Figure 15.7   Step response of the ASL regional warehouse model

because unsatisfied orders from retail branches were held on a backlog file until supplies were received. The forecasting was based on a weighted moving average rather than exponential smoothing. Hence, although the overall structure of the branch and regional models were similar, the details were completely different.

Figure 15.7 shows the output from the model when previously steady demand is increased by 5%. As at the branch level, stocks initially fall and the order rate overshoots the increased demand rate, but the different forecasting system leads to stepped increases in forecasts. Overall, the regional warehouse responds in a way which is qualitatively similar to the retail branch. However, the system takes over 12 months to settle down. The retail branch took about 6 months to settle down.

15.1.5   The central warehouse model

The management systems at the central warehouse were computer-controlled, although more sophisticated than in the regional warehouse. Orders from the regions were entered via data input terminals and interacted with the stock control systems to produce invoices, despatch notes and other paperwork. The demand forecasting used a double exponential smoothing system, allowed for seasonality in demand, identified outliers, etc. A full-scale production control and planning system placed orders with the factories as and when necessary. Overall, the systems were different from those employed at both branch and regional levels. Hence, the detail of the model differed from that of the earlier two.

Figure 15.8 shows the effect of increasing demand by 5% on the central warehouse after a previously constant demand. The demand forecast slowly rises to meet the new demand rate, and it takes over 12 months to do this because of the small constants used in the double exponential forecasting system. This forecasting system had been introduced to dampen out the effect of certain large customers placing orders only a few times each year. The rate

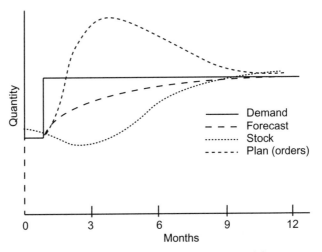

Figure 15.8 Step response of the ASL central warehouse model

at which orders were placed with the factories overshot by a large amount. The stock levels had still not settled down after 12 months of simulated time. The general manager's suspicions were beginning to look correct.

15.1.6 The total system model

It was also important to model the interactions of these three systems. Although the retail branches may experience a 5% step change in sales, their demand on the next level of the system will be amplified and delayed. As well as this amplification, the phasing of the new rates may differ somewhat. Hence, the already unsatisfactory state of affairs may look much worse after aggregating the three models. Figure 15.9 shows an outline influence diagram of this aggregate model. To make the model more realistic, the lead times experienced by the retail branches were no longer assumed constant. Increased demand on the regional warehouse from several retail branches would lead to a lengthening of the lead times. Similarly, service levels would change.

Figure 15.10 shows the result of subjecting the total system model to a step increase of 5% in sales at the retail branches. As might be expected from the three separate models, a familiar pattern emerges. The increase in customer

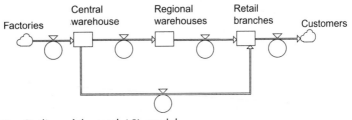

Figure 15.9 Outline of the total ASL model

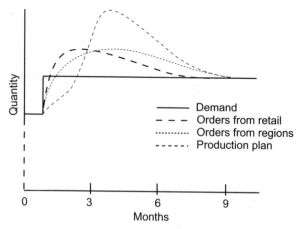

Figure 15.10   Step response of the total ASL model

sales leads to an overshoot in the demands placed by the retail branches on the regional warehouses. In turn, these increases lead to greater overshoot in the orders placed from the regions with the central warehouse. Finally, the central warehouse places orders with the factories at a rate way above the 5% step increase in customer sales. A 5% step increase in end user demand leads to the following maximum order rates within the system:

- Retail branch to regional warehouse: +8% maximum.
- Regional warehouse to central warehouse: +10% maximum.
- Central warehouse to factories: +23% maximum.

Thus changes in the market have been amplified up to four times within the system. The further away from the original change, the greater the degree of amplification. The various delays make such massive fluctuations inevitable because corrective action takes a long time to have any effect. There is also the risk that management may over-react if they see that their attempts to control things bring no immediate effect.

15.1.7   Some conclusions

The intuition of the general manager was clearly correct and he needed no persuasion of this for two reasons. First, most people love to be correct. Second, the stage-by-stage modelling had allowed him to keep continual contact with the progress of the study.

How could the operation of the system be improved? Many of the problems were caused by the interaction of the different systems found in the three levels of the hierarchy. Each of these systems made sense at its own level; put together, the effect was unfortunate. The first point is that the managers of the three levels were able to learn how their different policies interacted. It was clearly impossible to optimize the behaviour of the entire system;

however, each manager could now be made aware of the difficulties faced by others elsewhere in the system.

Given that the project was commissioned by the manager responsible for the central warehouse, it is fair to ask what benefits he received. As mentioned earlier, his intuition was proved correct. Also, the models clearly showed the effects of the delays within the system and identified the important interactions. In this sense, the 6 months of part-time work which went into the project could be viewed as problem structuring. The manager and the analyst were now aware of the weak points of the system and could now examine ways of improving its performance.

From the initial study, a further 18 months of part-time work was commissioned. Detailed investigations of various possible improvements were carried out. These were as follows:

(1) Operate without regional warehouses.
(2) Cut down information delays so that central warehouse could monitor end-user demand rather than simply using demand data from the regional warehouses.
(3) Modify the forecasting systems.
(4) Operate a stock control system not based on stock cover ratios.
(5) Change the parameters of the existing stock control systems.

Implementation of some of these followed.

15.1.8 A postscript

ASL hit a cash flow crisis shortly after the final meeting of this project and traditional remedies emerged from the directors' desks. One suggestion was that a 5% cut in stocks across the board would free the required cash. Thus a golden opportunity arose to use an existing model to see what would actually happen. What the simulations showed was that a 5% cut in target stock levels implemented simultaneously at all three levels would result in the following changes in actual stocks:

- A 6.7% drop at the central warehouse.
- A 10.7% drop at the regional warehouse.
- A 7.9% drop at the retail branches.

It would take the retail branches 4 months to reach this level whereas the central warehouse would take 6 months. For a substantial part of this 6 months, stocks would be rising at the central warehouse due to de-stocking lower in the system. This de-stocking would occur faster than schedules on suppliers could be cut.

Hence the directors were able to see that their notion of a 5% cut across the board would produce rather worse effects than anticipated. If stocks were to be rebuilt later, corresponding problems would arise. The 5% cut was not implemented.

15.2   DYNASTAT LTD

15.2.1   An expansion programme

Dynastat makes a range of electromechanical controllers for oil-fired heating systems. These devices use sophisticated electronics and are fitted to heating units for which Dynastat holds worldwide patents. Because of these controllers, the heaters use up to 15% less oil than competitive products. The rise in oil prices which occurred in the mid-1970s resulted in great increases in demand. At first, this increase was managed by using subcontractors to produce some units. But it became clear that Dynastat was stretched to its limits and large-scale investment was necessary.

The board agreed an investment programme costing about $70 million with the aim of doubling the output of the Dynastat factories. While planning the programme it became obvious that a key problem would be the need for more skilled manpower. A particular difficulty was the Rockingham plant near London. In the past it had been difficult to recruit enough skilled workers, and it seemed as if this could be a severe brake on the expansion programme.

15.2.2   The manpower problem

An analyst from the internal consulting group was asked to advise on this problem. At the first meeting, the personnel manager of the Rockingham plant said that he was convinced that the programme was impossible. His experience suggested that the skilled manpower targets were out of reach. As the meeting continued, it became clear that he had thoroughly analysed the recruitment potential—however, labour turnover seemed to have been forgotten. After a quick analysis of available figures, it became clear that the labour turnover for skilled workers was about 25% per annum (labour turnover being defined as the number leaving in a year divided by the average number of employees during the year). Later checks showed that 25% was typical for this type of industry.

In system dynamics terms, manpower can be regarded as a level fed by recruitment and depleted by labour turnover. Hence the simple model shown in Figure 15.11 was constructed. By using it, the recruitment rate to fill a specified number of jobs can be calculated. Remarkable as it may seem, Dynastat had previously been unable to relate labour turnover and recruitment to the expansion programme. But before this simple model could be used, appropriate functions for turnover and recruitment were required.

15.2.3   Recruitment

One fear was that the current high level of economic activity would make it even more difficult to recruit enough skilled workers. Analysis of available data showed that the numbers of skilled workers recruited in the past was positively correlated with the health of the economy. The apparently good

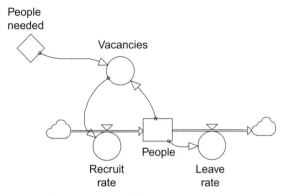

Figure 15.11   First simple Dynastat model

relationship is rather misleading, as it might suggest that recruitment is easier when the economy is booming. However, the reality is that more recruitment is necessary when the economy is booming and few recruits are needed when product demand is low. Hence some other way of modelling recruitment was needed.

A further complication was that Dynastat needed to model future recruitment rates and there was no guarantee that their economic cycles would coincide with the of the rest of the nation. Thus, the forecasts of hiring rates were produced by a combination of analysis and management judgement. To ensure consistency, the same forecasts of national economic activity produced for demand forecasting were used when predicting hiring rates and labour turnover. However, the forecasts were modified to allow for expected regional differences.

15.2.4   Turnover

Analysing historical leaving rates produced some interesting results. The leaving rate was very high immediately after joining Dynastat but was very low after 6 months. Thus, new recruits were highly likely to leave, but if they survived for 6 months then they were likely to stay for much longer. Hence for further analysis, the "attrition curve" could be simplified by considering skilled workers to be either "new" or "established". The modelling was made easier by the discovery that this simple model would suffice for all groups of skilled and semi-skilled workers in the factory. "New" workers were found to have a turnover of 170% per annum and the "established" turnover rate was about 10% per annum. These rates would not necessarily hold for the other Dynastat factories.

The effect of local employment levels on labour turnover was also investigated. It appeared that the leaving rate of "established" staff was not affected; however, it had a great effect on the leaving rate for "new" workers. This effect was incorporated within the model shown in Figure 15.12.

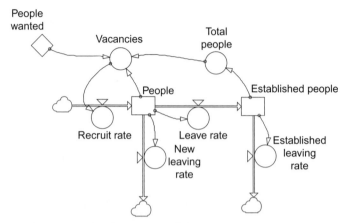

Figure 15.12   More complex Dynastat model

15.2.5   Some effects of this structure

If the model of Figure 15.12 is in a steady state, then the hiring rate must be positive, for the aim is to recruit enough workers to replace those who leave. However, there are delays in the system. As in most organizations, new workers were hired to fill existing vacancies (i.e., no hiring action was taken until some workers had left). Hence, steady state is possible only if vacancies exist to drive the recruitment rate. This means that there would always be a shortage of workers in the factory if current policies were followed.

Without even simulating with the model, a further problem was apparent. The overall average turnover was 25% per annum, represented by 170% for "new" workers and 10% for "established" workers. Suppose that Dynastat wish to increase the workforce from 4,000 to 6,000—a 50% increase. If the different rates are ignored, then the temptation is to recruit enough workers to fill the 25% overall turnover plus the 2,000 extra. However, this is clearly wrong. There will be a turnover of 170% among the "new" workers (if the economic conditions were unchanged) and thus the overall turnover will be much higher than 25% because the balance between "new" and "established" workers will have changed.

15.2.6   Validating the model

The principles of "white box" validity (see Chapter 12) were followed throughout the model construction. A "black box" check was now required. That is, could the model reproduce the past behaviour of the system? As the modelling occurred in 1977, the period 1971 to 1977 was chosen for this validation exercise. The results of initializing the model at January 1971 and running it until 1977 are shown in Figure 15.13. Statistical analysis confirmed that this adequately represented the actual system behaviour. Note, however, that this was not an entirely satisfactory check as the 1971

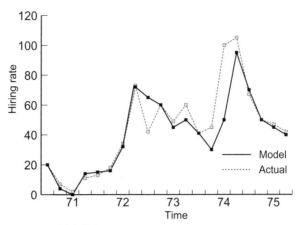

Figure 15.13 Dynastat initializing run

to 1977 data had been used to parameterize the model. However, some confidence was built up.

15.2.7 Simulation results

Figure 15.14 shows the results of the first run. It shows an enormous shortfall in available labour. This run assumed that previous policies were followed. The gap was so large that no conceivable increase in the hiring rate would close it. Hence attention was focused on the leaving rates and it was clear that reducing the 170% leaving rate of "new" workers was crucial.

To do this, the model had to be made more detailed by subdividing "new" workers. After some discussion and thought, it emerged that different factors caused workers to leave at various stages of their first few months at Dynastat. These were as follows:

- *FIRST MONTH.* "JOB SHOCK", could be improved by better selection, induction, training, etc.

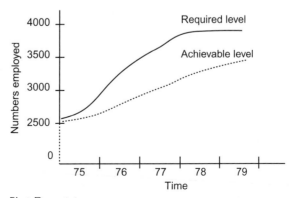

Figure 15.14 First Dynastat run

- *MONTHS 2 to 6.* "CULTURE SHOCK", could be improved by better supervision.
- *AFTER 6 MONTHS.* "NORMAL ATTRITION", affected by wage levels, the company image, motivation and other similar factors.

Using the model, the effect of improving these factors was investigated. Of course, for many of these the analyst had to rely on the judgement of the managers in order to incorporate appropriate functions into the model. Thus, the model was used to show the effect of improvements thought to be possible by the managers who would be responsible for their implementation. Some cross-checking of different opinions helped refine the process.

The complete model contained many more feedback loops, though was still simple. Many factors were inter-related (e.g., a high recruitment rate reduces the training available, which may affect the leaving rate of "new" employees). A range of actions that might reduce labour turnover were investigated, such as:

- Improved job descriptions.
- Improved selection procedures.
- A more professional approach to recruitment.
- Better training.
- Closer supervision.
- Retraining current workers.

The simulations showed that, based partly on the estimates of the managers, the expansion plan was feasible.

15.2.8   Predicting length of service

It seemed likely that some recruits might be classified as "high risk". To check this, the records of several hundred past employees were examined for obvious indicators. This showed that a simple system of weighting factors such as age, marital status and previous job history gave a good prediction of length of service. This prediction could easily be calculated at the time of a recruitment interview and used sensibly with other factors.

This was expected to produce a tangible payoff by reducing the "high risk" recruits. An individual leaving the company was estimated to have cost about $800 in recruitment and training. With an overall turnover of 25% and a labour force of 4,000, turnover was costing about $800,000 per annum. Reducing overall turnover to 20%, even ignoring the expansion programme, should therefore save about $160,000 per annum. This seemed a useful by-product of the simulation exercise.

15.2.9   The value of the exercise to Dynastat

As in the ASL case, the modelling was not very sophisticated and yet the benefits were high. The models were deliberately constructed in a parsimonious way. For example, the initial simple model of Figure 15.11 served to focus discussion on the leaving rates. This had not previously been a great concern to the company. Producing the results of Figure 15.14 led the management to give serious consideration to ways of reducing the turnover of "new" employees. Indeed, the idea of "new" and "established" workers entered the everyday vocabulary of the managers concerned. That is, they began to think about the problem in new ways.

A further advantage stemmed from the apparently unscientific way in which much of the model was parameterized. Despite much data analysis, many parameters could only be estimated by using the judgements of experienced managers who would have to operate the new policies. Because of their close involvement with the model, no solution had to be "sold" to them. Thus implementation was simply never an issue. Because simulation models, whether discrete or system dynamics, should be built in stages and can be shown as simple flow diagrams, this sort of commitment is possible. In this sense, simulation is not a last resort.

15.3 SYSTEM DYNAMICS IN PRACTICE

The ASL and Dynastat cases have been included for two reasons. First, they were successful exercises which led to distinct improvements within the organizations. Second, they illustrate important features of the use of system dynamics and of other simulation methods. These features are discussed below.

15.3.1 Simple models

Simplicity is not a virtue in itself, for over-simplification can clearly be disastrous. However, most analysts are beset by the desire to build all-inclusive models which are over-complicated. All management science models are simplifications. If a model could incorporate the full richness of the system being modelled then the model would be an exact replica of the system. This means that it would be just as difficult to control and, possibly, just as expensive to operate. Simplification is not disastrous, it is inevitable. Indeed, given that most management systems are in a constant state of flux, then an analyst would be totally occupied in keeping a replica up to date.

The approximations that make up the model need to be appropriate to the task in hand. Hence, in the Dynastat case, it was possible to consider the skilled workforce as a single homogeneous body. This was clearly a simplification, because not all the men and women would be equally skilled or equally productive. However, the model was not intended to reflect these individual differences, it was built to assess whether a sufficiently large labour force would be available to support an expansion plan. Given that the plan did not specify the precise set of skills required of the workforce and given that this was thought to be sensible, the model incorporated an appropriate level of complexity.

Chapter 5 discusses the "principle of parsimony". It suggests the development of models which are initially simple and include only the grosser, structural features of the system. Refinements are made as and when necessary, although the overall structure remains unchanged.

15.3.2   Communication

Given that most management scientists operate in consulting roles to managers, their methods need to be appropriate to that role. A consultant who maintains little or no contact with the client group is unlikely to make much impact. Discrete simulation and system dynamics offer great opportunities for the type of communication which leads to implementation. The secret lies in the use of flow diagrams, parsimonious models and graphical output.

Flow diagrams, whether activity cycles or influence diagrams, are simple to understand. Hence, the management science model need not remain a completely black box to the client. Through the sensible use of diagrams, the main structural features can be displayed, enabling the client to agree to them before detailed programming occurs. As the models are successively enhanced, much of this can also be displayed on the diagram. The Dynastat case illustrates this very clearly. The personnel manager had not thought to focus much attention on the question of the rate at which new recruits left the company. The flow diagrams showed the importance of this point and led to its incorporation into the study.

15.3.3   New thinking

This follows from the good communication produced by a simple approach to modelling. As an example, consider Dynastat, who gained three new insights from the system dynamics study. The first, as mentioned in Section 15.3.2, was the realization that keeping workers at Dynastat was as important as recruiting them in the first place. With hindsight, this does seem rather obvious, but in the hectic time following the announcement of the expansion plan other aspects preoccupied the managers concerned.

The second insight was the distinction drawn between new and established staff. The analysis of labour turnover figures clearly revealed the existence of these two groups of workers. Obviously, the consideration of only two groups was a simplification—yet it provided enough reality to enable the managers to control their system more effectively.

The third insight stemmed from the second. It was the realization, again after data analysis, that certain types of recruit were more likely than others to leave Dynastat not long after joining the company. This led to the development of a simple screening procedure which identified the "at risk" applicants. This again changed the managers' thinking about their recruitment practices.

15.3.4   Evolutionary involvement

Sometimes the client group may be able to specify exactly what they require of the analyst. Occasionally they are correct. More often, the call for help stems from a feeling that some improvement must be possible. In these cases, the modelling can only be exploratory at first. A feature of such exploration is the asking of sensible questions, "What if we try to ...?" From the answers to these questions comes the development of issues which require detailed research. This exploration approach to problem structuring (Pidd and Woolley, 1980) is well illustrated in the ASL case. Here the successive development of different models for the various sectors of the company led to more detailed questions being asked. Thus, system dynamics modelling led on to the detailed programme of work described in Section 15.1.7.

REFERENCE

Pidd M. and Woolley R.N. (1980) A pilot study of problem structuring. *Journal of Operational Research Society*, **31**, 1063–8.

Index